Bettina Bruns · Judith Miggelbrink (Eds.)

Subverting Borders

VS RESEARCH

Bettina Bruns
Judith Miggelbrink (Eds.)

Subverting Borders

Doing Research on Smuggling
and Small-Scale Trade

VS VERLAG

Bibliographic information published by the Deutsche Nationalbibliothek
The Deutsche Nationalbibliothek lists this publication in the Deutsche Nationalbibliografie;
detailed bibliographic data are available in the Internet at http://dnb.d-nb.de.

1st Edition 2012

Editorial Office: Dorothee Koch | Anette Villnow

VS Verlag für Sozialwissenschaften is a brand of Springer Fachmedien.
Springer Fachmedien is part of Springer Science+Business Media.
www.vs-verlag.de

Cover design: KünkelLopka Medienentwicklung, Heidelberg
Printed on acid-free paper
Printed in Germany

ISBN 978-3-531-17788-5

Contents

List of Figures[1]

---

1   As far as not marked differently in the legend, all pictures are taken by the authors themselves.

List of Tables[2]

---

2   As far as not marked differently in the legend, all tables are produced by the authors
     themselves.

Introduction

Bettina Bruns and Judith Miggelbrink

Small-scale trade and smuggling are part of everyday life at many borders. Whenever prosperity along the border differs leading to considerable price differences in the adjacent countries, the border may be used as an economic resource by inhabitants living nearby. Smuggling cigarettes, alcohol and fuel, illegal drugs and pharmaceuticals or the – at first glance – legal transport of commodities such as clothing or electronic devices: trading activities as the above mentioned often compensate for economic shortages that many households suffer from in consequence of difficult external conditions caused e.g. by economic crises or political transformation processes. Therefore, transborder small-scale trade and smuggling are possibilities to cope with stressful periods of biographic transition such as unemployment and poverty. At the same time, transborder small-scale trade and smuggling are an everyday border phenomenon which is part of the normal routine at many borders. Although there is no uniform definition of transborder small-scale trade applied throughout the different contributions to this book, the phenomenon can be approached by Williams' and Baláž's clarification which describes transborder small-scale trade as "(...) a form of arbitrage (Altvater 1998), understood as the exploitation of differences in prices and exchange rates over time and space via circulation activities" (Williams/Baláž 2002: 323). It is characteristic that small-scale traders operate with mostly limited economic resources and over relatively short distances. They rely on local knowledge and social networks in order to trade successfully. The same applies to smugglers. In theory smuggling and small-scale trade differ in accordance to their legal status. "Traditionally, 'trade' is the legal and 'smuggling' is the illegal means of moving items from one side of the border to the other" (Thuen 1999: 741). Legality respectively illegality thereby is not a natural feature of a person or a thing but the result of an external labelling process (see Singelnstein/Stolle 2008: 122) through which the attribute of being legal or illegal is applied. The status of (il)legality qualifies a relation between a trading activity and a state's law. Smuggling and small-scale trade are hence effects of state regulations (see Paul et al. 2002: 117). Table 1 shows this typology of transborder small-scale activities and their legal relation to the state.

Activity	Definition	Legal relation to the state
small-scale trade	"Applies to individual people crossing a border to purchase goods at a cheaper price" (Deflem/Henry-Turner 2001: 473)	legal
smuggling		illegal

Tab. 1: Typology of transborder economic small-scale activities

In praxis, however, the borders between legality and illegality while engaging in small-scale trade are fluid. The process of transporting goods contains mostly legal and illegal elements. For example it is possible that the amount of transported goods is fully legal, but that they were bought in an illegally functioning shop. Also it may be that goods were declared for own needs, although the goods were actually used as trading goods after crossing the border. Thus, legal formal trade and smuggling are often intertwined by small-scale traders.

Illegal elements of a transborder economic activity do not have to be automatically illegitimate. In the light of high unemployment and a high level of poverty, few decent paid working places or other alternatives, smuggling and small-scale trade are often highly legitimized among the population, although by state law labelled illegal and therefore forbidden. "Many transnational movements of people, commodities, and ideas are illegal because they defy the norms and rules of formal political authority", as Abraham and van Schendel put it, "but they are quite acceptable, 'licit', in the eyes of participants in these transactions and flows" (van Schendel/ Abraham 2005: 4). Legitimization does not necessarily derive from legality, but has its own sources.

Illegal markets bear some remarkable threats for those involved in them: In contrast to legal transactions, breaching contracts cannot be brought to court. This "opens the floodgates to informal rules or violence"[3] (Besozzi 2001: 14). Consequently, trust plays an important role in illegal markets. Furthermore, people engaged in the production of illegal goods and services face the risk of being controlled by the police at any time (see ibid.). This risk is not abstract but has to be regarded as a concrete element of the ongoing transaction and is therefore calculated by the traders anew time and again.

In case the traded goods are subject to certain restrictions or prohibitions (e.g. human beings, certain drugs, illegally produced cigarettes, items of historical and cultural interest) people have to face prosecution because of the illicit production

---

3   All quotes from German sources are translated by the authors.

and trade of certain goods. In other cases the kinds of goods are not problematic per se but the way how they come into circulation is against the law (handling stolen goods) or against the economic interest of the state or the private economy (avoidance of taxation, i.e. smuggling). However, these categories cannot be sharply distinguished as "the legitimisation of interdictions results from the interference of different rationales" (Besozzi 2001: 24). Therefore, traders involved in transborder trading practices may take a double risk regarding the ways they challenge the state or rather state authorities compared to those who take part into illegal markets within only one state: One source of risk derives from the illegality of markets. At the same time risk derives from the practice of transborder transactions: People who in order to bring goods from one side of the border to the other hide goods, declare them incorrectly or use unofficial routes have to face the risk of being detected by border authorities. With regard to the specificities of transborder small-scale trade in the broad field of informal economic activities, the risk of being detected by border officials always has to be weighed up against the potential profit.

Due to this risk of (partly) illegal economic transborder practices, people involved are understandably reluctant to share information to unfamiliar people such as researchers. Providing detailed knowledge about their transborder activities, which often represents their most important income source, may have most serious personal consequences. Therefore, research on smuggling and informal small-scale trade is a 'sensitive topic' (see Lee 1993) which means that it "present(s) problems because research into them [sensitive topics, B.B.&J.M.] involves potential costs to those involved in the research, including, on occasion, the researcher" (Lee 1993: 4). Obviously people are reluctant to share confidential information with unfamiliar researchers under these difficult conditions. Qualitative research – in contrast to quantitative methods – facilitates building trustful relations between the researcher and the researched. Furthermore, qualitative research allows for flexibility and openness in the research process which is essential when carrying out research in remote sites and in different cultural and linguistic surroundings as some of the authors in this volume did (see figure 1). With one exception, all contributions of this volume are based on qualitative empirical methods such as open interviews, participant observation and long-term fieldwork. Some contributors connect their central qualitative approach with quantitative analysis and document analysis.

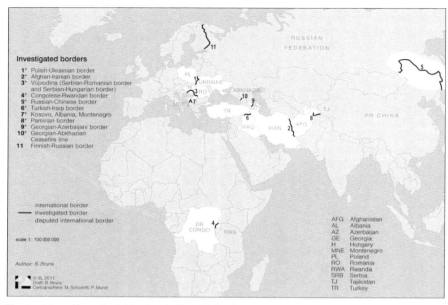

Fig. 1:   Map of investigated borders in the edited volume

In most of the cases discussed in this volume, the specific nature of the border regime plays an important role. Based on a series of case studies at the Georgian-Azerbaijani border, *Lale Yalçın-Heckmann and Nino Aivazishvili* discuss how people working in the informal economy and being dependent on border trade assess their cross-border trading for understanding the border regime. From the perspective of the people involved in the trading, the border regime becomes manifest through those officials who have to carry it out and therefore incorporate it. A similar detailed insight into the practices of transborder small-scale trade and smuggling is given by *Anna Stammler-Gossmann* who accompanied traders between Finland and Russia across the northernmost section of the border. She colourfully reports how she turned from a participant *observer* into a *participant* observer when asked in a taxi whether she could declare a winter tyre as her own. She also points out the importance of trust-based personal networks for the success of smuggling and transborder small-scale trade. Her empirical observations and findings are discussed within a broader framework of social change in Russia and the changing relation citizens build to 'their' state.

Small-scale traders and smugglers use borders as an economic resource. Its resource effect can derive from different sources such as differences in demand and supply, differences of taxation or differences in the legality of trading certain goods. However, the permeability of the border is a necessary precondition in order to use it as a resource. Using the concept of differential permeability, *Andrea Weiss* takes a close look at the permeability of the Georgian-Abkhazian ceasefire line. In doing so, she also takes into account the moral categories of licitness and illicitness involved in border permeability.

The use of the resource always presupposes illegality or informality. Nevertheless, there is a continuum of different kinds of cross-border trade that can be observed depending on how they are embedded into the changing nature of borders to which people react in one or the other way. The changing flows of cross-border activities due to border changes – the regime of control, visa requirements etc. – but also due to changing demands are demonstrated by *Rory Archer and Krisztina Rácz* who accompanied traders living in the Vojvodina on both sides of the Serbian-Romanian border. By using the example fuel trade between Turkey and Iraq *Gulcan Kolay* also demonstrates that smuggling is a flexible instrument taken as a means to survive and may be regarded as a taken-for-granted way of making a living in terms of moral judgement. Moreover, she argues that inhabitants of border regions always try to maintain a relationship between each other in a legal or illegal way and it is a question of circumstances if illegal trade dominates – as in her case – or trade turns into shopping as can be observed at many European borders.

One main topic is the relationship to the state and its sovereignty that is built by informal and illegal activities. Even though sovereignty does not necessarily rely on a bordered territory (see Agnew 2005), borders have been one of the most important media through which political rule has been exercised and stabilised throughout history. Thus, borders have to be seen "in the context of political rule" (Krämer 2009: 9) and, therefore, are a sensitive case in terms of being disregarded. As borders "define the territorial extent of a state's claim to sovereignty" (ibid: 10) all practices that challenge border control also challenge the state's sovereignty and can therefore be regarded as subversive. All articles deal in one way or another with the role of the challenged state but the way states are challenged and how this is related to social and political organisation differs. Based on fieldwork at the Polish-Ukrainian border, one interpretation is given by *Abel Polese* who understands a border as a site of conflict between citizens and the states because it explicitly limits circulation. The resulting artificial scarcity of goods and services has to be overcome by individuals – small-scale traders – who use deception as the 'first method' for commercial transaction. Though it might be taken for granted that deceptive tactics play an important role in cross-border small-scale trade and smuggling, *Just Boedeker* investigating the Afghan-Iranian border shows that smuggling is not necessarily a secret, clandestine or conspirative activity but is carried out more or less in public although it is prosecuted. The example of Baloch people living in the border region of Afghanistan and Iran and heavily involved in smuggling opium (heroine, morphine), cars, electronic devices and fuel illustrates the permanent struggle between states not fully capable to control their territory and a tribe that does not accept its living space divided by a national border. As a consequence, the tribe as whole is criminalized. Whereas in this case smuggling – be it large-scale or small-scale – is regarded as an expression of a long-lasting fight of a group against any superior power, *Martin Doevenspeck and Nene Morisho Mwanabiningo* argue that people trade across the Congolese-Rwandan border in order to cope with country-specific risks and uncertainties. It is not a specific strength or weakness of the states that motivates small-scale trade but specific situations people have to deal with in their everyday lives that persuade them to try to escape from their own state. In doing so, they subvert the state and re-confirm its territorial logic as Doevenspeck and Morisho Mwanabiningo conclude. *Tobias Kraudzun* emphasises the historical perspective with his fieldwork on the Eastern Pamir frontiers. He thereby shows what positive and negative effects emerging boundaries and reconfigured borders have had for the local population.

Cross-border small-scale trade – be it trading of illegal goods or be it trading of legal goods in an illegal way – is an economic activity that always builds a relationship with the state without necessarily indicating that state authorities are weak. The sheer existence of small-scale trade and smuggling does not necessarily indicate times or areas of limited statehood. How willing are state authorities to either prosecute or tolerate illegal and informal practices and if they are forced by the/an international community to fight against criminal acts? The 'shadow triangle' of Kosovo, Albania and Montenegro offers a good example to discuss a broad range of questions concerning the role of states and supranational entities (EU) in dealing with 'the illicit', as *Enza Roberta Petrillo* argues in her article. Illicit practices like smuggling and corruption affect the image of a state and have consequences for its international position and acceptance. Even though the existence of small-scale trade and smuggling does not always indicate a weak state this conclusion does not work in an international political context: Here, the existence of 'illicit activities' are very well regarded as an outcome of a state malfunctioning. This raises two further important questions: Given the different contexts in which small-scale trade and other activities are negotiated – what is an illicit act? The definitions vary according to the standards and traditions accepted in the respective context. And one may come to different conclusions depending on whether EU programmes to fight organized crime are applied or the 'Kanun', the Albanian Canon of Customary Law.

Almost all of the contributors highlight that small-scale trade serves interests beyond those related to supply and demand and beyond those of making a living. Moreover, they all acknowledge that social differences and identification in terms of ethnical and national ascription play a role in the way the economic activities and interactions are carried out. Doevenspeck and Morisho Mwanabiningo for example emphasise the role of cross-border activities in dealing actively with state-specific risks and uncertainties from an individual perspective. In contrast, Yalçın-Heckmann and Aivazishvili focus on the effects a shared economic activity has on processes of community building especially among women. *Kapitolina Fedorova* gives a deeper insight into problems and processes of interethnic communication that arise (unavoidably) from cross-border contacts between people who speak different languages. The 'imperfect Russian' developed in the Russian-Chinese border region is a very impressive example of how contacts predominantly economically motivated not only lead to new tools of interethnic communication, a so-called ethnolect, but can also show that relations between Chinese and Russian people are asymmetrical insofar as Chinese are treated as inferior to Russians'.

The short descriptions of this volume's contributions show that the phenomena of transborder small-scale trade and smuggling are very multi-faceted. This is reflected in their different labelling, e.g. 'contraband', 'suitcase trade', 'shuttle trade' or 'trading tourism'. Despite the diversity of transborder small-scale trade/smuggling and its wide dispersion, not only in Europe, its reception within social sciences is relatively low. Some researchers are focusing on smuggling and small-scale trade mostly in post-socialist countries in Eastern and Middle Europe (see e.g. Iglicka, 1999, 2001; Holtom 2003; Wallace et al. 1999; Hann/Hann 1992; Williams/Baláž 2002; Polese 2006). A coherent collection of this research can be found in the recently published edited volume by Mathias Wagner and Wojchiech Łukowski (2010). Also in the edited volume published by Winfried Heller and Mihaela N. Arambaşa (2009) the focus lies on informal practices in post-socialist European countries and includes economic activities across different borders, with a special focus on the Romanian-Moldovan one.

Nevertheless, this book seeks to go beyond a European frame and presents empirical studies on smuggling and small-scale trade in very different regions of the world. It sheds light on research in geography and neighbouring disciplines focusing on smuggling and transborder small-scale trade. On the basis of empirical research findings from borders all over the world, the publication strives to analyse mechanisms and conditions of informal activity and to detect parallels and differences of informal economic structures from different perspectives. The volume provides the reader interested in transborder small-scale economic activities with a comparative presentation of the same activity carried out very differently, depending on the respective external circumstances it is embedded in. Therefore it should be seen as a complement to existing studies.

The editors are grateful to Deborah Connolly who was responsible for the English proof-reading and to Lukas Schliephake for formatting the manuscript.

References

Agnew, J. (2005): Sovereignty Regimes: Territoriality and State Authority in Contemporary World Politics. In: Annals of the Association of American Geographers, 95, pp. 437-461.
Besozzi, C. (2001): Illegal, legal – egal? Zur Entstehung, Struktur und Auswirkung illegaler Märkte. Bern, Stuttgart, Wien: Verlag Paul Haupt.
Deflem, M. / Henry-Turner, K. (2001): "Smuggling". In: C. D. Bryant (ed.): Encyclopedia of Criminology and Deviant Behavior. Philadelphia: Brunner-Routledge, pp. 473-475.
Hann, C. / Hann, I. (1992): "Samovars and Sex on Turkey's Russian Markets". In: Anthropology Today, 8, 4, pp. 3-6.
Heller, W. / Arambaşa, M. N. (eds.) (2009): Am östlichen Rand der Europäischen Union: Geopolitische, ethnische und nationale sowie ökonomische und soziale Probleme und ihre Folgen für die Grenzraumbevölkerung. In: Potsdamer Geographische Forschungen, Band 28, Potsdam: Universitätsverlag Potsdam.
Holtom, P. (2003): "Coping with the Future of the Small-Scale Cross-Border Traders in Kaliningrad's Borderlands". In: H. Birkenbach and C. Wellmann (eds.): The Kaliningrad Challenge. Münster: LIT, pp. 152-168.
Iglicka, K. (1999): "The Economics of Petty Trade on the Eastern Polish Border". In: K. Iglicka and K. Sword (eds.): The Challenge of East-West migration for Poland. London: Macmillan, pp. 120-144.
Iglicka, K. (2001): "Shuttling from the former Soviet Union to Poland: from ‚primitive mobility' to migration". In: Journal of Ethnic and Migration Studies, 27, 3, pp. 505-518.
Krämer, R. (2009): Staatsgrenzen im Wandel: Eine theoretisch-historische Reflexion. In: R. Krämer (ed.): Grenzen in den internationalen Beziehungen. Potsdam: Welt Trends e.V., pp. 9-24.
Lee, R. M. (1993): Doing Research on Sensitive Topics. London: Sage.
Polese, A. (2006): Border-Crossing as a Strategy of Daily Survival: The Odessa-Chisinau Elektrichka. In: Anthropology of East Europe Review, 24, 1, pp. 28-37.
Singelnstein, T. / Stolle, P. (2008): Die Sicherheitsgesellschaft: Soziale Kontrolle im 21. Jahrhundert. Wiesbaden: VS-Verlag.
Thuen, T. (1999): "The Significance of Borders in the East European Transition". In: International Journal of Urban and Regional Research, 23, 4, pp. 738-750.
Van Schendel, W. / Abraham, I. (eds.) (2005): Illicit Flows and Criminal Things: States, Borders, and the Other Side of Globalization. Bloomington: Indiana University Press.
Wagner, M. / Łukowski, W. (eds.) (2010): Alltag im Grenzland: Schmuggel als ökonomische Strategie im Osten Europas. Wiesbaden: VS Verlag.

Wallace, C. / Shmulyar, O. / Bedzir, V. (1999): "Investing in Social Capital: The Case of Small-Scale, Cross-Border Traders in Post-Communist Central Europe". In: International Journal of Urban and Regional Research, 23, 4, pp. 751-770.

Williams, A. / Baláž, V. (2002): "International Petty Trading: Changing Practices in Trans-Carpathian Ukraine". In: International Journal of Urban and Regional Research, 26, 2, pp. 323-342.

Who has the right to forbid and who to trade? Making sense of illegality on the Polish-Ukrainian border

Abel Polese

1   Introduction[4]

> "We do not like to go to the capital. When he goes there, my husband is always nervous because of the traffic, because of the police's behaviour, because of people trying to rip you off. We need to go from time to time to get some documents but we try to avoid it. Once we could visit our relatives [on the other side of the border] by going on our ID [*grazhdanskii pasport*; A.P.] but to get a passport we have to go to the city."[5]

Limits to human action and interaction are detectable everywhere in a state (and not only). The state does not necessarily have a direct role in setting them, but they exist nonetheless. A local trader, from a village or another city, wishing to sell some products in another place must face a number of obstacles: finding the right place, entering a new zone, facing new competitors, finding new connections, affording travel costs etc. Likewise, somebody wishing to move from one city to another, temporarily or definitively, has to face a number of issues such as finding a place to sleep, earning the necessary amount of money, finding and trusting the right people. Even somebody simply wishing to visit a relative has to face issues like finding the way to the other town, affording the ticket and in general moving away from a comfortable environment to enter the unknown.

Borders, acknowledged or not (like in the case of unrecognised states), indicate separation between different geographical, administrative, social unities and actors; they also limit circulation of goods, people, ideas or money. In this respect, instead of using dualistic categories such as 'borders' (places where there is a real and tangible limitation to circulation) and 'non-borders' (place where there is no limitation to circulation) we could see a continuous line between different administrative entities and see that the number of obstacles to human action grows from a non-border, village to village, city to city, to a state one. As an intermediate situation we could think of de facto states where borders

---

4   This research was made possible thanks to a Marie Curie IOF Grant no: 219691.
5   Personal communication with a housewife from Kilye, Odessa oblast'.

do not exist but some control is applied, like on the Moldovan-Ukrainian border (see Polese 2006a).

Even in the case of 'non-borders', or former borders, like those among EU states, the end of a territorial competency generates some discrepancies that people are willing and able to exploit, the borders between Germany and Poland, where in theory free circulation of goods should level down differences, are an example. Price differences and labour costs are such that people move regularly across the border to buy cheaper goods or simply buy what is not available on the other side. The author of this paper, when living in Dresden, found it more convenient to cross the Polish border to buy a plane ticket than do things from and in Germany (internet tickets were less popular than nowadays).

There is, however, a substantial difference between non-state and state borders. Whilst with non-state borders the state tends not to put any direct limitation to the circulation of people or merchandise (there are of course exceptions), in state borders the state's claim to a monopoly of regulated predation (taxation, state expenditure) is based on the delegitimisation of other forms of predation (see van Schendel/Abraham 2005: 7). The state is the ultimate judge and has the right to set limits, to decide what is good and what is bad. Where its territorial competence comes to an end, the state feels the need and the right to regulate, to adopt a moral code, to suggest or better impose, what is right and what is wrong. What is legal on the one side of the border might not be on the other. If good relations with a neighbour state may be improved by tackling smuggling or migration, the state may be interested in finding an agreement with the neighbour state that will put local citizens' direct needs on a secondary level. When too many goods are smuggled through a border a state might come under pressure from neighbour countries. This may lead to a situation in which the state harms the citizens twice: first, by not creating the conditions for employment it prompts citizens to engage with illegal actions, such as smuggling, in order to survive; on the top of that it punishes the activities generated by state mismanagement. In that case not only the state cannot create the conditions to develop this area, but it is also punishes private initiatives that make up for state ineffectiveness or absence. In this respect the border is an interesting case, being the place where it is possible to see the potential conflict between the citizens and their state amplified to the maximum, thanks to the explicit limitations for the circulation of people, goods, capital, or even services.

Regional inequality is difficult to correct by national laws and people living in peripheral places, like border regions, might have to search for new resources and sources of income and borders will be a major opportunity for two reasons. The first is that borders, being points of discontinuity, provide opportunities for mediators, people matching a demand and supply on the two sides of the same border and earning money out of it. The other is that restrictions and prohibitions generate new demands. What becomes forbidden sees its price increase and the more a state prohibits a good, the more a good will be in demand. This generates new tensions on the one side, and new opportunities on the other. State morality might not overlap people's morality and socially backed rules (see Polese 2006a; van Schendel/Abraham 2005; Wanner 2005).

This makes borders places where people cross to buy cheaper tobacco and spirits, to get a cheaper and nicer haircut to places where such practices are consolidated and constitute a strategy of daily survival for many people, to situations in which such borders are a source of extremely high incomes and high economic interests.

It would be extremely difficult to find a moral threshold in such cases, and anthropologists have already warned about the difficulty to generalize moral standards everywhere and for everyone (see Humphrey 2002; Patico 2002; Polese 2008, 2010; Rasayagan 2005; Wanner 2005) so that the border between actions aimed at survival and those aimed at profit may be more fluid than one can imagine. If somebody decides to earn money by selling tobacco on the other side of the border because this may generate a profit there are two options. If s/he brings only one carton s/he is within the law, if two, this is already unlawful. However what is the difference between somebody bringing two cartons and somebody carrying one and asking a friend to carry the other carton through the border for him? And if somebody crosses the border 3 times per day with a single carton? They are still 'within the law' but what is the difference to one person taking 3 cartons at once? We tend to think in terms of lawful (bringing one carton) and unlawful (crossing in a car with 300 cartons) but there are millions of intermediate situations.

Whilst one may be more sympathetic towards those crossing the border with ripped clothes trying to make a living rather than somebody in an expensive car with gold chains and bracelets, both actions, in the end, are unlawful. The difference is that small traders use deception as a first method, whilst wholesalers may attempt deception but might also have the money to buy their way into or out of the country.

The questions about the functions, and uses, of a border, and the consequent switch in people's attitude, that move from a generalized moral standard to a contextual one is the main object of this paper. To do this the paper presents a case study of a border region, the L'viv, where dozens of people cross the Polish-Ukrainian border every day to make a living. The aim is to examine some of the issues related to business in border crossing from a closer perspective. We will look at them as forms of resistance, political participation but also as starting points to try to further blur the dividing line between legal and illegal, lawful and unlawful, to distinguish the legal and social approach to restrictions. How often should we buy tobacco for ourselves on the other side of the border to be lawful? If I buy for my neighbour is it illegal? Even if I buy it as a present? And if I accept a favour in exchange? It is all too easy, in the name of good governance, to condemn gift exchange and equate it to corruption. But what should be one's position if 'unlawful actions' are indirectly prompted poverty that may be seen as a direct result of state mismanagement?

Material for the paper was collected through intensive observation and informal interviews at border points from 2002 to 2006, when I happened to regularly cross the Ukrainian-Polish border (and being asked to carry cigarettes or alcohol for someone). Sources have been anonymised and all the sensitive information identifying the informants has been changed.

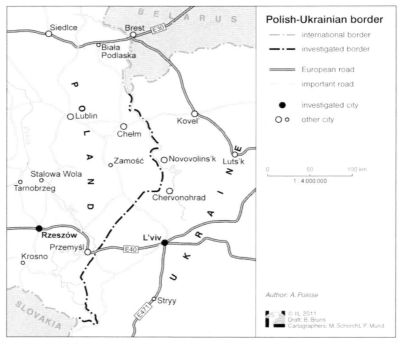

Fig. 2: Polish-Ukrainian border region

2   Redefining borders and their morality

Borders are places of great economic interest where goods are demanded and supplied. They are also areas of tension, not only physically but also symbolically, between the citizen and the state, and the ultimate evidence of limits of control over space by the modern state (see Lefebvre 1974). For the state, violation of the boundaries of legality becomes acute when we approach the political limits of the law or the geographic limits of the state (see Newman 2001). They are also places where individuals can renegotiate state policies that are not tailored for a given context in a way recalling the individual daily resistance conceptualised by Scott (1985). Starting from a perspective that borders, like all state institutions, are 'peopled' (see Jones 2007), this paper regards borders as areas of tensions between individuals and the state. Central to this discourse is the idea of representation. On a border some people may claim to represent the state and others not. However to draw a line between who is the state and who is not seems difficult. Availing the Foucauldian (1980) idea that power is everywhere, I see not only border officers but also common citizens as acting on behalf of the state and showing its multi-facetedness that makes it difficult to distinguish between those acting and those acted in the production of the political (see Navaro-Yashin 2004: 1f.).

The border, the borderland and the way of living it (see Gavrils 2005; Nugent 2002), become places for the production of the political, of actions that go beyond the mere economic interest of the actors (see Abbink 2001; Bruns 2009; Hoehne/Feyissa 2008) but have a political relevance and contribute to reshaping an economic policy. By studying the central role of the border in making and breaking ties between individuals one can shed some light on the way borders reshape human, social and economic relations in transitional countries. In doing so it becomes possible to challenge the notion of borders as monolithic entities to show their permeability and how their function may be affected by human agency. As border officers are also individuals with desires and needs not all decisions imposed from the top might suit them. They are part of a community and are, like others, subject to the social understanding of rules and impositions, of a local understanding of licit and illicit, suggesting that "what determines legality and illegality depends on the origin of regulatory authority, allowing the distinction between political (legal and illegal) and social (licit and illicit) origins of regulatory authority" (van Schendel/Abraham 2005: 17).

When unfavourable conditions apply, i.e. when the state proves unable to meet its citizens' necessities, informal transactions may become a way of engaging in politics (see Gupta 1995), to challenge political decisions that are not tailored for a given context. State impositions might even go against socially constructed habits and behaviours and conflict with them. The reason behind the survival of such habits is their broad social acceptability that conflicts with a legal logic bound to thinking in terms of 'yes' and 'no'.

As a result, more than their role, it may be interesting to concentrate on the function of borders, and living in borderlands (see Gavrilis 2008), and do this in a given context, rather than globally. This would mean concentrating on their narratives rather than their real function and how people perceive and report them (see Herzfeld 2005). In doing so it is possible to conceive borders as spaces, rather than simply as places.

Space may be limiting as a concept because it is often conceived in geography as a setting and scale for people's daily actions and interactions (see Castree 2009). This definition has geographical limits, not only given the role of place based agency, but also given that it varies from place to place (see Gregory 1982; Pred 1986). Such limits have been acknowledged to suggest that the global, the international and people's place based agency are interrelated in what Giddens calls 'structuration' (see Giddens 1984). This approach has shifted attention from an overemphasized historical dimension of phenomena to a more conscious awareness of how deeply dynamics of power, especially those created in capitalism, are inscribed in spatial relations (see Smith 1984; Soja 1989).

Space may be conceived as folded into social relations through practical activities (see Harvey 1996), paving the way to an idea of space as undergoing continual construction as a result of the agency of things encountering each other in more or less organised circulations. Space is no longer viewed as a fixed and absolute container, where things are passively embedded, but as a co-production of those proceedings, as a process in process and this is useful to understand the evolution of border relations and dynamics (see Thrift 2009: 86).

Space, in this case, fulfils two functions; one is to create a place for human interaction, the other to create a space for resistance to state measures. This interpretation of space is due to a misunderstanding between the state and the citizen. A state, to be respected, must not only be a state but also act as a state, that is to fulfil the functions its citizens expect them to (see Polese 2007). Should it fail to do so, people would act accordingly.

State authority lies on a compromise, *a do ut das* between the authorities and the citizens. If the state does not honour the contract, people might not be willing to respect it. As Bourdieu (1977) suggested, individual morality is also a matter of opportunities and people might be willing to forget 'state morality' in some occasions if they can see a benefit in this attitude. The fact that borders are places of high economic interest reshapes human relations. In the case of the border citizens may switch identities and identify with public zealous workers or with unsatisfied and underpaid officers depending on the situation. Some people tend to often change sides and boycott the state only when it is convenient, otherwise they simply exploit the state, and the power derived from it, for personal benefits.

Seeing borders as spaces can help us to overcome the simplistic version of borders as perpetrators of illegal transactions. In particular one can refer to the tendency, visible in scholarship and political circles to condemn, punish, repress informal transactions in any of their manifestations. Although informal economies, and informal payments with them, have long been acknowledged (at least since the ILO 1972 conference) a general tendency of international organizations operating in the region, and national governments, is to declare 'war on illegality' whatever form this takes. This is due to at least two reasons. One is that there is a part of scholarship that eventually supports such claims, i.e. no discount is applicable to a practice that is likely to put a country on its knees (see Papava/Khaduri 2002) and the simplistic statement that 'corruption is evil' (Transparency International USAID among others). The other is that transitional countries often depend on loans from FMI, assistance from the US or EU and other international bodies that urge them to tackle smuggling and corruption (the Ukraine is on the EU border) as soon as possible. If suggestions by international actors are translated into laws, they are better perceived than attempts to motivate unlawful practices and ascribe them to cultural or social factors. In addition figures are often exaggerated to serve parochial institutional interests (see Naylor 2002: x).

This may work in the short but not in the long run. Never in history has a black market been defeated from the supply side (see ibid: 11). In our case, once petty smuggling on the Polish-Ukrainian borders reached a worrying level for the EU, a decision was made not to allow more than 2 packets of cigarettes (instead of the internationally agreed 'one carton') through the border. There is no chance that this has liquidated the demand for income by people living in the border region, but it has changed the rules of the game (as we will see in one case study). Despite its real effectiveness, this sounds solid in the anti illegal trade reports in which it might be omitted, that because of increased border controls, the waiting time is exponentially rising at the border).

By concentrating on the social relations generated by the use of space, one can try to contextualize 'illegal' or 'extra-legal' practices that sometimes become legal in a different context (see de Soto 2001; Polese 2010). Recent empirical work from economists has highlighted the need to look behind informal payments to suggest that they depend, at least in part, on the incapacity of the state to act as a welfare dispenser (see Peter 2005). If state salaries are too low to secure the survival of public workers, they will look for an alternative source of income and this will most likely be in conflict with what the state rules, although it is generated by the fact that the state itself is unable to regulate such situations (see Polese 2006a, 2006b). What if unlawful actions are prompted by poverty that is, in turn, generated by state mismanagement? Informal transactions are strictly dependent on the very action of a state, its management and the kind of coercive power it may exert. This, in turn, also depends on the perception of the state, whether people agree with the devolution of power that many states (or rather their governments) take for granted, forgetting that, to be perceived as a state, one has to act as a state and fulfil its moral and material obligations.

In many cases people, and transactions, are not confronted with state morality until they come across it. Moving a good to sell it from a city to another is not a crime. But crossing a border with the same good might be, if the good is illegal somewhere else or if the quantity transported exceeds the permitted one and no declaration is filled. As a result, people living in places where the state has less influence might find easier to live according to their rules and engage with illegal actions without being aware of it. A teacher living in a remote village may offer private classes to his weakest students, helping them to pass the final test, and being rewarded with money or commodities. The same action in the capital city, where relationships are less personal and that is more under scrutiny from the international community is more likely to be perceived as illegal. Despite a recent ban, teachers continue accepting gratifications in the form of cognac or chocolates, at least until the state outlaws it. Those commodities, it has been shown, can be recycled and provide revenue (see Polese 2008, 2010; Wanner 2005) so that they are not very different from money, which in turn is officially banned and morally inacceptable. On borders, however, there is a direct confrontation with the law, things are either legal or not and this has to be decided quickly, to allow, forbid, or find a price for actions, goods, favours, connections. Due to this direct confrontation between individual morality, state laws and norms that are perceived as socially acceptable (or unacceptable), borders are a good environment for further investigating informal economies. However, because the concept and use of informal economies does not only depend on facts but on perceptions, the interest of borders is twice as high. On the one hand it is important to define what happens at the border and why it happens and on the other it is the perception of what happens, that is whether people think that 'it is wrong' but they do it nevertheless (see Fogarty 2005) or simply do not see this as wrong because a little corruption does not harm anybody (see Rasanyam 2011). Or perhaps they think it is wrong towards the state but they also feel the state is incapable of taking care of their needs and this is their response (see Polese 2006a, 2008).

3 Scenes from a border

L'viv bus station 8am. Groups of people are getting organized to head towards the Ukrainian borders, car drivers offer lifts, people negotiate with bus drivers and discuss among themselves. There are three main ways to cross the Ukrainian-Polish border: the slowest and most expensive is the train, where the wheels have to be changed, for the USSR railway (like the Spanish one) size differing from the Central European. Another way is to take a bus going to a main city, generally Lublin or Warsaw. The most exotic is to take a minibus to the border and cross it on foot. Those wishing to continue may take another minibus to the closest Polish city, Rzeszow, from where they continue their journey. The three ways are main channels of informal trade, though of different nature and modalities.

In many respects the Polish-Ukrainian border looks like a time boundary, with black leather jackets on the Ukrainian side and coloured sport coats on the other. Despite the EU recently investing a large amount of money in border security, also to increase the capacity of Ukrainian border officers, there is still a big difference in attitude between the two sides of the border and the amount of goods smuggled through the border is unknown to many.

The border is a sensitive one, in the sense that huge political and economic interests are at stake. On the one hand we have the European Union, with its desire to control the flux of people, and goods, through their borders, on the other we have the Ukraine that is seeking good relations with the EU, as this means assistance and support, in financial and material terms, and is willing to follow the EU's instructions. This means, conversely from the Moldovan-Ukrainian border, that the official version of the authorities matters. The border is not a no-man's land like Transnistria, on the contrary reports are filed, data recorded and the flux between the two countries monitored. With no responsibility (or even complicity) towards the neighbour country, Ukrainian border officers can allow themselves to simply ask for money, but with the EU controlling, petty negotiations are not in place here. Still, there is a way for most people to benefit from the border.

3.1 A false bottom train

There are few trains in Europe that offer such different conditions to the passengers, depending on the direction of the travel, other than the Berlin-Warsaw-Kiev. Passengers travelling from Berlin will enjoy a relatively smooth trip with Soviet courtesy at the Ukrainian border and elegant business manners from the train inspector to the Ukraine. The point here is not quantity, but quality. Few things are easily sold cheaper in Poland or Germany than in Ukraine so that trade is sporadic, if compared to the other way. Until a few years ago there was an agreement between travel insurance sellers and border officers, that they would send the sellers to compartments hosting foreigners, and then compel them to buy medical insurance to enter Ukraine. The habit seems to no longer exist and the worse annoyance now is the insistent offer of *vareniki*, fish or other eatable products. Smuggling in this direction is discrete, and one could say elitist, with computer accessories or some other small packets passed through the border.

What is more relevant for the researcher, and even more for border officers, is the petty smuggling starting from Kiev and continuing all the way to the Polish border. In that case passengers might face a sleepless night, with energetic ladies jumping across the car, hiding goods and moving them from place to place until the border has passed. They first have to convince the Ukrainian border officers that they are not worth paying attention to. After all, it is known, everyone starting from the *provodnik* (train inspector) is involved in some kind of business. The mere fact of going onto the other side of the border is a potential gain so every chance has to be used. Who does not need some extra money? This is why the train is the festival of short-term benefits.

Ladies aged from 30 to 60 show their vitality and move boxes as big as they are before getting to the Ukrainian border. The kind of movements varies depending on how tough they expect Ukrainian, and then Polish officers to be. To this we can add the variable unemployment and inflation, with people happier to engage in transactions once they need more money. Professional 'traders' have a key to open most doors and a screwdriver to open walls and ceilings like a tin can. The Ukrainian side of the check is normally made by the nose by officers seeking extra revenue in exchange for a blind eye. Thanks to the need to change the wheels time is not short, but never enough to check everybody. Officers might want to look for bigger businessmen, those who expect most of the gain from the trip, often leaving people with small quantities of goods alone. Occasionally, they might want to detain someone just to fill the reports with something.

People who expect big gains from the border crossing on their side also know that such gains do not happen without taxes and partial losses and they will be more than happy to negotiate with Ukrainian border officers.

For this reason the traders have to pack their goods in a way that they seem harmless, dividing big boxes into small bags, distributing them among several compartments or hiding them in other places. The compromise is for traders not to bring 'too much', in the eyes of border officers. The *provodnik* will then negotiate a price with them or the conditions to have a light inspection. Custom officers have to find a way to integrate their income and also have a certain plan to fulfil but, conversely from their Polish counterpart, their main concern is their superiors, who will demand a part of their extra incomes. Thus their task is to check the right people, who can present them with enough money, for money needs to be shared with their superiors. There seems to be little of the civic engagement to the state and the sense of duty that pushes them to act. This 'uncivic' approach has been explored by anthropologists like Roitman (2005) redefining the way people live their citizenship and engage in civic actions or their denial like in the case of fiscal disobedience. Likewise Kyle and Siracusa (2005) also show how failed-to-meet expectations can alter the relationship of citizens with domestic and international laws, prompting them to break laws in search of welfare their country is unable to grant. In such cases social rules come to overlap legal ones and the border between the legal and the licit becomes fluid. Control over the situation is not assured by laws but by informal norms like in the case of traffic police fines that regulate the behaviour of drivers. In the West it would be 'if you do not want to pay a fine, drive consciously' whereas in the Ukraine 'if you want to lower the risk of being harassed by traffic police drive consciously'. The result might be very similar (see Polese 2008) with the difference that in this second case the state loses the extra revenues coming from fines.

The level of prohibition and control the state imposes does nothing but alter the supply-demand relationship and the income of the actors involved. Tougher border controls will not discourage the daily traders but change the prices to be paid at the border, with seasonal higher revenues for custom officers or traders, depending on the context. The only hope for the state may be that controls become so tough that it will not be economically convenient for traders to smuggle cigarettes or alcohol and cease. However, even if this becomes highly burdening, if traders have no other option can they really let things be? Not only their income, but also custom and border officers' income as well as that of their superiors and their families depend on their activity. Border smuggling does not end at the border but benefits a whole set of people from those buying goods to those selling to those who accept bribes and smuggling and corruption will not be eliminated by stopping the trader. This will just change the rules of the game. If smuggling is tackled the state will have to face the issue of low salaries for border officers and unemployment in border regions, which might make things even worse.

Once the Ukrainian side has been passed, the train becomes even more evanescent as the Polish officers are supposed to come and they will apparently show no mercy for petty smugglers. Immune from any bribe attempts, they have a reputation of being insensitive to personal problems and have a black and white approach: either you pass or not. Despite being a common perception among petty traders, this is only half of the picture. True that EU pressure on external borders is such that Poland has seen itself implementing a number of reforms unthinkable some years ago. True also that internal control is such that small bribes will not buy your way into the country. Also true perhaps that custom officers have become much worse since 2004, when Poland joined the EU. In this respect, seeing so many possibilities to earn easy money and not being able to take advantage from might affect their attitude towards petty smugglers.

However Polish custom officers might not be as bad as they are depicted in the account of many Ukrainian 'border traders' I have listened to. The Polish-Ukrainian border is a hot spot, it is well-known that smuggling passes through it and the EU has asked for effective measures to be taken. Due to the level of control, officers are more reticent to accept bribes, although this does not mean that there are no informal agreements. If one has to take a risk at this border, they will not do it for 5 USD as on the other side. They would go for more substantial sums.

Polish officers have something in common with their Ukrainian counterparts. They have to confiscate a quantity of goods big enough to make their superiors happy but will not be rewarded financially. They, in turn, can use the records of confiscated material to show that their controls are effective and they are indeed fighting smuggling through the border. There are no official figures on how many goods are smuggled through the border (if they were available the EU or Poland would be happy to use them to crash such flows) so that a good way to show zealous inspection is to confiscate enough goods. This means no bribes at the Polish borders but tributes to the EU. Custom officers may also understand that those traders have children, need revenue, and not necessarily all of them might be willing to show scorn for their poorer neighbours but also custom officers need to eat, and to do this they need to show some results. The compromise is to confiscate enough goods to show some work has been done, but leaving enough to the traders to make their border crossing worthwhile. Time at the border is also limited, especially on a train, but the quantity of goods found is also seasonal, depending on the expectations of high-level officers and the EU. The train might be opened as a bean can, checking ceilings, walls, toilets or rubbish bins and all parts that could be used to hide goods, or the control will be a fast one, supposing the period of the year, or day of the week, is a quiet one.

Border officers, like other people, seem to incarnate the drama of dual identities. They are individuals and fellow citizens, but also representatives of the state, and this demonstrates a conflict between professional tasks and individual choice that is proper to the state-citizen relationship (see Jones 2007).

4   Alternative ways of crossing

Besides the train, I crossed the border on foot and by bus. Walking through the borders is difficult and not worthwhile for the case study. First of all it is harder to find alliances at the border and everything is done on a personal basis, people are searched individually and they have few places to hide the goods, in addition, they prepare themselves well before the border, so that I could not observe the dynamics I had the chance to observe in other situations. The second hurdle is that this is physically proving. One has to work one's way through using elbows and knees and the concept of a line is an abstract one here. Once you cross you see a settlement grown on informal trade, where people buy the cheapest cigarettes and alcohol in Poland. There is a service for the next city, from where you can reach most Polish destinations, but many people stop here, sell, and return to their place on either side of the border. Not only Ukrainians go to Poland to sell, also Polish cross the border and return to Poland to sell, crossing the border as many times as they can during the day.

Informal trade is all the more visible when crossing by bus. On the way to the border the ladies in the bus start rushing around and open the cigarette cartons to hide single packets wherever they can. Some squeeze 3 or 4 of them into black stockings and hide this 'black sausage' behind the bus curtains. Some others remove the pillow from the seat and hide some underneath it. All places with little light are particularly appreciated, be this the overhead compartment (where the black stockings are hidden as deeply as possible) or other small sections between a seat and the bus walls. Almost everybody changes their clothes to be able to hide some cigarettes under the new, and wider, ones and everybody only keeps the maximum quantity of alcohol and cigarettes allowed in their hand bags ready for inspection.

The border approaches and we queue for inspection. The ladies make their final checks to make sure the cigarettes will not fall out at the wrong moment. Once the time has come, passengers may be asked to leave the bus and take out their personal belongings. The inspection has two dimensions. On the one hand they check every passenger and how many goods they have with them. On the other they check the bus full of nobody's goods, cigarettes that nobody will claim back and that will be confiscated without punishing those trying to pass them through the border. Controls on people and hand luggage have got tougher so the strategy has evolved to become impersonal with teams working together. Everybody hides goods in the bus and remembers where. Some bags are eventually found and taken away. Once back in the bus, traders check who has lost what for the good of the community. Having to find a quantity of cigarettes means the Polish officers will not look at whose they are but go for a certain quantity. Those who have the highest losses will find consolation in that next time it might not be their turn to lose that much and their profit will be higher. I talk of teams because, especially in some buses (like the L'viv-Lublin one) people get into the bus at the same point and come from the same village, showing solidarity with each other. The question of whether what they were doing was acceptable or never arose. As in other cases (see Fogarty 2005; Rasayam 2004; Polese 2006a; van Schendel/Abraham 2005) the boundary was between licit and illicit, leaving the judgement on legality to the officers. As long as we have children, need money and the state does not provide us with enough access to resources, what we are doing is simply to make up for a lack of action of the state. Local moralities overlap, conflict, and partially replace state morality. However local moralities are also subject to certain rules, as the follow-up of this case shows.

Passengers go back into the bus and wait. Only one young lady is sent for and disappears into a custom barrack. Along with alliances and rivalries, sometimes also love, hand in hand with money, is a main feature of daily survival. One of the ladies turns out to have a lover at the border crossing point and is with him while everybody waits for them. Thanks to this asset, other say, she is the bravest one in the bus, carrying far more goods than she would be allowed and securing much higher revenues than the others. This has allowed her to buy some land and build a house where she lives comfortably enough, whilst her village mates struggle to survive.

Most ladies acknowledged that team work is needed to cross the border. Belonging to the same village was another reason to cooperate and no one ever mentioned what they were doing as something they perceived as 'illegal'. However, the relationship with the young border officer put this lady in an ambivalent position. She seemed to be outside the team, able to carry more things but being only partially accepted as part of the village, as some people considered she was selling her body for money. The fact that she enjoyed a higher economic status in some cases was not enough to justify her 'low moral level' and some ladies mentioned they would not do this even if they had the possibility.

There seems to be a dividing line between what you are allowed to do and what is socially acceptable and the above lady seemed to have crossed it. Whilst engaging in an activity widely justified by local norms, she was deliberately violating some principles of her community. The question is what the border was. Was she judged because of making much more money than the others and thus envied? Or because she was mixing love and money? What principles was she violating? They were all going beyond legality but she seemed the only socially stigmatisable. Apparently she was not only violating legal rules but also the principle of licitness existing among her fellow villagers.

After the border was crossed nobody hurried to retrieve their goods. There was still a chance of a hidden control before the first village. Once the chances lowered, they set out to check who had lost what and changed back into "normal" clothes. Normally the driver stops the bus and they buy huge nets of onions, that for some reason are cheaper in Poland than in the Ukraine and can be sold back home. Meat is another of the goods to buy in Poland and sell in the Ukraine but it is riskier. First of all transporting meat is not permitted across the border, secondly meat is a perishable good and it might go off (especially in the summer) or be confiscated whereas onions are more innocent in many respects.

Such buses and ways to cross the borders are quite frequent along the Polish-Ukrainian border and people do this on a regular, often daily, basis. A question that is still puzzling is the gender dimension, for most of the traders were ladies. To conduct a study on the gender dimension of this trade would be extremely interesting. At this stage I can only speculate on the fact that this job requires little physical efforts (although high levels of stress), whereas men can be employed in construction or agricultural works. Another point might be the social status of those women and that they only engage in such transactions if their husbands' revenues are not enough, this may imply that the husband is not working, has problems with alcoholism, or is gone.

5   Concluding remarks

The trade in the proximity of the Polish-Ukrainian border described in this paper seems in contrast with the values a state, and in this case the Ukraine, is willing to propose and accept. However, despite an official discourse condemning contraband, the petty trade in which people engage is often perceived as something socially acceptable by the traders themselves and, in some respect, even by border officers. The Bourdieuan (1977) gap between state and individual morality finds empirical application in this research, where people choose to subscribe to a state or individual moral code depending on the opportunities they offer. Underground economies are related to institutional failure (see Bovi 2003). A weak state means uncontrolled revenues, no income taxes paid and, even more importantly, a distorted perception of the role of the state. In such cases the state may be perceived as limiting initiative and activities whilst bringing no real advantage to the loyal citizen. As Bovi (2003: 67) and Layoza (1996) noticed, where the state is able to protect its citizens and offer some advantages, or at least perspectives of change, people would be more willing to act in the frame of legality. In the case above people might not want to abide because control is only partially enforced. However, this also happens because allowing people to survive on the verge of illegality is a way to make up for ineffective economic reforms that affect some regions in particular. Owing to necessity, people seem to have constructed a grey area between legality and illegality in their narrative when they use expressions already present in other geographical contexts such as 'signs of attention' (see Patico 2002), 'little corruption' (that does not hurt anyone; see Rasanayagam 2003, 2011) or construct social norms to survive legal impositions (see Harrison 1999).

In such a context informal payments are not necessarily an example of the degradation of society. On the contrary, they participate in creating an independent – and possibly uncontrollable – economic system in which the state officially forbids, but in reality allows, and the people officially abide by the rules, but also know how to increase their revenues. All actors are satisfied, limiting economic discontent and avoiding social tensions. Such petty trade may be seen as the solution, rather than the cause, to problems such as high unemployment and low revenues. When few people are willing – or allowed – to invest in domestic companies, goods are hard to find and money scarcely circulates, informal payments, networks, *blat'* seem a possible solution. This situation is also convenient for political elites, especially when they are unable to engage in effective reforms. Border officers will not object since they can top up their salary and ordinary people can break up a vicious circle preventing them from earning money and access some goods at a price cheaper than the domestic one.

References

Abbink, J. (2001): "Creating Borders: Exploring the Impact of the Ethio-Eritrean War on the Local Population". In: Africa (Rome), 56, 4, pp. 447-458.

Abraham, I. / van Schendel, W. (2005): "Introduction: The Making of Illicitness". In: W. van Schendel and I. Abraham (eds.): Illicit Flows and Criminal Things: States, Borders, and the Other Side of Globalization. Bloomington: Indiana University Press, pp. 1-37.

Bovi, M. (2003): "The Nature of the Underground Economy-Some Evidence from OECD Countries". In: JIIDT, 7, pp. 60-70.

Bourdieu, P. (1977): Outline of a Theory of Practice. Cambridge: Cambridge University Press.

Bruns, B. (2009): Grenze als Ressource: Die soziale Organisation von Schmuggel am Rande der europäischen Union. Wiesbaden: VS Verlag für Sozialwissenschaften.

Castree, N. (2009): "Place: Connections and Boundaries in an Interdepent World". In: N. Clifford, S. Holloway, S. Rice and G. Valentine (eds): Key Concepts in Geography. London: Sage, pp. 153-172.

Fogarty, P. (2005): 'We all do it and we all think it's bad': Discourses and Practices of Corruption in Moldova. Paper presented at the Workshop: Emerging Citizenship and Contested Identities between the Dniester, Prut and Danube Rivers, 10 and 11 March, Max Planck Institute for Social Anthropology.

Foucault, M. (1980): Power/Knowledge: Selected Interviews and Other Writings 1972-1977. Ed. and transl. by C. Gordon. New York: Pantheon.

Giddens, A. (1984): The Constitution of Society. Cambridge: Polity Press.

Gregory, D. (1982): Regional transformation and industrial revolution: A Geography of the Yorkshire Wollen Industry. Minneapolis: University of Minnesota Press.

De Soto, H. (1989): The Other Path: the Economic Answer to Terrorism. New York: Basic Books.

De Soto, H. (2000): The Mystery of Capital: Why Capitalism Triumphs in the West and Fails Everywhere Else. New York: Basic Books.

Foucher, M. (1991): Fronts et frontiers. Paris: Fayard.

Gavrilis, G. (2008): The Dynamics of Interstate Boundaries. Cambridge: Cambridge University Press.

Gorodnichenko, Y. / Peter, K.S. (2006): Public Sector and Corruption: Measuring Bribery from Micro Data. IZA Discussion Paper No. 1987, URL: http://www-personal.umich.edu/~ygorodni/private-public-Gorodnichenko-Peter-2006-01-25.pdf (last access: 13.03.2010).

Gupta, A. (1995): "Blurred Boundaries: The discourse of Corruption, the Culture of Politics, and the Imagined State". In: American Ethnologist, 22, 2, pp. 375-402.

Harrison, G. (1999): "Corruption, development theory and the boundaries of social change". In: Contemporary Politics, 5, 3, pp. 207-220.

Harvey, D. (1986): Justice, Nature and the Geography of Difference. Oxford: Basil Blackwell.

Herzfeld, M. (2005): Cultural Intimacy. Cambridge: Harvard University Press.

Hoehne, M. V. / Feyissa, D. (2008): Resourcing state borders and borderlands in the Horn of Africa. Working papers, Max-Planck-Institute for Social Anthropology.

ILO (1972): Employment, Incomes and Equality: A Strategy for Increasing Productive Employment in Kenya. Geneva: ILO.

Jones, R. (2007): People, States, Territories. Oxford: Blackwell.

Lefebvre, H. ([1974] 1991): The Production of Space. Oxford: Blackwell.

Miller, W. L. / Grodeland, A. B. / Koshechkina, T. Y. (2000): "Victims or Accomplices? Extortion and bribery in Eastern Europe". In: A. Ledeneva and M. Kurkchiyan (eds.): Economic Crime in Russia. London: Kluwer Law International, pp. 113-128.

Navaro-Yashin, Y. (2002): Faces of the State. Princeton/NJ: Princeton University Press.

Naylor, R. T. (2002): Wages of Crime: Black Markets, Illegal Finance, and the Underworld Economy. Ithaca/NY: Cornell University Press.

Newman, D. B. (2001): "Borders and Barriers: Changing Geographic Perspectives on Territorial Lines". In: M. Albert, D. Jacobsen and Y. Lapid (eds.): Identities, Borders, Orders: Rethinking International Relations Theory. Minneapolis: University of Minnesota Press, pp. 137-151.

Nugent, P. (2002): Smugglers, Secessionists and Loyal Citizens on the Ghana-Togo Frontier. Athens: Ohio University Press.

Papava, V. / Khaduri, N. (1997): "On the Shadow Political Economy of the Post Communist Transformation, an Institutional Analysis". In: Problems of Economic Transitions, 40, 6, pp. 15-34.

Patico, J. (2002): "Chocolate and Cognac: Gifts and the Recognition of Social Worlds in Post-Soviet Russia". In: Ethnos, 67, 3, pp. 345-368.

Polese, A. (2006a): "Border Crossing as a Daily Strategy of Post Soviet Survival: the Odessa-Chisinau Elektrichka". In: Eastern European Anthropology Review, 24, 1, pp. 28-37.

Polese, A. (2006b): Paying for a Free Education. Transitions On Line, Prague (08.08.2006).

Polese, A. (2007): Ukraine: the State is Public, the Private Sector is Private, the Public Sector is…?. Presented at the Workshop on Property in Eastern Europe, New European College, Bucharest 14 and 15 June 2007

Polese, A. (2008): "'If I Receive it, it is a Gift; if I Demand it, then it is a Bribe': On the Local Meaning of Economic Transactions in Post-Soviet Ukraine". In: Anthropology in Action, 5, 3, pp. 47-60.

Polese, A. (2010): At the origins of informal economies: some evidence from Ukraine (1991-2009). Friedrich Schiller University of Jena, Working Paper.

Pred, A. (1986): Place, Practice and Structure: social and spatial transformation in southern Sweden. Cambridge: Polity Press.

Rasanayagam, J. (2003): Market, State and Community in Uzbekistan: Reworking the Concept of the Informal Economy. Max Planck Working Papers no.59.

Roitman, J. (2005): Fiscal Disobedience: An Anthropology of Economic Regulation in Central Africa. Princeton/N.J: Princeton University Press.

Scott, J. (1985): Weapons of the Weak. Heaven, London: Yale University Press.

Smith, N. (1984): Uneven Development: Nature, Capital, and the Production of Space. Oxford: Blackwell.

Soja, E. (1989): Postmodern Geographies: The Reassertion of Space in Critical Social Theory. London, New York: Verso.

Temple, P. / Petrov, G. (2004): "Corruption in Higher Education: Some Findings from the States of the Former Soviet Union". In: Higher Education Management and Policy, 16, 1, pp. 83-99.

Thrift, N. (2009): "Space: The Fundamental Stuff of Geography". In: G. Valentine, S. Holloway and N. Clifford (eds.): Key Concepts in Geography. London: Sage, pp. 85-95.

Wanner, C. (2005): "Money, Morality and New Forms of Exchange in Postsocialist Ukraine". In: Ethnos, 70, 4, pp. 515-537.

Cross-border trade and identity in the Afghan-Iranian border region

Just Boedeker

1   Introduction

During research among the Baloch people in the Afghan-Iranian border region it became apparent that many of the tribesmen were engaged in illicit trade. For this reason, this article deals with cross-border trade among the Baloch confronted with the institutions of territorial nation states. It should demonstrate why illicit trade is considered legitimate from a Baloch perspective while it interferes with the territorial demands of the bordering nation states. In this context these practices cannot be reduced to a purely functional meaning as they are not just a coping strategy for economic constraints. As I will underline, socio-cultural and historic aspects should be included in the discussion. It will be shown that the neighbouring states were not able to establish their institutions and national boundaries beyond a certain degree of indirect rule until recently and are still perceived as a quasi colonial power interfering in Baloch affairs.

This article mainly deals with the following questions: Why does smuggling play such a major role in this area? Why are Baloch identities so determined by disobedience and rebellious concepts against institutions of nation states and border control? Which consequences does this have for the perceptions of national boundaries?

In the first two parts I will present the concept as well as the methodological approach and the circumstances of the fieldwork. Then, I will introduce some aspects of the recent history of the borderlands and some socio-cultural aspects to explain why national boundaries did not play a crucial role until recently. Thereafter, I will present three examples of illicit trade I was confronted with during research. In the description of the contrasting perspectives on illicit trade of the Baloch interlocutors and the representations of nation states there is a focus on the Baloch point of view as research was not been conducted among representatives of the border regime. Finally, I will outline the interrelations between the historic and socio-cultural circumstances with the current practices of cross-border trade. As from a Baloch perspective the word 'smuggling' gives a pejorative meaning to a business which is perceived as a legitimate activity, I will avoid this term in the description of their activities.

2   Concept

As Donnan and Wilson underline in their work on 'borders', an anthropological focus on international borders illuminates the exercise of political power between supranationalism from above and ethnonationalism from below (see Donnan/Wilson 1999: 1). This article on cross-border trade in the Baloch borderlands exemplifies two different images of frontiers and the surrounding borderlands struggling for dominance: On the one hand two different nation states with more or less pronounced national boundaries underlining national territorial integrity, on the other hand Baloch people living in the borderlands with a high degree of mobility in the framework of plurilocal and transnational kinship networks (see Schindler 2008). Consequently there are two different spatial perceptions interfering on the matter of cross-border trade both symbolizing different exercises of political power. The main focus is on the meaning of cross-border trade for the network-orientated highly mobile Baloch society and some of its cultural practices confronted with a frontier representing the territorial requirements of apparently foreign powers. In this context cross-border trade exceeds the perception of cross-border trade as a strategy for coping with poverty or the prevention of poverty and some historic and cultural aspects affecting the perception of illicit trade as a part of a Baloch identity have to be involved.

While the national frontier marking different exercises of customs and subsidies are the precondition for at least part of this trade, the territorial claims of the bordering nation states are neglected by most of the Baloch traders. This paradox results partly from the historical background of this certain area, which served as a kind of shatter zone or refuge area between the bordering imperial powers.

3   Methodological approach and circumstances of fieldwork

During my research on transnational identities of the Baloch people in the Afghan-Iranian border region, I conducted three fieldworks in Kabul and the Baloch areas in southwest Afghanistan and southeast Iran in 2008, 2009 and 2010. During these ethnographic fieldtrips I adopted the methods of participant observance, living in Baloch families to "grasp the native's point of view" (Malinowski 1922: 25)[6] and to study their perceptions of the international border

---

1   This famous citation of Malinowski who established the method of participant observance in
       Ethnology indicates the final goal of which an Ethnographer should never lose sight: „This
       goal is, briefly, to grasp the native's point of view, his relation to life, to realise *his* vision of

between Afghanistan and Iran. The dominant question of this research was how Baloch identities are built in an area mainly populated by Baloch people but separated in different state structures.

I lived in different Baloch households located in Kabul, the province of Nimruz in south-western Afghanistan and in the Iranian province of Sistan and Balochistan mainly in the surrounding area of the cities Zabul and Zahedan. In Afghanistan my main informants were activists of a recent Baloch national movement. On the Iranian side of the border my hosts were active in the transport and trade of fuel on different levels. Apart from my own hosts I had the opportunity to speak to a number of Baloch individuals active in opium trading or transferring Afghan workers to their Iranian destinations. Talking about these businesses considered as smuggling from the perspective of the Iranian authorities is hardly a secret matter and not even very conspirative. Evidence of these unofficial trades is easily seen when taking public or private transport between different cities in the Iranian border region; obvious instances of transportation of Afghan workers on pickup trucks between Iranian army checkpoints and long rows of oil drums of unofficial fuel traders on both sides of the border are clearly visible. Even for the people involved in this business talking about their work is hardly a matter of concern but rather a theme that is proudly presented during a friendly conversation. As recorded interviews tend to generate a more formal atmosphere among the interviewed I preferred to take written notes and minutes from memory on this matter.

4   Introducing the Baloch settlement areas

Today the Baloch people live in a closed settlement area in the border regions of the nation states of Pakistan, Iran and Afghanistan. In the course of their history this region has been at the crossroads of the powers of Iran, India and Afghanistan, a kind of shatter zone between the great powers. National frontiers were demarcated by the British at the end of the 19th century (Durand Line and Goldsmid Line between 1894 and 1896) however the border areas were hardly controlled by any national authority until recently. Between 1666 and 1947 parts of the Pakistani area were ruled by the Baloch kings of Kalat (khanate of Kalat). However, these rulers barely managed to govern the whole area, which was mainly under the control of several local leaders. Even under British rule from 1839, control was basically gained through subsidies for the tribal chiefs and indirect rule. As Brian Spooner showed, the scarce Baloch settlement area acted

his world. We have to study man, and we must study what concerns him most intimately, that is, the hold which life has on him."

for centuries as a hideaway for different threatened tribes from the neighbouring political powers of Afghanistan, Iran and India. Yet due to the natural conditions no political centres were established in this territory. The Baloch have subsumed and incorporated these later immigrant groups who accepted the Baloch language as a lingua franca. So in a way these groups became 'Balochised' without the establishment of any superior political structure. Being a Baloch traditionally meant that "no group allowed themselves to become subordinated to non-Baluch" (Spooner 1969: 149). Therefore this region became the 'lands of dissidence' a kind of 'shatter zone' between the great powers (see Spooner 1983). As the following historical descriptions from outsiders illustrate, great parts of the Baloch settlement areas were not under any direct control and were perceived as lawless regions.

Land of the disobedient

At the end of the 19th and the beginning of the 20th centuries, representatives of the British army and the colonial government in India described Balochistan and especially the Sarhad, a mountainous region south of Zahedan, as a mainly lawless and wild region. Curzon, who was viceroy of India between 1898 and 1905, mentions that in 1885 Captain R.H. Jennings, an officer deputed by the Indian Government and the first (European) to penetrate the region, refers to the term Yaghistan, the country of the Yaghis, for this region and further denotes that the inhabitants of the Sarhad basically obtained their subsistence by rapine (see Curzon 1892: 262/263). The term $Y\bar{a}\dot{g}\bar{\iota}$ can be translated as disobedient or rebel. The term Yaghistan is equivalent to "land of the disobedient" (Nölle-Karimi 2005: 177). But this term is also applied in the discussion on the complex relation of the Pashtun Ghilzai tribes in Afghanistan with the concepts of government or state. Anderson describes this relationship as "a continuous play of integration and disintegration". He further denotes: "What they put in opposition are the activity and seats of government (hokumat, where governing takes place) to the land of freedom or unrestraint (yaghistan), as points on the plain. Yaghistan is where no man is above another, in contrast to hokumat where there are governors and governed" (Anderson 1983: 125).

The 'wild Baloch marauders' and social banditry

In other descriptions the region of the Sarhad is denominated as a "nest of robbers" (Sykes 1902: 93). And Baloch tribes of this region were portrayed as bandits "constantly raiding across the frontier" (Sykes 1902: 230 N.1) and General Dyer of the British army even wrote "the tribes literally live by raiding" (Dyer 1921: 42). A decade later Coleridge Kennard mentions a "Baluch raiding army" (Kennard 1927: 185) consisting of about a thousand men. And the famous British travel writer Rosita Forbes wrote in a book published in 1931 about the "wild Baloch marauders" (Forbes 1931: 142).

Beside these historic perceptions of Baloch tribes by Europeans, raiding and forms of rebellions against superior powers from the outside have played a major role for Baloch identities and their cultural memory to this day. Predatory raiding has been an important issue for Sarhadi tribes for their subsistence. According to Salzman, "the exploitation of these 'resources' of the socio-cultural environment provided substantial income for the tribesmen. This raiding fitted with the tribesmen's self-conception as warriors rather than labourers" (Salzman 1971: 442). "Furthermore," he specifies, "the Sarhadi adaption, with its dependence upon territorial mobility, resulted in a population less vulnerable to political or military control. Consequently, political authority on the Sarhad Plateau was highly restricted; authority status was that of the first among equals, and leadership was based upon consent" (ibid: 443). This correlates with egalitarian concepts among the Pashtun neighbours of the Baloch, as the founder of the Durrani rule in Afghanistan, Ahmad Shah Durrani (1747-73), was designated as *primus inter pares* (*durr-i durrān*, pearl of the pearls) (see Glatzer 1983: 226).

The historical topos of the 'wild Baloch' depending on rapine and raiding can be partially explained by the tough ecological conditions of Balochistan. Its hostile deserts and dangerous mountains and the "dependence of the tribesmen upon scanty and erratic rainfall for local production, and their vulnerability in the face of frequent, recurrent, and serious droughts" (Salzman 2000: 135) certainly often forced them to raid. On this matter Salzman notes for the Sarhad: "The Sarhad could not sustain pastoralism and runoff cultivation as anything but the riskiest adaptations, unless there was a reliable inflow of resources. Raiding guaranteed that inflow" (ibid.). Likewise the Baloch engagement in illicit trade in the area of research can be partly explained by a serious drought which destroyed large parts of the agricultural lands coinciding with the Taliban rule.[7]

However, apart from these ecological constraints there also exists another motivation among the Baloch for ignoring the rules of the bordering nation states: The topic of the Baloch combatant fighting for his freedom against a superior power plays an important role in their cultural memory. The incident of Dadshah exemplifies the image of this kind of Baloch rebel (*Yāġī*) or Bandit

---

7   This drought is perceived by many Afghans as the divine Nemesis for the crimes committed by the Taliban (see Rzehak 2004: xxi, FN14).

(*šarīr*) (see Šahbaxš 1994/1995: 52). He was a lineage leader of the Mobareki[8] tribe who started a rebellion resulting from a tribal conflict of two Baloch confederations struggling for the political power in the southeast area of Iranian Balochistan. In the context of this conflict he opposed the Iranian authorities in the middle of the 1940s. While from the point of view of the Iranian authorities he was nothing more than the leader of a 'bandit gang' terrorizing rich and poor alike, according to the Baloch legend he carried out his exploits in a Robin Hood fashion, "harassing Iranian police and army outposts and robbing rich Baluch feudal lords to help the impoverished nomads" (Harrison1981: 104). The conflict escalated on March 24, 1957, when Dadshah and 24 of his men killed an American military aid official, his wife and an American contractor (Kevin and Anita Caroll, Brewster Wilson). This happened at the gully of the river Sarhe on a mountainous track leading from Iranshahr to the southern coast of the Gulf of Oman. As Dadshah later described this killing was a mistake because he and his group thought they were attacking a party of Iranian officials. "In American eyes, however, the case had disturbing and sinister aspects that made it a front-page sensation until Dadshah was killed in gun battle with Iranian police ten months later" (ibid.). As Dadshah conducted daredevil skirmishes with his pursuers during these ten months and he died in battle refusing to surrender, he became a legend. Nevertheless during his rebellion his followers never numbered more than forty or fifty. Many stories were written about him, poems composed and fairytales and proverbs about this theme are still recited (see Šahbaxš 1994/1995: 53).

Baloch perceptions of national frontiers

In the spatial perceptions of many Baloch the Iranian-Afghan frontier has merely a divisive rather than a seperative meaning. As I realised during my fieldwork most Baloch do not experience their living space separated by national boundaries, as many of them have travelled to Afghan or Pakistani Baloch areas to visit their relatives or for trading purposes. They did not think of geography in terms of national entities such as Iran and Pakistan with clear-cut borders; they experienced the territory inhabited by the Baloches as 'Balochistan' referring to national membership only by phrases like: *e ša āškā āt-ā* (Balochi: 'He came from the other side'). Consequently identification with the bordering nation states and their administrative centres like Tehran, Islamabad or Kabul is less distinctive than their identification with lineage networks which might reach to

---

8   The tribal centre of the Mobareki, a south-western Baloch tribe, is located in Fanuj.

places as far as Muscat, Nairobi or London. Family networks are expanding across national frontiers and identification with the own patriline is considerably more pronounced than the acceptance of nation state institutions.

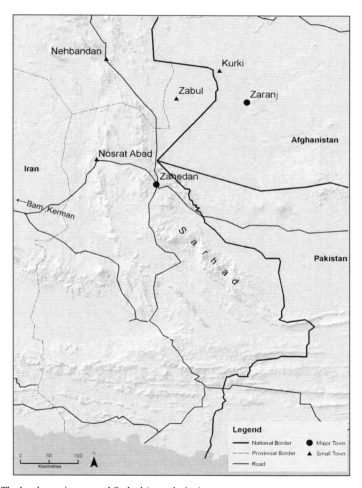

Fig. 3:   The border region around Sarhad (own design)

An experience of Philipp Carl Salzman during his fieldwork in the 1970s in the border region of the Sarhad illustrates this spatial perception vividly:

"Upon my arrival in Pushti Kamal, I told people, that I came from America. Halil, the headman of the Dadolzai camp, at that time located next to the Halki Ja'far; asked if America was as far as Tehran. At first I took this to mean that Halil wondered if America would be as close as Tehran, but I later understood that what he meant was what he said: he wondered if America was as far as Tehran. For Halil and most other Sarhadi Baluch, Tehran was a vast distance in space and also in culture and ethnicity. So when Sarhadi Baluch thought of leaving the Sarhad to work for wages, they usually thought of Pakistan, the southern coast of Iran, and the Arabian emirates." (Salzman 2000: 138)

Therefore, mobility plays a dominant role in the border region and many Baloch associate themselves with a number of locations corresponding to their plurilocal (see Schindler 2008) lineage networks. This mobility mainly takes place within an area which is perceived as Balochistan resembling a kind of spell or 'security circle'. As in former times Baloch nomads accomplished judiciary and executive functions in an area perceived as a 'security circle' (see Scholz 1974a: 40/59). This concept is expanded on the border region of Iran, Afghanistan and Pakistan. Within this area the Baloch way of life predominates, which for example, is expressed in Iran through a Baloch dress code (*lebās-e Balōčī*).

An unofficial border crossing which is illegal according to Iranian law makes social and economic resources accessible that are denied to the populations remotely located from the border regions. According to this, both of my host families in Iran had relatives on the Afghan side of the border who they visited more or less regularly. For the general transit over the border between Iran and Afghanistan my informants generally preferred to use illegal side routes instead of the official border crossing. In their perception the Baloch as a border tribe are entitled to cross the border without being controlled by the border police and without any international permits. When I was approaching the Afghan-Iranian border from Afghanistan it was obvious that the illegal passages next to the official border crossing were used more frequently than the official one.

By cultivating cross-border lineage ties the Baloch put themselves in the position to gain both social and economic resources. So, one member of the Narui[9] tribe who held the position of a tribal elder expanded his influence by resolving tribal affairs in the border region. For example, he organised the transfer of the corpse of an Afghan Pashtun to Afghanistan who died in Iran or he negotiated compensation payments for an Iranian Baloch who was killed in a conflict with a Pashtun over smuggling matters. Similar to their Pashtun neighbours tribal elders seem to enlarge their reputation among the tribesmen through successful negotiations with state institutions (see Glatzer 1977: 172).

---

9   Narui is a comparably populous Baloch tribe settled particularly in Iran and Afghanistan, but also in Pakistan. Nosrat Abad is perceived as their tribal centre, today, although parts of the tribe are scattered in many different regions.

As this tribal elder had both Baloch and Pashtun origin and as he had tribal brothers on both sides of the border he was suitable for solving these transborder affairs thus gaining social prestige in his lineage and tribe and even among the neighbouring tribes in the border region. As this example and the following examples of cross-border trade illustrate, national frontiers are to all intents and purposes a source of social and economic resources. In contrast to this implication the separating effect of these boundaries is widely neglected and any form of border or state control is perceived as an illegitimate intrusion in Baloch affairs.

5   Different kinds of unofficial trading

Fig. 4:   Close to the border, 2008: Children conveying Iranian cement

The region of my research is considered to be the gateway of smuggling between Afghanistan and Iran. There are a variety of contrabands traded in this region. From Afghanistan the most prominent export product is opium and its derivatives heroine and morphine. Another important area of cross border trade is weapons. To that effect you can find illegal firearms in many Baloch households mainly imported from Afghanistan. In addition there is a large range of traded products the Iranian government imposes import tariffs on, such as cars or electronic devices. Many of these products are imported through Iranian ports, brought to Afghanistan in sealed containers and then re-imported by Baloch traders bypassing or bribing the Iranian customs police. There are also some animate imports like large herds of camels bought in Afghanistan to sell at a much higher price in Iran. Apart from this, work migration from Afghanistan is organised through people smuggling in the border region. From Iran, the main contraband goods bypassing the Iranian customs laws are cheap and often subsided goods produced in Iran. The most obvious goods imported from Iran are fuels. In the following I will describe three fields of unofficial trading I was confronted with during my fieldwork and some dimensions of their impact.

Fuel trade

Illegal fuel trade was most obvious on both sides of the border. In Afghanistan you could see long rows of oil drums in one of the central streets of Zaranj, a small city close to the Iranian border. The number of these barrels was completely oversized for this small settlement in the south-western periphery of Afghanistan. Close to the border crossing pickups could be seen coming from Iran bringing large amounts of 20-litre cans which were reloaded on the donkeys of children bringing them to Zaranj.

On the other side of the border unofficial fuel traders sitting under their umbrellas were also selling fuel either to traders bringing it in the direction of the borders or to motorists who had used up their allocated ration of subsidised fuel. Recently a rationing system was setup whereby motorists receive a determined monthly allocation of subsided fuel stored on their magnetic strip petrol cards (*kart-e benzīn*). As this ration is not sufficient for many motorists, they have to cover their consumption partly from the illegal market. The reasons for fuel trading become abundantly clear when you have a look at petrol or diesel prices while approaching the border. In the vicinity of the Afghan or Pakistani frontier, prices rise considerably. Therefore, unofficial trade even starts in Iranian territory at a certain distance from the border.

One of my hosts worked in this business supplying the diesel trade from the provincial capital of Zahedan to the border town of Zabul. He had a dumper truck with a secret fuel tank between the double bottom of his vehicle. This way he and his driver could convey two thousand litres of diesel twice a day with an apparently empty truck. So he earned more than the equivalent of two hundred Euro a day and more than four thousand Euro a month. Fuel trade also takes place on a smaller scale: another host had a small bus for public transport. He received highly subsidised fuel from the government as he was apparently conducting public services. As there were not many customers while I was there he sold his fuel on the black market and generated a daily income of 13.20 Euro. Compared to the first example this is not very lucrative but it is less risky. At the end of my stay the owner of the dumper truck was caught by the police at a checkpoint and they confiscated his truck. He managed to get it back thanks to a bribe of some thousand Euro, sold the truck and was thinking of buying a bus since public transport was the current camouflage for fuel trading. This trend resulted in extremely regular public transport between Zahedan and Zabul. There were countless buses starting every few minutes not waiting until they were completely loaded with passengers as it is common in other Iranian regions. After the passengers had disembarked in Zabul at the bus terminal they turned right into a neighbourhood where workshops specialised in unloading buses and trucks. Mainly Afghan migrants live and work in these workshops. They pumped portions of fuel out of the tanks of the vehicles and unloaded twenty-litre cans by hand in oil barrels similar to the ones I saw on the Afghan side of the border one year earlier. The dangers of using public transport for fuel smuggling also became apparent during my stay when one bus caught fire because of its inflammable load and completely burnt out. Luckily none of the passengers were injured or died; they just lost their luggage.

A Baloch fuel trader I met in Kabul in 2010 proudly described how he was circumnavigating the checkpoints of the Iranian forces at Nosrat Abad and 25 kilometres northwest of Zahedan with his Toyota pickup through side roads in the mountains. At the same time he was bringing fuel from Bam to the Afghan side of the plain of Sistan. His old pickup was upgraded with a stronger engine and the gearbox of a new Toyota model to make it more suitable for the tracks which were off-road for the main part. Baloch traders always drive in convoys of several cars each loaded with about 1400 litres of fuel to help each other in case of a breakdown. The trip lasts up to two days with a profit of about 200 US Dollar. He himself had several serious accidents leading to the destruction of his vehicle but never to personal injury. He and many others said a very large number of Baloches involved in this business had died as a result of accidents. Nevertheless, these stories were proudly presented and my informant even showed me a self-made film of dozens of Toyota pickups loaded with contraband in the Afghan border village of Kurki underlayed with a Baloch song.

People 'smuggling'

According to a current UNHCR (United Nations High Commissioner for Refugees) report there are about 930,000 registered Afghans living in Iran[10] and according to an estimate by the Afghan Research and Evaluation Unit (see AREU 2006: 2) there were about 500,000 single Afghan labour migrants in 2004. This number has probably not changed considerably since. The gateways for this migration are the Iranian provinces of Khorasan and Sistan and Balochistan. As there are several army checkpoints in these areas bypassing them has to be organised by local population groups.

Fig. 5:   2008: Afghan work migrants approaching the Afghan-Iranian border

On the Afghan side of the border Afghans from different tribes and areas of the country come to the vicinity of the international frontier to wait for their transit to Iran. Baloch tribesmen organise their transit from the Afghan city of Zaranj. The prices depend on the distances of the final destinations from the border: In 2008 crossing the border cost about 150 Dollar and the transfer to more distant

---

10   See http://www.unhcr.org/pages/49e486f96.html (last access: 08.04.2010).

places like Kerman and Tehran were accordingly more expensive, up to several hundred dollars.

During my residence in Iran I travelled several times between the cities of Zabul and Zahedan. During these trips I saw several pickups loaded with a number of more or less hidden people, especially at night. Close to the army checkpoints they jumped out of the cars, ran in the direction of the mountains to bypass the checkpoint on side paths and after the mountains their transport was waiting to bring them to Zahedan. On another occasion I took the bus from Zahedan to Kerman. After half of the distance I was confronted with the most conscientious army checkpoint I ever experienced in Iran: policemen searched the luggage of every single passenger and checked all passports. Yet just a few hundred metres after this checkpoint motorcycles were bringing migrants through small tracks in the mountains. After their arrival, people waited for transport to the next destination. One of my acquaintances in Zahedan also told me about his transportation of several Afghans from Zabul to Zahedan and he proudly described how he and his companion circumnavigated a checkpoint close to Zabul through remote tracks in the desert, escaping from persecutors and bypassing the checkpoint close to Zahedan on mountain tracks. He was impressed by the strength of about twenty Afghans sitting on the platform of their pick-up enduring all the strains of their journey. He accentuated that Iranians would not be able to stand these tough conditions. The driver of my host working in the fuel trade, decided after the confiscation of the dumper truck to restart smuggling Afghan work migrants from Zahedan to Kerman. As he had a fast Peugeot car he could transport four or five workers for the price of two or three hundred dollars each.

Opium trading

The production of opium in Afghanistan has been rising constantly since the invasion of the Soviets in 1979 as it was important for financing different rebellious groups especially in the southern provinces of Afghanistan bordering the Baloch settlement area. In 2007, according to the World Drug Report 2009, the world's largest quantities of opium (427mt or 84% of the global total) and heroine (16mt or 25% of the world total) were seized in Iran and the world's second largest morphine seizures were also reported by the Islamic Republic (10mt, following Pakistan with 11mt or 40% of the global total; see UNODC 2009: 41). Therefore, the United Nations Office on Drugs and Crime estimates that 83% of the opium exports from Afghanistan cross the border into the Islamic Republic of Iran either directly from Afghanistan or via Pakistan (see ibid.: 44).

Iran has one of the highest consumption prevalences of opium in the world. According to the UNODC (United Nations Office on Drugs and Crime) the estimate is 1.5-3.2% compared to the German estimate of 0.14-0.29% (see ibid: 235ff.)[11].

In Afghanistan the province of Nimruz with its centre Zaranj is one of the most important intersections for the distribution of opium and its derivates. Under Taliban rule the Baloch tribe of the Brahui[12] managed to become one of the major players in this business. Until the 1970s the Brahui had played a marginal role in this region as a result of their nomadic lifestyle and their specialization in camel breeding in remote desert areas of Nimruz. According to one of my informants in Iran this lifestyle was even a reason for their advancement during the Taliban regime. According to him the Brahui had a strong commitment to Baloch customary law thanks to pastoral nomadism, which resembled the customary law of the Pashtun Taliban, the Pashtunwali. Hajji Jom'a Khan, a member of this tribe, is said to have established a network moving an estimated one billion dollars worth of opium a year (see Peters 2009: 26ff.). According to this source, his network included a force of 1,500 armed men, he maintained a network of corrupt government officials in Afghanistan, South Asia and the Persian Gulf, he moved a fleet of cargo ships between the Pakistani port city of Karachi and the United Arab Emirate of Sharjah and he maintained about 200 residences in Afghanistan, Pakistan, United Arab Emirates and Iran. In Zaranj he owned a heavily palatial compound next to the governor's mansion. According to an article published in New York Times in December 2010 Central Intelligence Agency (CIA) officers and Drug Enforcement Administration (DEA) agents relied on him as a valued source for years and were also paying a large amount of cash. This source even indicates that "Mr. Juma Khan was secretly flown to Washington for a series of clandestine meetings with CIA and DEA officials in 2006" (Risen 2010). At the end of my stay in Afghanistan in October 2008 he was lured to Indonesia where he was arrested and handed over to U.S. authorities. Among the tribesmen – especially among his own, the Brahui – Hajji Jom'a Khan still holds a reasonable reputation. Thanks to him and his career the tribe of the Brahui advanced to one of the important players in the province and even in national policy. As a result,

---

11   Although the age range of the estimations of prevalence differs for some years (Iran: 14-64 years; Germany: 18-64) the difference in numbers is still significant.
12   Apart from Balochi members of this Baloch tribe or tribe confederacy speak Brahui, a Dravidian language, which in contrast to Balochi is not associated with the Iranian languages. The Brahui tribes are spread all over the Baloch areas but they also live in a closed settlement area in the district of Kalat in Pakistani Balochistan. A more or less independent government of the Ahmadzai Khans (Ahmadzai is one of the Brahui tribes) who ruled the Khanate of Kalat between 1666 and 1947 settled in this region.

one of Hajji Jom'a Khan's cousins who had held the title of provincial governor in Mujaheddin times occupied two different ministries in the Afghan cabinet after the fall of the Taliban rule and is now again the governor of Nimruz.

Fig. 6: Zabol 2008: Opium consumption with *wāfur* (the traditional pipe) is widely common in Iran

Apart from this large scale business in the opium trade a lot of small scale traders can be found in Zaranj who send their contraband by car or on camels to Iran. As the price for one kilogramme of opium was about 70 dollars in 2008, a fraction of its price in Tehran,[13] there is a high profit margin on its trade but also a high danger. One of my acquaintances brought 200 kilograms of opium from Zabul to a destination in the north of Khorasan close to Nehbandan and the profit per kilogramme was about 7 Euro. In Sistan and Balochistan drug traders are regularly sentenced to death and executed in public. But according to my informants most of the executed are poor unofficial traders not having the financial resources to bribe the officials. In Kabul I was told by a Baloch involved in this business that as a rule unofficial traders who are not armed are not sentenced to death but imprisoned for several years. The different

13   In 2010 the price for one kilogram was considerably higher: I was told that the price rose to about 300 Euro in Nimruz, to 350 Euro in Zahedan and to 720 Euro in Tehran.

dimensions of opium consumption on both sides of the border were quite remarkable: While in Afghanistan consumption was comparably uncommon during the gatherings I attended, consumption in Iran was common and some of my acquaintances smoked opium on a regular basis.

6   Different perspectives on illicit trade

As these examples demonstrate, smuggling – or trading as it is seen from a Baloch perspective – is not an embarrassing and clandestine activity that enables participants to cope with poor living conditions. The protagonists operating in this domain appreciate the (illegal) cross-border trade as a legitimate source of income and regard the counteractive measures of the Iranian state as a repression of the Baloch tribes. It is rather a prestigious profession preferred to manual work and the source of adventure stories attesting courage and manliness. This positive connotation of illegal cross-border trade results from different social and culture-historic factors which I discussed above.

Due to the Iranian official perspective of Baloch trading activities, which are perceived as smuggling and undermining the Iranian nation state, Baloch people are criminalised as a whole and excluded from any official posts for the main part. Consequently, the Baloch settlement areas are perceived as a vastly wild area where the territorial claims of the central government are hardly accepted by a bunch of smuggling tribes. A similar perspective became apparent when I told some of my Iranian acquaintances that I was planning to go to the area inhabited by the Baloch. They warned me about the 'dangerous Baloch' mostly involved in kidnapping foreigners.

The occurrence of death penalties in the Sistan and Balochistan provinces is one of the highest in Iran and many of my interlocutors had been in jail for a period in their lifetimes and often sentenced for crimes they had not committed. In Afghanistan, I was told that people crossing the border were shot by Iranian forces on a weekly basis. As a measure against Baloch cross-border trade the Iranian authorities have built a wall and trenches separating the Iranian territory of Sistan from the Afghan province of Nimruz. This physical obstacle has not had any effect on illegal transit – yet. But when one of my contacts was talking about this wall he became upset as he regarded an unmolested crossing of the border as an ancestral right of the Baloch people. This wall was – although it is bypassed in several ways – rejected by many of my interlocutors and often compared to the Berlin Wall.

Compared with the Iranian side of the frontier almost no interventions of Afghan national institutions exist in Baloch trading practices. Currently this region serves as an area of retreat and shelter for Baloches fearing political persecution or criminal proceedings in Iran and Pakistan despite its economic problems. There, feasibilities for cultural evolvement and political freedom as well as illicit trade are generally warranted, especially in the 'Baloch' province of Nimruz where no international forces are garrisoned and no PRT (Provincial Reconstruction Team) is based. Accordingly most of my interlocutors perceived the Afghan side of the border as an area with vast possibilities of self-fulfilment. Only the comparably minor Baloch influence on Afghan political decision-making processes and the low living-standard there were sometimes brought up.

For the economy of the region unofficial trading does play a major role as there is hardly any industry nor sufficient natural resources for agriculture or pastoralism due to a severe drought during the last twenty years. But these economic reasons are not adequate to explain the prominence of unofficial trade among the Baloch. I would like to highlight that among the Baloch social and cultural aspects play a crucial role for the general acceptance of unofficial trade as an honourable practice. In this framework cross-border affairs do not simply serve economic requirements but are a potential source of social and political influence. Therefore, considering 'smuggling' in this region, social and economic factors have to be treated as intermingled motivations challenging the administrations of the bordering nation states.

7   Conclusion

In the previous paragraphs I have attempted to demonstrate that in the history of the Baloch settlement areas, the territorial demands of the bordering nation states did not succeed until recently and no centralised political power has been established beyond a certain degree of indirect rule. As a result the paradoxical situation meant that one of the main sources of income is national boundaries while their separating effects are neglected by most Baloch traders. One of the main reasons for the disobedience against state control seems to be the perception of this area as a shatter zone without any rules by the outside powers – a perception which is adopted by its inhabitants.

To answer the introductory questions on the importance of smuggling in the area, the reasons for the popularity of rebellious concepts among the Baloch and the consequences for the perceptions of national boundaries, I would like to present the following conclusive remarks:

First of all, in the spatial perceptions of my Baloch informants their settlement region is not seen as a remote area on the periphery of nation states demarcated by borders, but as an area with its own centres and lineage networks crossing national frontiers. As a consequence, nation states ruled from centres located a vast distance in space and culture are perceived from their perspective as a threat from outside. It is possible that the hostility towards representations of nation states is one of the most uniting factors of the heterogeneous Baloch tribal identities and results from the permanent incorporation of immigrant groups hiding from neighbouring political powers. As a result, disobedience and the image of the heroic social bandit fighting against subordination are seen as representations of the traditional social order. In this context smuggling as an illegal but legitimate activity is an honourable profession.

Second, the Baloch perceive their inherited living space as at the crossroads of the nation states. Within this area mobility is a common social practice not only assuring social and economic resources but also effecting a consistent flow of people and goods. Customs laws or border restrictions are seen as obstacles to their ancestral law of an unmolested border crossing. This mobility takes place along their plurilocal lineage networks within the security circle which is perceived as Balochistan and, at least in Iran, delineated by the Baloch dress code.

Third, the topos of a Baloch fighting with a far more powerful opponent is celebrated in many legends. It stylises the Baloch conflicting with national institutions as a culture hero. Consequently rebellion and insubordination against the superiority of nation states and its governments are seen as part of Baloch freedom. Unofficial trade is perceived as an uprising against customs, laws and the determinations of the bordering states. It is a coping strategy for Baloch life in the border region resulting from the former pastoral nomadism and its inflow through raiding and trading. The smugglers' impetus is comparable to the 'social banditry' described by Eric Hobsbawm (1972: 73) as a rebellion against the forces considered being destructive for the traditional social order. As this traditional social order has been the game of integration and disintegration in the land of the disobedient, almost any representation of a superior nation state is perceived as destructive for this order. Hence, in this context, smuggling cannot be explained merely by its functional meaning as "part of a strategy for coping with poverty or prevention of poverty for the individual and his household" (Bruns 2010: 60).

This form of cross-border trade can hardly be compared to the border context between well-established nation states as we come across in most European contexts. Perhaps the most comparable situation to the Baloch example is the 'Pashtunistan'-question (see Khan 1981) and the social situation in the Afghan-Pakistan border area where we find similar requirements: a heterogeneous tribal ethnic group, influenced by the concepts pastoral nomadism and weak structures of nation states.

References

Anderson, J. W. (1983): "Khan and Khel: Dialectics of Pakhtun Tribalism". In: R. Tapper (ed.): The Conflict of Tribe and State in Iran and Afghanistan. London & Canberra: St. Martin's Press, pp. 119-149.

AREU (2006): Continued Protection, Sustainable Reintegration: Afghan Refugees and Migrants in Iran, URL: http://www.unhcr.org/refworld/country,,AREU,,IRN,,47c3f3c51a,0.html (last access: 08.04.2010).

Bruns, B. (2010): Grenze als Ressource: Die soziale Organisation von Schmuggel am Rande der Europäischen Union. Wiesbaden: Verlag für Sozialwissenschaften.

Curzon, G. N. (1892): Persia and the Persian Question. Vol. II. London: Longmans, Green, and Co.

Donnan, H. / Wilson, T. M. (1999): Borders: Frontiers of Identity, Nation and State. Oxford: Berg.

Dyer, R. E. H. (1921): The Raiders of the Sarhad: Being the Account of a Campaign of Arms and Bluff against the Brigands of the Persian Baluchi Border During the Great War. London: H.F. & G. Witherby.

Forbes, R. (1931): Conflict: Angora to Afghanistan. London, Toronto, Melbourne, Sydney: Cassell.

Glatzer, B. (1977): Nomaden von Gharjistan. Aspekte der wirtschaftlichen, sozialen und politischen Organisation nomadischer Durrani-Paschtunen in Nordwest-Afghanistan. Wiesbaden: Steiner.

Harrison, S. S. (1981): In Afghanistan's Shadow: Baluch Nationalism and Soviet Temptations. New York/NY: Carnegie Endowment for International Peace.

Hobsbawn, E. J. (1972): Die Banditen. Frankfurt a.M.: Suhrkamp.

Khan, K. M. (1981): "Der Paschtunistan-Konflikt zwischen Afghanistan und Pakistan". In: K. M. Khan and V. Matthies (eds.): Regionalkonflikte in der Dritten Welt: Ursachen, Verlauf, Internationalisierung, Lösungsansätz. München, Köln, London: Weltforum-Verlag, pp. 283-384.

Kennard, C. (1927): Suhaïl. London: The Richards Press.

Malinowski, B. (1922): Argonauts of the Western Pacific: An Account of Native Enterprise and Adventure in the Archipelagoes of Melanesian New Guinea. London: George Routledge & Sons.

Nölle-Karimi, C. (2005): „Die paschtunische Stammesversammlung im Spiegel der Geschichte". In: M. Kemper and M. Reinkowski (eds.): Rechtspluralismus in der Islamischen Welt. Berlin, New York: Walter de Gruyter, pp. 177-194.

Peters, G. (2009): "How Opium Profits the Taliban". Peaceworks 62, Washington D.C.: United States Institute for Peace.

Risen, J. (2010): "Propping Up a Drug Lord, Then Arresting Him". In: The New York Times, 11. December 2010, URL: http://www.nytimes.com/2010/12/12/world/asia/12drugs.html?_r=1 (last access: 20.05.2011).

Šahbaxš, 'aḏīm (1373): Māǧarā-ye Dādšāh: Pažūhešī dar tārīx-e moʿāṣer-e Balūčestān, Šīrāz: Entešārāt-e Navīd.

Salzman, P. C. (1971): "Adaption and Political Organization in Iranian Baluchistan". In: Ethnology 10, 4, pp. 433-444.

Salzman, P. C. (2000): Black Tents of Baluchistan. Washington, London: Smithonian Institution Press.

Schindler, D. (2008): "Plurilocality in Balochistan: A Case Study of Kinship, Marriage and Belonging". In: C. Jahani, A. Korn and P. Titus (eds.): The Baloch and Others: Linguistic, Historical and Socio-Political Perspectives on Pluralism in Balochistan. Wiesbaden: Reichert Verlag, pp. 235-246.

Scholz, F. (1974): Belutschistan (Pakistan): Eine sozialgeographische Studie des Wandels in einem Nomadenland seit Beginn der Kolonialzeit. Göttingen: Erich Goltze KG.

Spooner, B. (1969): "Politics, Kinship, and Ecology in Southeast Persia". In: Ethnology, 8, pp. 139-152.

Spooner, B. (1983): "Who are the Baluch? A preliminary investigation into the dynamics of an ethnic identity from Qajar Iran". In: E. Bosworth and C. Hillenbrand (eds.): Qajar Iran, social and cultural change 1800-1925. Edinburgh: Edinburgh University Press, pp. 93-110.

Rzehak, L. (2004): Die Taliban im Land der Mittagssonne: Geschichten aus der afghanischen Provinz. Wiesbaden: Dr. Ludwig Reichert Verlag.

Sykes, P. M. (1902): Ten Thousand Miles in Persia or Eight Years in Iran. London: John Murray.

UNODC – United Nations Office on Drugs and Crime (2009): World Drug Report 2009, URL: http://www.unodc.org/unodc/en/data-and-analysis/WDR-2009.html (last access: 20.05.2011).

Šverc and the Šinobus: Small-scale smuggling in Vojvodina

Rory Archer and Krisztina Rácz

1   Introduction

The flat lands of Vojvodina, the northern province of Serbia, are the preserve of the *šinobus*, a metal railcar resembling a bus on wheels. The *šinobus* travels on decaying single rail tracks and is usually unfeasibly slow, bouncing through cornfields from town to village to town. When the train tracks run parallel to a road, as they do between Subotica in Serbia and the Hungarian border, the cars appear to race by at breakneck speed. They mostly travel under the 80 km per hour speed limit but the *šinobus* reaches peak speeds of 30 km per hour on this line. Passengers may notice this as the speedometer is visible to those sitting in the front seats behind the driver. The atmosphere in the *šinobus* reflects its leisurely speed – sitting close together in a small, enclosed environment passengers tend to interact more than on Vojvodina's far more comprehensive bus network or faster inter-city trains.

The *šinobus* (Hungarian *sínbusz*) is a colloquial term for the class 812 railcar made in the Goša factory in Smederevska Palanka, Serbia since 1958. An ancestor of the German Dmot railcar Class 126, acquired by the Socialist Federal Republic Yugoslavia in lieu of post World War II war reparations, it was used on smaller non-electrified branch lines in Yugoslavia.[14] The service has been reduced in recent decades and most of the remaining routes are in Vojvodina. Two routes traverse the Serbian border to Jimoblia in Romania and Szeged in Hungary. Such journeys have a strong multilingual and multinational character. They are associated with (often grey or illicit) transborder activity at a local level and they form our entry point for the exploration of such phenomena.

We explore the continuing changes since the 1980s in illicit cross-border trade (i.e. largely unsanctioned transnational activity) to and from North-eastern Serbia to Romania and Hungary through the Vojvodina region, an area trisected by Serbian, Romanian and Hungarian state borders and linked by *šinobus* routes. Our focus is primarily on the embedded socio-cultural nature of the illicit trade – how it is experienced and represented at the micro-level. Investigating how narratives of the economic 'golden age' of Serbia (as a component of socialist

---

14   See http://sinobus.webs.com/infohistory.htm (last access: 20.05.2011).

Yugoslavia) are pitted against the socially and economically challenging period of the 1990s and the current ambiguous stage of European integration, one should gain insight into the strategies that are put to work to position oneself individually and collectively in the border region – meaning not only the state border but also the border between nations, social groups and between legal and illicit. The border region and smuggling are constitutive of the dynamism between the citizen and the authorities, the legal and illegal, sellers and buyers, Serbs and Romanians, Serbs and Hungarians. Exploring *šverc*[15] (petty smuggling) in Vojvodina by looking at how smuggling and the social interactions it involves are articulated also demonstrates how small-scale smuggling has created social networks leading to the accumulation of social capital and how, on the other hand, cultural capital is made use of in order to facilitate illegal trade and thus accumulate economic capital. The *šinobus,* a railcar that crosses the borders in question represents a *lieu de mémoire* of small-scale smuggling and localised transborder activity and formed a key means of transport during our fieldwork.

On the basis of fieldwork conducted in the border region of Northeast Serbia, Western Romania and Southern Hungary in 2010 we explore narratives of Serbia as the exporter of economic, cultural and social commodities in the case of smuggling into Romania, and Serbia as dependent on another country's resources in the case of smuggling of household necessities and fuel from Hungary and Romania. Imagined hierarchies between the states involved in smuggling were inverted at different points in recent decades – since the 1980s ever-changing visa requirements and divergent economic conditions prompted various flows of grey economic and cultural activity across state borders. We demonstrate the fluidity and context dependent nature of illicit cross-border transactions between Serbia and Romania and Serbia and Hungary from the 1980s to the 2000s, depicting how the specific dynamic socio-economic and political conditions of the three states and the specific local dimensions of the Vojvodina border region contributed to the rise of informal cross-border (grey) economic activities. In addition to the economic rational of *šverc* we also explore the cultural legacy of these cross-border interactions and normative attitudes towards *šverc* that we encountered.

---

15   The Serbian word for smuggling also used by local Hungarians, in Vojvodina.

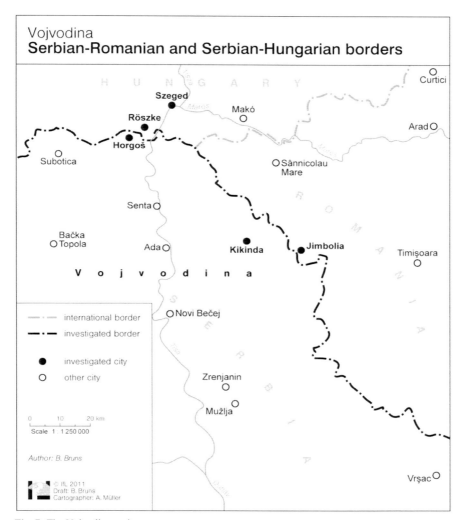

Fig. 7: The Vojvodina region

2   Positioning the research

The term *šverc* originates from the German word *Schwarzhandel* (black market) and is used to describe the informal, open-market trade in contraband, cheap commodities in Serbo-Croatian (see Jašarević 2007: 279). *Šverc* predates the wars and crises of the 1990s – during Tito's Yugoslavia massive amounts of commodities were smuggled in and out of the country and sold at markets. In Serbia of the 1990s war and sanctions changed the role of *šverc* – smuggling was encouraged by the regime fostering what Andreas (2005: 337) terms an "uncivil society – reflected in a higher level of public tolerance for lawbreaking and an undermined respect for the rule of law". Smuggling became not only to be perceived by many as socially acceptable rather than deviant, but even celebrated as patriotic (see ibid: 337-341; see also Antonić 2002).

After the collapse of Yugoslavia, Vojvodina, like the rest of the former state, was faced with severe socio-economic depression and high unemployment rates – a result of the economic crisis that had begun in the 1980s, the warmongering policy of the Milošević regime and the international sanctions that had been imposed on Serbia/Yugoslavia since 1991 (see Judah 2000; Thomas 1998; Ramet/Pavlaković 2005). These factors contributed to smuggling ('sanctions busting') becoming an important factor of economic survival. Indeed the Milošević government deliberately fostered black markets and smuggling networks as a means to prevent social unrest (see Dimitrijević/Pejić 1993; Dinkić 1995: 229). In the Balkan context transnationalism in the 1990s has come to refer to foreign interventions or organised crime, a particular concern of the 'international community' actors (see Hožić 2008). Phenomena like small-scale smuggling are thus articulated as problems that require a firmer establishment of legal authority rather than accepted as a logical consequence of post-socialist socio-economic precariousness. Perhaps the most notable example of *šverc* for certain international actors in former Yugoslavia is the 'Arizona' marketplace in Bosnia and Herzegovina which has been fostered and represented by such actors as a means to encourage inter-ethnic cooperation in Bosnia (see ibid.; also Jašarević 2007). Ethnographic research by Jašarević however suggests that "[w]hat is at stake at Arizona is not primarily a negotiation of (multi)ethnicity" but rather the "differentiation between subsistence and an unchecked accumulation of profit" (2007: 275).

The case of small-scale smuggling in Vojvodina, as in the rest of former Yugoslavia calls for a broader contextualisation in the social sphere. As *šverc* is largely particular to border areas, only by understanding the characteristics of these regions is it possible to account for the dynamism between states, nations, and the border, and the role of *šverc* and the actors engaged in it. As Wilson and Donnan (1998) argue in their work on border identities, borders are cultural constructs that give meaning to the boundaries between nations. States control border areas as their first lines of defence, but informal networks at the border areas often compete with the state power, therefore border areas cannot be considered as mere extensions of the state. All the more as people may construct their identities differently at the border regions than they do elsewhere in the state often being connected to the other side of the border by ties of ethno-national unity (see ibid.). Various practices such as smuggling can thus be seen as a way to undermine the efforts of the state to control identities of the people in the border areas. By studying the border area, it is possible to simultaneously explore the flexibility of people in border areas to adapt to culturally diverse environments, and the rigidity of states to ideologically control their cultural space (see ibid: 4). This is particularly resonant in liminal border areas of Vojvodina where there is no precise fit between nation and state; the border goes against the logic of supposed ethnic, linguistic and cultural homogeneity. Vojvodina offers an interesting case study for questions of diversity and ethnicity. Officially, more than 20 national minorities live alongside Serbs in Vojvodina; the most numerous being Hungarians, Roma, Romanians, Slovaks, Croats and Ruthenians (see Ilić 2001). Thus it is to be expected that such an area has a longstanding tradition of cross border and inter-ethnic networks. Stereotyped narratives of multicultural Vojvodina exist (see Korhec 2006; Devicé 2002) alongside evidence of strained ethnically framed cleavages (see Bieber/Winterhagen 2006).

Wilson and Donnan (1998, 1999) advocate for an anthropology of borders that integrates the study of visible and symbolic borders between states. Besides this distinction between the real and the imaginary border, they also maintain a clear-cut distinction between nations and states, a distinction that is the most visible in border regions (ibid. 1998: 2). Other works also emphasize the role of borders in ethno-national division, the fostering of conflict and inequalities (see Holly et.al. 2003; Meinhof 2003). Although our research looks at state borders as frontiers that exhibit political and social features (see Wilson/Donnan 1998: 5), instead of focusing on the separation and demarcation of separate states, cultures and peoples, we rather explore its characteristic to connect, to transport and to transform culture, and to create social ties between those on the "opposite sides" of it as well as imagined geographical hierarchies.

Serbian migration to Vojvodina has occurred in different waves (the most recent by Serbian war-time refugees in the 1990s) and in-group socio-cultural cleavages demonstrate that commonality and difference is not exclusively ethnically framed but can relate to the duration of residence in the region and alleged cultural and civilizing difference (see Živković 1997, 2001). A body of literature explores imagined geography and representations of Eastern Europe (see Wolff 1994) with a particular focus on the Balkan Peninsula from the perspective of the European problematising civilizing discourses (see Todorova 1997; Goldsworthy 1998; Bjelić/Savić 2002). Such representations have long been internalised within the region (see Todorova 1997) conceived by Bakić Hayden (1995) as 'nesting orientalisms': patterns of perceived Europeanness vis-à-vis a less European internal or nearby other. Research by Jansen suggests that such representations can be enacted retrospectively in the Serbian context in which positive narratives of socialist Yugoslavia focus on the relative Westernness of Yugoslavia compared to other socialist states – "For them we were the West!" (2009: 828).

Differentiation between the in-group and the other (side of the border) has been a traditional means of identity creation and central feature in the construction of ethnicity (see Holly et.al. 2003). Neighbouring states and the status of their inhabitants are perceived as asymmetrical, and this inequality is expressed in the way people formulate their attitudes towards their neighbours. This imagined hierarchy is not stable, though: stereotypical views of the Other are often negotiated and conflicted, and expressed through various discursive strategies. At various times, under various conditions 'unequal' neighbours are seen differently (see Galasinska/Galasinski 2003; Meinhof/Galasinski 2002). Divergent economic circumstances, political affiliations and social conditions greatly contribute to how people in border areas refer to themselves, their neighbours, the border and their transborder experience.

In our research we use the concept of narratives to explain the way people in border areas construct their identities across the dimensions of time and space: the way they recreate their memories of the time when Serbia was the exporter of popular cultural goods versus when it was an importer of economic goods such as food, petrol, textiles etc. We understand narratives to be a repertoire of verbal instances through which people constitute themselves as parts of social networks, through which they create their identities in a social sphere (see Somers 1994). Narratives give the means to individuals to understand and make sense of the social world in which they live. This narrative constitution of identity is made possible by the characteristic features of narratives: they connect parts of a story into a chronological order, create causal relationships between the parts of a story, people appropriate narratives that they identify themselves with selectively and they provide events with a temporal and special dimension. Therefore people don't invent narratives on their own, but derive them from an already existing limited repertoire (see ibid.).

Two key methods were used in our field research, participant observation and informal semi-structured interviews – both classical ethnographical methods in the sense that we were concerned with the informants' interpretation of the theme of our study: grey cross-border activity. Having the *šinobus* as an introductory focus enabled us to make initial contact with informants more easily by forming a logical starting point to discuss sometimes delicate matters like smuggling and other cross border dynamics, as a cognitive association exists between the *šinobus*, *šverc* and a regional sense of identification. In 2009 and 2010 we crossed the Serbian-Romanian and Serbian Hungarian borders by train, car, bus and on foot at several border crossings between Serbia and Romania and Serbia and Hungary. Our research in North-western Vojvodina focuses on two *šinobus* routes; from Kikinda (Serbia) to Jimbolia (Romania) and from Subotica and Horgoš (Serbia) to Röszke and Szeged (Hungary) and the surrounding road borders.[16]

Fig. 8:   The *šinobus* at Subotica station

During our travels in the towns and villages in the border area we observed and interviewed local residents, passengers, traders, buyers, border guards, conductors and customs officials about travelling by *šinobus* and other means of

---

16   Kelebia (Serbia) – Tompa (Hungary), Horgoš (Serbia) – Röszke (Hungary), Kiszombor (Hungary) – Cenad (Romania), Srpska Crnja (Serbia) – Jimbolia (Romania), Vatin (Serbia) – Moravița (Romania)

transport, the border, the business across it, passenger traffic and the nature of smuggling and of smuggled goods. Research was conducted in Serbian, Hungarian and English. Naturally we are aware that this methodological approach has its limitations: the choice of informants is random, restricted to passengers and local people who happened to be in the vehicle or at a certain place at the same time as us. However, travelling with other passengers through the border also provided valuable sources of information as we could observe and to a certain extent participate in the activities that were the focus of our research. We assume that "experience (...) is always embedded in and occurs through narrative frames" (Olick/Robbins 1998:110), therefore the way for us to grasp the memories of small-scale trade in the last decades is through narratives and articulations of it. We drew upon these narratives in order to arrive at some conclusions about the nature of the grey trans-border practices, actors and its regional meaning. In addition to drawing upon secondary literature relating to smuggling and borders in general and the Vojvodina region we paid attention to newspaper sources to provide empirical weight to discussions and to familiarise ourselves with the localised media discourses in regard to smuggling.

3   Three decades of *šverc*: narratives of smuggling in Vojvodina from the 1980s to the 2000s

Yugoslavia as Romania's window to the west

At least since the emergence of market influences in the Romanian cultural sphere from 1978 (see Verdery 1995:96) the illicit consumption of Yugoslav cultural products has become a dominant practice in Timişoara and the surrounding region. As a result of this legacy, and the native 15,000 strong Serbian minority in Timişoara, Serbian popular culture remains visible (and audible) in the city. During our fieldwork visits to Romania respondents consistently mentioned Serbian music (in particular Lepa Brena, a pop-folk performer) and maintained that Romanians in the border region (the city of Timişoara and its environs) have been consuming Yugoslavian/Serbian mass cultural products since at least the 1980s, chiefly newly composed folk music[17] (henceforth NCFM) through illicitly accessing Serbian radio and television

---

17   Newly composed folk music (Serbian: *novokomponovana narodna muzika*) was a style which
developed from the 1960s in Yugoslavia merging folk styles from various regions of
Yugoslavia and the wider Balkan region with modern music styles (rock, pop etc.). The 1990s
variant is known as *turbofolk* or *neofolk* (see Vidić Rasmussen 1995, 2002).

stations during the 1980s and later through the distribution of pirated music cassettes.

A Romanian student from the east of the country recalling a summer spent with an aunt in Banat in the early 1990s, remembers Serbian vendors selling pirated cassettes of Lepa Brena and other musicians and "Serbian grannies hawking *anti-bebi pilule*" (oral contraceptives) on the streets of Timişoara.[18] Serbian/Yugoslav mass culture like Lepa Brena had an edge over Romanian modern musical forms having developed in the image of Western performers with a strong Balkan vernacular under the comparative liberty of the Tito regime. In Romania (like Bulgaria) ethno-pop musical forms arose in tandem with glasnost and perestroika in the mid-1980s and signified "an emergent sense of regional Balkan consciousness within the European continent" (Buchanan 2002: 4f.). "This musical style became an icon of the possibilities of personal freedom and expression within a totalitarian regime and a harbinger of the political changes to come" (Rice 2002: 27; see also Buchanan 1996). Đorđe Matić, writing of Lepa Brena's performances in 1980s in neighbouring Romania and Bulgaria in front of 100,000 person crowds noted the enthusiasm of the audience as Brena sung *Živjela Jugoslavija* ('Long Live Yugoslavia' – an ode to Tito's Yugoslavia):

> "We all got the message from the television, without words, that slaves in the neighbouring darkness experienced our country as freedom, and Tito's name as its symbol. Without force, without anyone having to suggest it, they simply thought so. A few years ago I saw the same footage again – it is still one of the most fascinating things I have ever seen." (2004: 226)

Serbian NCFM began to 'sneak' into Romanian Banat from Yugoslavia as Serbian musicians performed at weddings and their music was circulated through pirated cassettes (see Beissinger 2008:106). In the border zone Romanians were able to tune into Serbian television and radio which disseminated pop-folk styles. NCFM was not aired on Romanian media nor officially sold. Timişoara became a centre for the unauthorised production of a Romanian variant of NCFM with a Romani imprint that became known as *muzică sîrbească* (Serbian music) which from the perspective of the communist government violated the model of a homogenous Romanian national culture requiring measures to eradicate it (ibid.: 107). Despite official bans on Balkan ethno-pop in Romania during communism and widespread disapproval of the post-Ceausescu phenomenon of *muzică orientală* these music styles have thrived (see Voiculescu 2005).

---

18   Personal correspondence with authors, February 2010.

Fig. 9:   The 'Lepa Brena Pizzeria'

As well as the legacy evident in *muzică orientală*, physical reminders of Yugoslav/Serbian cultural influences are manifest in the city. Timişoara boasts a 'Lepa Brena Pizzeria', 'Restaurant Yugoslavia', 'Restaurant Karađorđe' and 'Restaurant Pljevlja'[19]. The 'Lepa Brena Pizzeria', a bold four-storey edifice in the eastern periphery of the city decorated in pictures from the Yugoslav performer's 1980s heyday boasts three kinds of pizza in honour of the folk music queen and regularly hosts live Serbian and Romanian pop-folk acts. The upmarket 'Restaurant Karađorđe' in the city centre, named after the leader of the first Serbian national uprising, adheres to specifically Serbian culinary traditions while 'Restaurant Yugoslavia' falls into a Yugo-nostalgic category (similar to Tito-themed establishments in former Yugoslavia [see Velikonja 2009]) with various Tito-themed memorabilia celebrating the former republic. Upon our arrival in 'Restaurant Yugoslavia' a christening party was in full swing taking over most of the restaurant. The waitress apologetically explained in Serbian "we

---

19   Plevlja is a town in Montenegro.

usually only play Serbian music but because of this christening party we are playing some Romanian [*manele*[20]] tonight".

'Sanctions busting': Serbia as an illicit importer

The end of the socialist regime in surrounding states and the international embargo of the 1990s suddenly changed the notion of Serbia/Yugoslavia as a regional hegemon in terms of cultural commodities – it became dependent upon *šverc* goods from neighbouring Romania and Hungary. The shortage of basic household goods, petrol, tobacco and textiles, led to the development of extensive and specialised trading networks across the borders. In the case of both Romania and Hungary, petrol is the most widely remembered item that was smuggled to Serbia, like the *šinobus*, fuel smuggling became emblematic of the era of the sanctions. Although Serbia was relatively self-sufficient in food as an agricultural country (particularly the fertile Vojvodina region) the state relied heavily upon fuel imports.

As for small-scale smuggling between Serbia and Hungary, the usual pattern was the following: smuggling alcohol and cigarettes to Hungary from Serbia, where they were cheaper, and selling Hungarian petrol in Serbia, where it lacked. Smugglers were both Serbian and Hungarian, although Serbian citizens engaged in it more, especially Hungarians from Serbia. This category was particularly well-placed to engage in cross-border transactions as many had pre-existing networks of acquaintances and relatives in Hungary and knowledge of the Hungarian and Serbian language.

Small-scale smuggling networks often connected relatives and friends living on different sides of the border but it also took place between random business partners. For example a former resident of Kelebija, a village on the Serbian side of the border with Hungary, recalled how

> "a Hungarian [citizen] who had come to Serbia to sell petrol, equipped with a specially enlarged petrol tank in his car for the purpose, would simply knock on the door of a random house in Kelebija, and ask if the household deals in petrol. The trade was therefore profitable to both parties, and it knew no ethnic boundaries. Serbian businessmen were as much involved in the trade as Hungarian housewives."

Women played a key role in the small-scale trade between Serbia and Hungary, both travelling to and from the country supplying, transporting and selling goods, and also acting as intermediaries, for a certain amount of money allowing the

---

20   Romanian ethno-pop, a sister style of Yugoslav NCFM.

petrol or the food and textiles to be stored at their homes until the customer came to pick it up. Smuggling as a social practice both supported and subverted traditional gender roles: During the bombing of Serbia in 1999, as men were prohibited from leaving the country, women would cross the borders in their place to buy goods and sell them back home. Yet, larger-scale illegal smuggling has remained reserved for men -- a differentiation of practices by no means unique in the history of transborder activity (see Cheater 1998). Also, the type of items traded by women were characteristically associated with the domestic sphere assigned to women, taking for granted that they are better at choosing the type of food, clothes etc. that is most demanded and profitable in Serbia - only to support a male/female dichotomy of *šverc*.

The small town of Jimbolia in Romania is located four kilometres from the Serbian border in Srpska Crnja and forms the railway terminus for the *šinobus* from Kikinda. During the 1990s it became a centre for trade (sanctions busting) in petrol and household goods. Surrounded on two sides by the Serbian border, according to two young male informants, "everybody in Jimbolia sold petrol". Towns like Jimbolia enjoyed an economic boom – petrol could be sold in Serbia for three times the Romanian price (see Andreas 2005: 345f.). Jimbolia remains a relatively wealthy town with low unemployment – residents pointed out that before the impact of the global economic crisis, factories in Jimbolia imported workers from Serbia to cover labour shortages.

Although Romania publicly supported the UN sanctions regime, violations were directed from the highest political level according to former intelligence chief Virgil Magureanu. Romanian investigation estimates that 695 train cars carried 36,000 tons of fuel into Serbia during the sanctions period escorted by the secret service (see ibid.). When Serbian males were unable to leave Serbia due to regulations imposed because of war at various points during the 1990s (1991-1994; 1999) Romanian men crossed the border to sell fuel directly in Serbia.

One bakery worker estimated half the town's adult population sold goods in Serbia, including his mother and grandmother. "People used to cross the border just to use the [Serbian] duty free shop, to legally buy cartons of cigarettes and then sell them in Jimbolia in cafes". He pointed out that many families have kin on opposite sides which served as go-betweens in markets and ad-hoc petrol stations as well as a social function. During the pig slaughtering season, a student from Jimbolia mentioned "all were together, Serbs, Romanians and Hungarians". Other inhabitants of the town also mentioned that the 1999 NATO bombing generated a degree of solidarity as the bombs were felt in Jimbolia and intruded on everyday activities "the planes were overhead while we were swimming and fishing, we felt the ground shake, literally", the student remembered.

Since the end of sanction regimes against Serbia the illegal petrol trade has diminished (though reports of illegal selling of fuel on the street do surface from time to time [Lj.B. 2008]). Passengers on the *šinobus* between Kikinda and Jimbolia have reduced in numbers. A Serbian border guard in Kikinda station recalled "before there were much more passengers [on the Kikinda-Jimbolia railbus] for economic reasons – three full wagons. Those who still go, those with family connections, go by car now. Serbs don't buy in Romania anymore because it's too expensive". In April 2010 on the *šinobus* only two other passengers were in the wagon along with the driver and conductor. At the open market in Jimbolia some Serbian (and Hungarian) goods were on display but no Serbian registered cars were visible – nor did we hear the Serbian language being spoken. One informant did mention a Serbian man who sells household goods informally, "*Vegeta*[21] and that type of thing" in cafes in Jimbolia.

Making a profit from smuggling as a full time job was considered by most informants to be rational given the massive unemployment of the time. An artist speaking about his home village in Serbia describes:

> "While local men were doing the petrol business in the yards of private homes with the driver and the passengers of buses from South Serbia that came to buy petrol in Kelebija and sell it at home in the South of the country, women were serving coffee to the 'guests', and after the transaction both parties shook hands, satisfied with the outcome."

He stresses, "There was no one I knew who would reject the business for nationalist reasons". Networks were formed, friendship-like relations were born, all in order to subsist or make a profit.

Smuggling was not a taboo topic; on the contrary, it was a fully visible everyday practice, a new layer of society, those who earned a fortune out of the petrol business, was created. These *nouveau rich* became visible by building eclectic bright-coloured huge villas and driving expensive cars. Yet, they were rather the exception than the rule, and smuggling remained a survival mechanism for most of the citizens of North Vojvodina, with only a few of those who "could afford to look down on their neighbours who engage in *šverc*".

As for the other smuggled goods, such as textiles and footwear, they were brought from Hungary together with petrol (sometimes worn in layers during the customs inspection by the smugglers themselves) then stored in improvised warehouses or private homes, and sold in the flea market in Subotica. As the arrangement of the customs inspection when travelling by train is such that customs officers enter the train after the vehicle has already entered Serbian territory as far as the first railway station, another option for their transport was

---

21   A vegetable-flavoured additive ubiquitous in former Yugoslav kitchens.

to bring them by *šinobus* or regular train from Hungary and throw them out through the window into the fields before the customs inspection where it was arranged that someone would pick it up. We heard anecdotes of people from the area going out to the fields near the border in search of goods thrown from the train before the interlocutors had time to retrieve them.

European integration in the Pannonian plain – current opportunities and constraints for the cross-border informal economy

Improvement in socio-economic conditions and a levelling in prices between Hungary, Romania and Serbia since the 2000s render *šverc* a less important survival mechanism for Serbian citizens. Several informants noted, with a few exceptions, prices are more or less the same in Serbia, Romania and Hungary. "It is not worth doing it anymore". Cheap household goods and textiles are now commonly sourced from Turkey and China – sold in the so-called China shops, found all around in Vojvodina even in the small villages. Shops that used to sell smuggled clothes and shoes have been replaced by Chinese immigrants now who sell a range of Chinese manufactured items.

However, due to large price gaps between Serbia and EU states (including Romania and Hungary) in terms of cigarette prices and insufficient border controls cigarette smuggling is still big business with Serbia allegedly the leading state in the region (see Stanimirović 2010).[22] Reports have noted that Serbia remains a source of illicit cigarettes for Romania and most further EU markets and in particular the borders in Banat (see NUNS 2010).[23] Illicit cigarette trade is conducted so openly it is difficult for the casual visitor not to notice it.

At the Serbo-Romanian road border at Srpska Crnja/Jimbolia a new 'duty free shop' has been built tucked away discretely to the side of the Romanian customs buildings. The interior is stacked from floor to ceiling with cigarettes yet a Romanian border guard seated behind the counter told us upon entry that the cigarettes were not for sale. When we inquired why the shop displays hundreds of cartons of cigarettes with prices attached without selling them we were given a shrug and told "*reklame* – advertising purposes". A Serbian border guard later explained more frankly the purpose of the shop. "It's organized crime. They only sell in bulk to truck drivers and the like; they can't sell in

---

22   See   http://www.blic.rs/Vesti/Drustvo/194802/Srbija-prva-u-regionu-po-svercu-cigareta   (last access: 20.05.2011).
23   See   http://www.vesti.rs/Blogovi/Vrsac-novi-centar-sverca-cigareta.html   (last   access: 20.05.2011).

smaller quantities. A criminal organised it for them. Now that they are in the EU and they can do anything they like", she responded cynically.[24]

Crossing the same border a few months later early on a Friday night, the queue of cars moved at a snail's pace through the Romanian side of the border. All the cars waiting were Romanian with Timişoara (TM) licence plates. Many of the passengers (the majority males aged 20 to 40) appeared to know one another and fraternised beside the parked cars. As the queue slowly moved towards customs some cars turned back into Romania either through their own accord or under the instructions of police and customs. Approximately 100 meters after the Serbian border controls over 15 cars and over 30 people loitered outside a solitary grocery shop in the otherwise empty countryside. A couple of men were loading boxes into a car boot carried from the premises of a long deserted motel. Most cars had Romanian licence plates – only two were from Serbia. Upon our entry to a bar in a nearby village the customers and waiter were speaking about the smuggling operation. "It's a bad shift for them [smugglers]" the waiter commented. He explained that Romanians obtain cigarettes in Serbia and transport them across the border. Some Serbian citizens also participate. This is done by making a deal with certain border guards – thus the cigarette smugglers have to wait until a suitable permutation of border guards are on duty on both the Serbian and Romanian sides of the border post until they can transport their goods from Serbia to Romania. The group must wait until shifts change necessitating hours of waiting in cars until they can securely pass the border. "So šverc is back to life in these parts?" – "Yes it is", the waiter responded with a bemused and slightly proud expression.

4 Interpreting *šverc*: Morality, social and cultural capital

Moral šverc?

Exploring the social dimensions of *šverc* in heterogeneous border regions we found that there was indeed a high tolerance for smuggling and the practice is very much embedded in the realm of the ordinary and the everyday. We did not encounter patriotic interpretations of cross-border grey transactions – in border areas of Vojvodina ethnic categories are quite blurred and flexible. From the perspective of Belgrade, Budapest and Bucharest the border areas in question and towns like Kikinda, Jimbolia, Subotica, Timisoara and Szeged do not fit

---

24 Duty free shops were part of a significant organised crime network in Serbia during the 1990s with a chain operated by Marko Milošević (son of Slobodan). See also: http://www.politika.rs/rubrike/Hronika/t31880.lt.html (last access: 20.05.2011).

comfortably into proscribed national categories. Thus 'patriotism' is confused –
to which nation-state would (could) patriotism be directed? Our research finds
that practical categories and rational motivations such as visa regimes, police and
state regulations, supply and demand, price differentiation held more weight than
ethno-national categories. A significant amount of *šverc* involved the formation
of interethnic 'circumstantial coalitions' (see Monterescu 2009), embedded
multiculturalism detached from the normative weight that the term implies. By
and large our informants articulated ethnicity as a social fact and were cynical of
(often externally driven) normative multiculturalism.

The state itself (represented by sets of institutions and individual politicians)
is commonly viewed as ambiguous at best, deeply immoral and dysfunctional at
worst, justifying *šverc*, at least on smaller scales. A great amount of discourse on
smuggling from the perspective of North Atlantic states focuses on concepts like
'rule of law', and 'corruption'. However many Serbian citizens (and Hungarians
and Romanians) are acutely aware that the upper echelons of power in the state
do not pay much more than lip service to such principles and thus *šverc* becomes
legitimised on the basis of survival. (If the state does not function according to
the rule of law why should cross-border transactions?). Public perception of the
state in Serbia holds it to be extremely weak in delivering basic rights for its
citizens (see Kostovicova/Bojičić-Dželilović 2008: 12, 15; Krastev 2002).
Recent survey data shows that more people consider criminals to rule Serbia (23
percent) than state institutions of governance (18 per cent) (see Cvejić 2010).

We found that many informants' narratives of small-scale smuggling were
delineated from mass smuggling, organised crime or the smuggling of narcotics.
In the border regions of Vojvodina smuggling was commonly conceived in two
normative streams. On the one hand what could be termed 'subsistence
smuggling', the smuggling of items used for personal use or for selling in small
quantities at markets, is an embedded phenomenon with a long precedent and to
a large degree socially acceptable. For instance a passenger on the Subotica -
Szeged *šinobus* told us that even though she did not participate in the illegal
trade going on between Szeged – Subotica, but being from Szeged, she had
naturally heard stories about it and described it in blatantly obvious terms. "Of
course people were smuggling, they [the customs officers] didn't let them take
stuff over the border legally so they had to". On the other hand organised crime -
for example the large-scale smuggling of cigarettes, alcohol and narcotics is
considered a criminal act and a social taboo; widely reported in news media in
these terms (see Stanimirović 2010; NUNS 2010; Danilović 2007). These
notions of morality cohere with Jašarević's research which is also concerned
with *šverc* in a multiethnic setting. She finds that for its traders, the Arizona
market is a "negotiation of customary, normative claims to subsistence against

neoliberal claims to profit" (Jašarević 2007: 282-283). In the case of borderland Vojvodina such claims were levelled against the state and 'organised' criminals who were frequently deemed to be in cahoots against the ordinary people ('*narod*').

Šverc as capital

In the classical Marxian sense of the term, capital means both a surplus value and an investment with expected returns in the market. Also, capital is associated with the production as well as the exchange of commodities; it is a process rather than a commodity or a value, and it involves social activities (see Lin 2001). If we explore small-scale trade between Serbia and Romania and Serbia and Hungary, we observe that making money was possible only through investment, and not only financial, but also investing in human relationships that were necessary to start and to sustain business. It is obvious that profit was only possible through a social activity where two parties exchanged goods, and what was exchanged varied in the two cases. On an abstract level we can see the exchange between Serbia and Romania in terms of cultural capital (see Bourdieu 1982), while the exchange between Serbia and Hungary as an exchange where social capital (see ibid.) was made use of.

Using the neo-capital theory of cultural capital in its broadest sense and stripping it from its focus on class relations, we can conceptualise it as the process whereby a group establishes its culture to be the dominant one, which is in turn internalised by the group lower in the imagined hierarchy. Cultural capital can be converted into economic capital, i.e. it is invested in order to make profit (see Lin 2001). To Bourdieu (1982), culture is a system of symbols and meanings. Therefore cultural elements imposed by one group and accepted by the other are the symbols and their interpretation by the dominant group. We can understand the trade between Serbia and Romania in the 1980s, even though not fully equate it to the concept, using the term cultural capital: dissemination of the elements of Serbian culture through the media into Romanian society and utilising this cultural capital in later instances of trade.

For instance Serbian sellers assumed it to be natural that some knowledge of the Serbian language existed on the Romanian side of the border, and thus they could communicate with their buyers in their own language. Also it was taken for granted that Romanian customers had some knowledge of certain Serbian products. The demand for certain Serbian items in Romania was utilized by Serbian smugglers/sellers as a kind of cultural capital that they possessed, that was exchanged for financial gain.

In the cases of smuggling to and from both Hungary and Romania we can see the illegal activities and the networks formed by it as positioning the participants in a social space that is only partly defined by nationality and/or citizenship. Rather, *šverc* gave the actor means to survival strategies and ways to make money, change their status and accumulate what Bourdieu defined as social capital:

> "[T]he aggregate of actual or potential resources which are linked to possession of a durable network of more or less institutionalized relationships of mutual acquaintance or recognition (...) which provides each of its members with the backing of the collectively owned capital, a 'credential'." (ibid: 51)

Social capital is always embedded in exchanges, material or symbolic, and needs constantly to be invested in to be transformed into economic capital (see ibid.). This is not only true for the new criminal elite associated with the Milošević regime who made a fortune but also to the 'common' people for whom *šverc* was a survival strategy (or at least a means of mitigating a difficult economic situation) and who actually made use of their relationship networks, their knowledge of Hungarian, or strategic information about the border area as resources in order to make profit ("I know people there"). For instance, having a relative who deals in petrol in Kelebia is by all means a resource for a small-scale smuggler from Szeged, or a family friend who works as a customs officer at the border definitely makes the illegal exchange easier. In other words, social capital is the "investment in social relations with expected returns in the marketplace" (Lin 2001: 19).

Šinobus and šverc as cultural commodities

"Everything is more relaxed", a traveller on the *šinobus* between Horgoš and Szeged commented. The same person, upon mentioning the possibility that the line is about to be closed, shrugs her shoulders, expressing apathy towards the future of the 'grey lightning'[25]. Like the conductor on the Kikinda – Jimbolia railbus, she recalls the 1990s when the train had not one but two or three carriages, all of them full, unlike today which sees less than a dozen passengers per journey.

As several *šinobus* lines have ceased[26] and the *šinobus* of the Serbian Railways became incompatible with EU standards the railbus is becoming a

---

25   The nickname for the *šinobus* of the Serbian (Former Yugoslavian) Railways.
26   The *šinobus* lines Ruma (Serbia) – Zvornik (Bosnia) and Šid (Serbia) – Bijeljina (Bosnia) have already been closed.

remnant of the past. However, there are indications that the *šinobus* might actually survive – at least in a recontextualised cultural form. It has been commodified culturally by a couple of regional artists. In 2010 the third festival called *Kultúrcsempész*[27] ('Culture Smuggler') boarded the Szeged – Subotica *šinobus* alongside the real ticket-inspectors, the audience and other passengers. Festival organiser, writer Roland Orcsik describes the festival as a means of "decontextualising the *šinobus* as a symbol of smuggling, using the concept ironically, and building on its narrative"[28]. Participants travel from Szeged to Subotica on the *šinobus* spending the night and returning the next day. Contemporary Serbian and Hungarian poetry and short stories are read on the railcar and participants socialise in the tatty train stations bars along the way[29] during the two hour ride, exhibitions are opened and concerts are held in Szeged and Subotica. The festival is supported by organisations and cultural groups on both sides of the Serbo-Hungarian border.

Orcsik and the other organisers frequently travelled by *šinobus* with other students and smugglers, watching how the customs officers "tore the railcar apart" in search of contraband. For him, like for many young people from Vojvodina who have studied in Hungary, the *šinobus* and the border are a "symbol of his poetry and his life". The idea for the festival originated during a period in the mid 2000s when a number of ethnically framed violent incidents occurred in Vojvodina (see Hagan 2009: 625ff.; HRW 2005; Bieber/Winterhagen 2006). Serbian media mostly ignored the incidents while Hungarian press frequently labelled Serbs as '*četniks*'[30]. Feeling bad about these negative processes as a Serbo-Hungarian, Orcsik decided to do something positive in the region – 'smuggling culture'. Smuggling is meant ironically, as a means of distance from clichéd terms like 'multicultural' or 'interculturalism'. He adds that 'although the *šinobus* is a symbol of smuggling for us, for the smugglers it's a symbol of survival'. The *Kultúrcsempész* festival removes the idea of smuggling from its usual context and sets it in a new one, but does it through retaining one of its symbols, turning the *šinobus* into a *lieu de mémoire*, the embodiment of memory at a certain site. One of the conditions of a *lieu de mémoire* to exist is its capacity to change and to recycle meaning, and its goal is to capture memory (see Nora 1989). We see the main idea of the festival, to emphasize the long-lasting intercultural and regional relationships (see Berényi

---

27   *Kultúrcsempész* website: http://kulturcsempesz.blogspot.com/ (last access: 20.05.2011).
28   Personal correspondence with authors, September 2010.
29   *Krčme* (Sebian), *kocsma* (Hungarian).
30   *Četnik* – a violent royalist Serbian national movement from World War II. The term gained renewed notoriety in the 1990s wars with the formation of *četnik* paramilitary groups. It is used as a derogatory term for Serbs.

2009) as an attempt to conserve the memory of the 1990s through its re-contextualization. The festival has been attended by a Novi Sad based band, active since 2001 who call themselves '*Šinobusi'* in honour of the railbus. Former participants of the 'culture-smuggling' festival, the band makes visual use of railway imagery and incorporates it into its songs (titles like 'Endless tracks' and 'Silver arrow'[31]).

Fig. 10: *Kultúrcsempész* - the *šinobus* festival[32]

5   Conclusion

We have sought to examine three broad flows of the informal cross-border economy in Vojvodina. In the 1980s Yugoslavia was a source for material goods and cultural products for its poorer and more isolated socialist neighbours. Simultaneous to the rise of nationalism in Serbia and other republics, Yugoslavia

31   'Beskrajna pruga' and 'Srebrna Strela' – another nickname for the Serbian Railways' *šinobus*.
32   Source: Edvárd Molnár. In: Magyar Szóe, URL: http://www.magyarszo.com/fex.page:2009-10-19_A_II_Kulturcsempesz_Sinbusz_Fesztival_margojara.xhtml (last access: 30.06.2011).

witnessed a 'last cry' of pan-Yugoslav pop-culture.[33] We examine how part of this culture, newly composed folk music, made its way illicitly into Romania through the Banat region. The legacy of this music is evident in the visual and audible traces of Serbian pop-culture in the city of Timişoara and the impact of Serbian pop-folk on contemporary Romanian ethno-pop, *muzică orientală*. The 1990s saw a massive change in the relationship between Serbia and its neighbours – the end of communism saw regime changes in Hungary and Romania, the availability of consumer goods with the adoption of the market economy. The cold-war geopolitical hierarchy which saw Serbia/Yugoslavia hold a more prestigious position than its Warsaw Pact neighbours was inverted by the early 1990s. War and sanctions in Serbia rendered Vojvodina poor and isolated. Serbia became dependent upon the resources of Hungary and Romania. As part of this process we have examined narratives of the smuggling of household necessities and fuel into North-eastern Vojvodina from Hungary and Romania. The post-2000 era is characterised by processes of European integration. 2000 marked the end of the Milošević regime in Serbia and the beginning of meaningful democratisation and the relative normalisation of public life. Hungary and Romania became EU member states in 2004 and 2006 respectively. As the shortages and crises of the 1980s and 1990s receded so did *šverc* to a certain degree. With the equalisation of prices for many goods at three sides of the borders there is less incentive to smuggle – cultural products and other goods are freely available through legal channels. However, as we have demonstrated by reference to our own research in Banat, cigarette smuggling is still big business driven by a gap in the price between Serbia and bordering EU states and ambiguous standards of border regulation.

Other than tracing the dynamics of small-scale smuggling chronologically we sought to observe the practice from the normative perspectives of informants we communicated with. What can be observed is that unlike bigger-scale smuggling or the trade of illegal weapons, narcotics or human trafficking, *šverc* is not a social taboo. Rather, it is embedded in the everyday practices of the actors involved in it and viewed by them as one of the many strategies of surviving economic difficulties and ubiquitous to border life in this particular area. The immorality of the state as represented by institutions and public figures is considered a key justification for *šverc*. Search narratives sharply contrast with concerned actors who fret about the negative impact of smuggling upon processes of Europeanization. Widespread smuggling visible to passengers and officials alike at the Hungarian and Romanian side of their borders with Serbia

---

33   This is embodied by the Yugoslav New Wave (Idoli, Azra), pop stars like Lepa Brena and
      Tajči, and events like the 1984 Sarajevo Winter Olympics, the 1987 Zagreb Universiade and
      the 1989 Yugoslav win in the Eurovision Song Contest with the band Riva.

surely negate the notion of European integration as a departure from the grey economy. In fact as one Serbian border guard drolly commented to us, neighbouring states to Serbia now in the EU can 'do what they want' without major consequences. In this case she was referring to a major smuggling ring operating at the border post by organised criminals.

One may expect a study of a multi-national, multi-lingual border region to revolve around ethno-national categories, particularly in a state like Serbia where nationalism remains an extremely tangible element of socio-political life. However, we found that in the border regions of the Serbia, Hungary and Romania a certain degree of cultural heterogeneity and ambiguity violates a Gellnerian model of nationalism which presupposes cultural homogeneity as contingent for the political principle of nationalism (see Gellner 1983, 1997). While ethno-national categories were resonant, evident by the casual reification of many informants who spoke of 'the Serbs' and 'the Hungarians' as bounded homogenous groups, the actions of most respondents did not cohere with such narrow ethno-national conceptions. Ethno-national belonging appeared to be more or less accepted as a social fact by informants but did not represent a touchstone which would dictate *šverc* and other cross-border activities. Many categories were posited as sources of difference not only ethnically but socio-economically, regionally and morally and thus demanding a less 'ethnicised lens' of the researcher.

References

Andreas, P. (2005): "Criminalizing Consequences of Sanctions: Embargo Busting and Its Legacy". In: International Studies Quarterly, 49, pp. 335-360.

Antonić, S. (2002): Zarobljena Zemlja: Srbije za Vlade Slobodana Miloševića [A Captive Country: Serbia under the Rule of Slobodan Milošević]. Beograd: Otkrovenje.

Bakić Hayden, M. (1995): "Nesting Orientalisms: The Case of Former Yugoslavia". In: Slavic Review, 54, 1, pp. 917-931.

Beissinger, M. H. (2008): "Muzică Orientală: Identity and popular culture in Postcommunist Romania". In: D.A. Buchanan (ed.): Balkan Popular Culture and the Ottoman Ecumene: Music, Image and Regional Political Discourse. Lanham/MD: Scarecrow Press, pp. 95-142.

Berényi, E. (2009): A II. Kultúrcsempész Sínbusz Fesztivál margójára [On the margins of the second Culture Smuggler Festival]. In: Magyar Szó, 19 October (Művelődés) 2009, URL: http://www.magyarszo.com/fex.page:2009-10-19_A_II_Kulturcsempesz_Sinbusz_Fesztival_margojara.xhtml (last access: 21.09.2010).

Bieber, F. / Winterhagen, J. (2006): Ethnic Violence in Vojvodina: Glitch or Harbinger of Conflicts to Come?. ECMI Working Paper, 27.

Bjelić, D. / Savić, O. (eds.) (2002): Balkan as Metaphor: Between Globalization and Fragmentation. Boston: MIT Press.

Bourdieu, P. (1982): "The Forms of Capital". In: J. E. Richardson (ed.): Handbook of Theory of Research for the Sociology of Education. New York: Greenword Press, pp. 46-58.

Buchanan, D. (1996): "Wedding musicians, Political transition, and national consciousness in Bulgaria". In: M. Slobin (ed.): Retuning culture: Musical changes in central and eastern Europe. Durham/NC: Duke University Press, pp. 200-230.

Cheater, A. P. (1998): "Transcending the state? Gender and Borderline Constructions of Citizenship in Zimbabwe". In: T. W. Wilson and H. Donnan (eds.): Border identities: Nation and state at international frontiers. Cambridge: Cambridge University Press, pp. 191-214.

Cvejić, B. (2010): "Građani i dalje najviše cene Tita [Citizens still regard Tito most highly]". In: Danas, 1, pp. 4-5.

Danilović, J. (2007): "Novi putevi šverca cigareta [New routes for smuggling cigarettes]". In: Politika, 19 June (Hronika) 2007, URL: http://www.politika.rs/rubrike/Hronika/t31880.lt.html (last access: 01.09.2010).

Devicé, A. (2002): Nationalism, Regional Multiculturalism and Democracy. Bonn: Zentrum für Europäische Integrationsforschung.

Dinkić, M. (1995): Ekonomije Destrukcije [The Economics of Destruction]. Belgrade: VIN.

Dimitrijević, V. / Pejic, J. (1994): The Effects of UN Sanctions Against Yugoslavia (Serbia and Montenegro): Theory and Conventionalism in the Current Context, URL: http://www.kent.ac.uk/politics/research/kentpapers/diumitri.html (last access: 26.04.2006).

Galasinska, A. / Galasinski, D. (2003): "Discursive strategies for coping with sensitive topics of the other". In: Journal of Ethnic and Migration Studies, 29, 5, pp. 849-863.

Gellner, E. (1983): Nations and Nationalism. Oxford: Blackwell.

Gellner, E. (1997): Nationalism. London: Weidenfeld and Nicolson.

Goldsworthy, V. (1998): Inventing Ruritania: The Imperialism of the Imagination. New Haven: Yale University Press.

Hožić, A. (2008): "The Balkan Merchants: Changing Borders and Informal Transnationalization". In: D. Kostovicova and V. Bojicic-Dzelilovic (eds.): Transnationalism in the Balkans. Abingdon: Routledge, pp. 27-40.

HRW – Human Rights Watch (2005): Dangerous Indifference: Assaults on Minorities in Vojvodina. URL: http://www.hrw.org/de/node/11582/section/8 (last access: 01.09.2010).

Holly, W. et.al. (2003): "Unequal neighbours: coping with asymmetries". In: Journal of Ethnic and Migration Studies, 29, 5, pp. 819–834.

Ilić, V. (2001): Minorities and refugees in Vojvodina. Belgrade: Helsinki Committee for Human Rights in Serbia.

Jansen, S. (2009): "After the red passport: towards an anthropology of the everyday geopolitics of entrapment in the EU's 'immediate outside'". In: The Journal of the Royal Anthropological Institute, 15, 4, pp. 815-832.

Jašarević, L. (2007): "Everyday Work: Subsistence Economy, Social Belonging and Moralities of Exchange at a Bosnian Black Market". In: X. Bougarel, E. Helms and G. Duijzings (eds.): The new Bosnian Mosaic: Identities, Memories and Moral Claims in a Post-War Society. Aldershot: Ashgrave, pp. 273-294.

Judah, T. (2000): The Serbs: History, Myth and the Destruction of Yugoslavia. Ithaca: Yale University Press.

Krastev, I. (2002): "The Balkans: Democracy without Choices". In: Journal of Democracy, 13, 3, pp. 49-51.

Korhec, T (2006): Unikatna regija u Evropi. Belgrade: Limes plus.

Kostovicova, D. / Bojičić-Dželilović, V. (2008): "Europeanising the Balkans: Rethinking the Post-Communist and Post-Conflict Transition". In: D. Kostovicova and V. Bojičić-Dželilović (eds.): Transnationalism in the Balkans. Abingdon: Routledge, pp. 9-25.

Kultúrcsempész [Culture Smuggler] (2001): Festival website, URL: http://kulturcsempesz.blogspot.com (last access: 10.09.2010).

Lin, N. (2001): Social Capital: A Theory of Social Structure and Action. Cambridge: Cambridge University Press.

Lj.B. (2008): "Nema ulične prodaje benzina [There are no street sales of petrol]". In: Zrenjaninski List, 12 June 2008, URL: http://www.listzrenjanin.com/index.php?option=com_content&view=article&id=1213:svratite -za-beskunike-prestaje-da-radi&catid=133:hronika (last access: 01.09.2010).

Matić, Đ. (2004): "Lepa Brena". In: I. Andrić, V. Arsenijević and Đ. Matić (eds.): Leksikon Yu Mitologije [The Lexicon of Yu Mythology]. Zagreb and Belgrade: Rende and Postscriptum, pp. 223-226.

Meinhof, U. H. / Galasinski, D. (2002): "Reconfiguring East-West identities: cross-generational discourses in German and Polish border communities". In: Journal of Ethnic and Migration Studies, 28, 1, pp. 63-82.

Meinhof, U. H. (2003): "Migrating borders: An introduction to European identity construction in process". In: Journal of Ethnic and Migration Studies, 29, 5, pp. 781-796.

Monterescu, D. (1999): Relational Sociology and the Fallacies of Methodological Nationalism: Theorizing Urban Space and Binational Sociality in Jewish-Arab "Mixed Towns". URL: http://web.ceu.hu/soc_ant/faculty/monterescupub/Monterescu%20Spatial%20Heteronomy%20 in%20Ethnically%20Mixed%20Towns%20Ashgate%202007.pdf (last access: 10.09.2010).

Nora, P. (1989): "Between Memory and History: Les Lieux de Mémoire". In: Representations, 26, pp. 7-24.

NUNS (2010): "Vršac novi centar šverca cigareta [Vršac the new centre for cigarette smuggling]". In: Vesti.rs, 10 August 2010, URL: http://www.vesti.rs/Blogovi/Vrsac-novi-centar-sverca-cigareta.html (last access: 09.09.2010).

Olick, J. K. / Robbins, J. (1998): "Social Memory Studies: From Collective Memory to the Historical Sociology of Mnemonic Practices". In: Annual Review of Sociology, 24, pp. 105-140.

Ramac, M. (2001): Vojvodina Autonomy Drive: The province of Vojvodina is demanding that the Serbian authorities restore its former autonomous status. URL: http://iwpr.net/report-news/vojvodina-autonomy-drive (last access: 20.05.2011).

Ramet, S. / Pavlakovic, V. (eds.) (2005): Serbia since 1989: politics and society under Milošević and after. Seattle: University of Washington Press.

Rice, T. (2002): "Bulgaria or Chalgaria: The Attenuation of Bulgarian Nationalism in a Mass-Mediated Popular Music". In: Yearbook for Traditional Music, 34, pp. 25-46.

Šinobusi (2010): Official website. URL: http://www.sinobusi.com/ (last access: 20.09.2010).

Somers, M. R. (1994): "A narrative constitution of identity: A relational and network approach". In: Theory and Society, 23, 5, pp. 605-649.

Stanimirović, S. (2010): "Srbija prva u regionu po švercu cigareta: rast ilegalnog tržišta [Serbia first in the region for cigarette smuggling: the growth of the illegal market]". In: Blic, 21 June 2010, URL: http://www.blic.rs/Vesti/Drustvo/194802/Srbija-prva-u-regionu-po-svercu-cigareta (last access: 01.09.2010).

Thomas, R. (1998): Serbia under Milošević: Politics in the 1990s. London: Hurst and Co.

Todorova, M. (1997): Imagining the Balkans. Oxford: Oxford University Press.

Velikonja, M. (2009): Titostalgia: A Study of Nostalgia for Josip Broz. Ljubljana: Peace Institute.

Verdery, K. (1995): National ideology under socialism: identity and cultural politics in Ceausescu's Romania. Berkeley, Los Angeles: California University Press.

Vidić Rasmussen, L. (2002): Newly Composed Folk Music of Yugoslavia. New York, London: Routledge.

Vidić Rasmussen, L. (1995): "From source to commodity: newly-composed folk music of Yugoslavia". In: Popular Music, 14, 2, pp. 241-256.

Voiculescu, C. (2005): "Production and Consumption of FolkPop Music in PostSocialist Romania: Discourse and Practice". In: Ethnologia Balkanica, 9, pp. 261-283.

Wilson, T. M. / Donnan, H. (1998): "Nation, state and identity at international borders". In: T. M. Wilson and H. Donnan (eds.): Border identities: Nation and state at international frontiers. Cambridge: Cambridge University Press, pp. 1-30.

Wilson, T. M. / Donnan, H. (1999): Borders: Frontiers of Identity, Nation and State. Oxford, New York: Berg.

Wolff, L. (1994): Inventing Eastern Europe: The Map of Civilization on the Mind of the Enlightenment. Stanford: Stanford University Press.

Živković, M. (1997): "Violent Highlanders and Peaceful Lowlanders: Uses and Abuses of Ethno-Geography in the Balkans from Versailles to Dayton". In: Replika: Hungarian Social Science Quarterly (Ambiguous Identities in the New Europe, Special Issue), URL: http://www.c3.hu/scripta/scripta0/replika/honlap/english/02/08zivk.htm (last access 27.06. 2011).

Živković, M. (2001): "Nešto između: simbolička geografija Srbije [Something in between: the Symbolic Geography of Serbia]". In: Filozofija i društvo, 18, pp. 73-112.

Navigating uncertainty: Observations from the Congo-Rwanda border

Martin Doevenspeck and Nene Morisho Mwanabiningo

1   Introduction

This article concentrates on how people make use of the state boundary between the cities of Goma, Democratic Republic of Congo (DRC), and Gisenyi, Rwanda to cope with specific uncertainties on either side, how these borderlanders, by doing so, expose themselves to new uncertainties and how they at the same time subvert and perpetuate the border through their activities. This tension-filled state boundary separates two countries that, after fifteen years of war, proxy warfare and mutual allegations of supporting militias and rebel groups, have only very recently started hesitant efforts towards a political rapprochement. Despite the long-lasting ethnic and identity conflicts in this region and remaining tensions (for overviews see Mamdani 2001; Lemarchand 2009; Prunier 2009) this border, situated between the Congo Basin and the densely populated highlands of Uganda and Rwanda, has always kept its function as a transit point for long-distance trade connecting the east and the west of Central Africa (see Tegera/Johnson 2007). Additionally, the Goma-Gisenyi border posts were always and still are busy places of daily commuter transit. Thousands of small-scale traders and day labourers, but also students and teachers, come and go between the two towns. Different taxation laws in the two countries foster widespread small-scale smuggling, the *chora chora*. Many consumer goods for instance, such as electrical appliances, alcohol or construction materials are cheaper in the DRC, and are unofficially re-exported to Rwanda, from where they came.

All these people use the border to cope with different country-specific risks and uncertainties in their everyday life by engaging in different border-related activities. The spectrum of these risks and uncertainties ranges from crime and lack of legal certainty in Congo to economic patronizing and excessive control and policing in Rwanda. With regard to strategies for coping with risk and uncertainty, there are three main types of border-related activity we will focus on: small-scale trade, smuggling and commuting. We argue that analysing the motivations and strategies of these border crossers, and their encounters with representatives of the border regime, by drawing on the concepts of risk and uncertainty can provide precious insights into state-society relations and an understanding of the state's legitimacy. After presenting the analytical framework and methodological background of the study, and contextualizing the border, the empirical chapter analyses different patterns of coping with risk and uncertainty connected with the border, before the paper ends with some reflections on the methodological, contextual and theoretical contributions of this research.

2   Linking border studies and risk research: the analytical framework

Our approach is supported by social anthropology, political geography and social theories of risk and uncertainty. Focusing on border economies marked by small-scale cross-border trade and smuggling reflects a turn in geography and other disciplines within border studies, away from descriptive approaches to state boundaries and towards the analysis of agency and processes in borderlands (see Kolossov 2005; Paasi 2005; Newman 2006). It furthermore recognizes that state boundaries have always been, and often still are, shaped by trade and a range of illicit activities that constitute important livelihood strategies for the border populations who make use of the special opportunities the border creates, just as much as by geopolitics and processes of globalization and regional integration (see Thuen 1999; Girtler 2006; Golub/Mbaye 2009). However, the various practices utilizing the border cannot be studied in a political vacuum. Rather, the motivations for engaging in a border-related activity, be it illicit or not, must be considered and linked to the wider political economy and the condition of the state on either side. By motivations we do not imply incentives such as price and tariff differences, which should be regarded as prerequisites rather than driving forces for cross-border trade. Instead, we focus on the impacts of a "permeation of stateness into the everyday" (Painter 2006: 753), which we perceive as risks for and uncertainties of borderlander's livelihoods. Hence, when linking the concepts of risk and uncertainty to the study of cross-border agency we are not primarily interested in the sheer economics of smuggling (see for example Bhagwati/Hansen 1973; Slemrod/Yitzhaki 2002) and the associated strand of risk analysis of smuggling situations (see e.g. Sheikh 1989). Accordingly we neglect the different demand and cost functions of smuggling and unofficial trade highlighted in this literature, and use these terms synonymously. In the study area, both activities are carried out with the objective of evading taxes and fees by importing undeclared goods, and, as we will show later, both transpire at customs stations as well as along unauthorized routes between the checkpoints. We conceptualize small-scale cross-border trade, smuggling and other cross-border activities as a means of dealing with risk and uncertainty arising from the specific pattern of statehood on the respective side of the border. People attempt to escape, at least temporarily, from their own state, while sometimes exposing themselves to risks and uncertainties linked to the state of 'the other'.

Nevertheless, crossing the border to cope with the risks and uncertainties of everyday life arising from the performance of the state, does not necessarily embody political resistance. As in other parts of the world (see Donnan/Wilson 1999), research on unofficial cross-border trade that incorporates the complicity of state agents in Africa suggests an ambivalent relationship between illicit border activities and state-society interactions, and points to the paradox that these activities subvert the nation state and at the same time seem to continually reconfirm its territorial logic, as they depend on the border for its perpetuation (see Flynn 1997; Nugent 2002). Roitman (2004, 2005), in her study on the border economy of the Chad Basin, describes the outcome of this contradictory relationship not as a parallel or alternative political order, but as a 'dislocated political system'. Despite subversive border practices, this dislocation is considered as being entrenched in the logical order of the nation state, which it ultimately confirms and perpetuates. The author suggests that the key to understanding the paradox between the "increasing intensity of unregulated activities and the persistent efficacy of state infrastructure" (Roitman 2004: 194) is to distinguish between state power and pluralized state regulatory authority. This means that the state, represented by border officials, may not prevent smuggling, but may extract fees from the smugglers. Drawing on the work of Roitman and using a case study from a borderland not far from our case area, Raeymaekers (2009) describes the establishment of new forms of political interaction along the Congolese-Ugandan border, through an analysis of unofficial cross-border trade.

In this article we intend to shed light on the relationship between cross-border activities and state-society relations by concentrating on the border crossers' motivations, which are, as we argue, linked to risks and uncertainties that are rooted in the two specific patterns of statehood on the two sides of the border. Contemporary risk concepts are first of all applied to describe the particular development stage of modern or post-modern societies, reflected not least in the title of Ulrich Beck's seminal book on reflexive modernity (see Beck 1986). Though the reflexive modernization approach (see also Giddens 1991) is only one of several theoretical approaches to risk in the social sciences (for a comprehensive overview, see Zinn 2008), most of these approaches share more or less the same deep-rootedness, both philosophically and empirically, in the Western experience of the successful use of risk for economic progress in the modernization process. Another commonality is that they broaden the perspective by referring to the social construction of risk, thus highlighting its mental and selective dimension. In this regard, Deborah Lupton (1999: 35) distinguishes epistemologically between realist, weak constructionist and strong constructionist approaches, according to the degree to which they accept that risks are objectively given. Since construction implies agency, the concept of risk should be applicable to a study of human agency in general, be it in modern or allegedly pre-modern societies. In this regard, we refer to the distinction between hazard as a fact independent of human agency, and risk as an outcome of a decision by actors or society, which emphasizes the relevance of social action (see Luhmann 1993). In this perspective, risks are socially constructed since, based on calculation, they are translated hazards. Risk is therefore a relative category, linked to and determined by particular actors.

A broader approach aiming at a societal perspective of risk reveals the importance of the more general concept of uncertainty (see Bonss 1995; O'Malley 2004, 2008). We understand uncertainty as a concept of managing everyday life in a politico-economic environment that is highly dynamic and therefore difficult to assess both in the present and in the future. Thus, if we agree that uncertainty is in one way or another a fundamental experience of people all over the world today who have to accept some degree of uncertainty and instability, and that risk research is therefore also an attempt to understand the life worlds of people in precarious livelihood contexts, then it becomes clear what Macamo (2008: 258) means when he considers Africa as an ideal empirical background for following a risk perspective. This involves an attempt at loosening a certain epistemological wedge that has resulted from making a distinction between concepts of risk in modern to late-modern societies and those in the rest of the world, which implies a predominant focus on vulnerability and natural hazards in risk research in Africa. Instead, the entire complex of 'old' and 'new' empirical and epistemological objects of risk research should be considered, which in our case includes the danger constituted by the state itself.

To put it simply, we seek to understand how borderlanders describe the uncertainties and specific risks they face in their respective country, how far the Goma-Giseny state boundary constitutes a source of certainty for border crossers, and what kind of new risks emerge from border-crossing. We argue that this analysis of interpretations and activities can help to shed light on the nature of contemporary state-society relations in this borderland.

3   Methodological approach

In order to gain insights into the strategies of border crossers and their encounters with the respective state, we opted for a mix of methods. This consisted of observation at different places on the border, interviews both at the border and in the homes of the interviewees, and a standardized questionnaire, which together with secondary data from reports of customs authorities in Congo and Rwanda gave an idea of the nature and quantity of commodities traded officially and unofficially. For this paper, we drew on data gathered during several field trips to the Congolese-Rwandan borderland between March 2007 and September 2010. Interviews and informal conversations were conducted in French, Swahili and Kinyarwanda with different individuals from both sides of the border. Not all interviews are audio recordings, since many Rwandans were scared of the Rwandan secret service, which is omnipresent but hardly visible to outsiders, both at the border and in the two towns. To observe the various border practices, we stayed at the border on a regular basis and often crossed it several times a day. This allowed us to follow the daily negotiations of official and unofficial border crossings, particularly on the Congolese side, and the strict checks people are exposed to in Rwanda. While it was fairly easy to approach small-scale traders and commuters, it was much more difficult to gain the trust of smugglers. Ironically, it was one of our interview partners at the Rwanda Revenue Authority who put us in contact with a smuggler who was well-known in the milieu. This young woman, who was born in Congo and raised in Rwanda, accepted to be part of our team as a research assistant and helped us to get in contact with other smugglers from both sides. Her presence during the meetings was a kind of guarantee for our respondents that we were not working for the border authorities or the police. Moreover, as a key informant, she opened our eyes to smuggling practices that were otherwise invisible. Yet, even if our respondents were not involved in trafficking illicit goods such as drugs or weapons, and we avoided touching upon the sensitive issue of smuggling petroleum and minerals, our research and in particular our regular border crossings, sometimes four or five times a day, gave rise to suspicions on both sides. It was much easier to handle the Congolese authorities, who gradually became familiar with us, than the strict Rwandan border security. Two short-term arrests by the latter only temporarily interrupted our research.

4   Conflict, trade and merging cities: The Goma-Gisenyi border in context

The geopolitical setting

Goma and Gisenyi were founded as Belgian and German colonial military posts respectively, and, as in so many other parts of Africa, a new border suddenly separated local life worlds that had until then been closely intertwined. After the First World War, the Belgians took over Gisenyi together with the rest of the German colony of Rwanda-Urundi (see Bindseil 2008). From independence in 1960 until the 1990s, the border was characterized by lax controls, which reflected the close relationship between Zaire's long-time dictator, Mobutu, and the Rwandan president, Habyarimana, who were close allies in the politics of the Great Lakes region. An important rupture occurred in 1994, when, after the end of the civil war in Rwanda and the genocide as its horrible culmination, more than one million refugees, including well-armed soldiers and militias, crossed the border into Goma, fleeing reprisals by the troops of Rwanda's former rebel chief and current president, Paul Kagame. Virtually overnight, the border became a border between two enemies, since the Zairian authorities did not prevent the exiles from launching attacks on the Rwandan side of the border. These attacks triggered the invasion of the new Rwandan army, which, together with the rebel movement of Laurent Desiré Kabila, the father of Congo's current president, Joseph Kabila, spearheaded the overthrow of Mobutu in 1997. During the following years, Goma was the headquarters of a Rwandan-backed rebel movement which contested the new regime in Kinshasa (see Tull 2005). During the de facto occupation of Eastern Congo by Rwanda from 1998 to 2003, there were virtually no border controls. The border regime changed again when Rwandan troops retreated in 2003. With the elections of 2006, and the political decline of the Rwandan-backed rebellion, the Congolese state regained a certain degree of control of its borders in the east. At the same time the insurgency of dissident General Laurent Nkunda, who was perceived as Rwanda's proxy, against Joseph Kabila (see Stearns 2008), gave rise to a distinct militarization of the border and rigid controls. With Nkunda's arrest in 2009, the Rwandan government reacted to harsh allegations by the international community of fuelling the war, and opened the door for a political rapprochement. This also found expression in a relaxing of the rules for border crossers and less rigid controls.

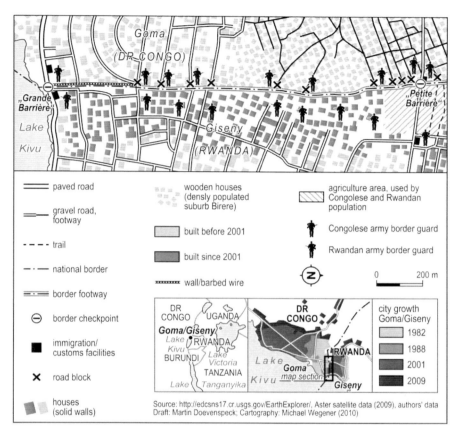

Fig. 11: The border area between Goma (DRC) and Giseny (Rwanda)

A fragmented urban borderland

From the beginning of violent conflict in Eastern Congo in the early 1990s, Goma's population increased fourfold to an estimated 800,000 in 2010. Refugees from the war-torn rural areas, and migrants attracted by the new job market created by the construction boom, where a lot of money from mineral exploitation (especially cassiterite and coltan) is reinvested, but also by the concentration of international humanitarian organizations, poured into the city (see Vlassenroot/Büscher 2010). Gisenyi, with about 100,000 residents, is far smaller, although it has experienced steady but more modest growth during the past two decades. Beside cross-border trade the city depends economically on a modest tourism industry, a brewery and some banks. The westward extension of the city towards the border has led to significant densification. Here, the two cities almost physically merge, due to extensive construction activities in a strip between the two official border checkpoints Petite Barrière and Grande Barrière (fig. 11).

This area was seen as a neutral zone until the Rwandan authorities made a dirt road in the late 1990s to definitely fix the boundary line, which now runs between the poor but lively district of Birere, with its wooden houses, and the Rwandan-occupied area with high-class real estate. Today, most buildings along the border are only separated by no more than five metres (fig. 12).

Fig. 12: Buildings along the border: The new construction is on the Rwandan side, the corrugated-iron house on the Congolese

Despite the spatial proximity and intensive economic interactions, little prepares the visitor to this borderland for what is waiting on the other side. Gisenyi is a calm, well-organized and tidy city, well-equipped with infrastructure, where plastic bags are forbidden for environmental reasons, and where one can feel safe strolling about at night. By contrast, the first impression one gets of Goma is usually that of a chaotic, stirring and vibrant place with hardly any basic infrastructure or public services, except in the city centre, and an extremely high crime rate. This reflects real asymmetries and inequalities: economic opportunities in unsafe Goma, in contrast to visible urban governance and security in Gisenyi, where local markets are much smaller. It mirrors the completely different paths of development followed by the two states since the mid 1990s, with the result that this border is not only one between former warring parties, but also between two very diverse political orders and societal projects. On the one side Rwanda, ostensibly the 'strongest' state in Africa with its obsession for security and control and an impressive development in terms of macroeconomic indicators (see Goloobo-Mutebi 2008; Ansoms 2009). On the other side, the DRC with weak and dysfunctional, if not completely absent, state institutions, partly under the custody of the UN and the international humanitarian industry, and partly at the mercy of politico-economic adventurers (see Kodi 2008; Prunier 2009).

The border regime

The DRC and Rwanda share two main border checkpoints: Goma/Gisenyi on the northern shore of Lake Kivu, and Bukavu/Cyangugu on the southern shore. With more than 15,000 people crossing the border officially every day, the Goma-Gisenyi borderland is considered as the most integrated in the region (see INICA 2006). These border crossers are not only traders and day labourers but also students and teachers who come and go between the two towns. There are two main official border posts linking Goma and Gisenyi: Grande Barrière, also called Corniche, which is situated on the lakefront, and Petite Barrière which links Goma's commercial centre and the Gisenyi market. Most cross-border trade takes place at Grande Barrière, since this is the customs post for cars and trucks. The staff of international organizations use this border post for immigration procedures. Petite Barrière is usually closed to personal vehicles and large trucks, and it is rare to see foreigners at this checkpoint where only pedestrians can cross. A third but less frequented border post is called Kibumba-Ruhuna and serves the people living in the more rural areas north of Petite Barrière. The three border posts open at 6 am. As an expression of the political rapprochement between the DRC and Rwanda, Grande Barrière was kept open until midnight from September 2009, and since April 2010 it has been open daily for 24 hours, whereas the two others still close at 6 pm. Officially it is unproblematic for local residents to cross the border as they only need to show their identity card to the immigration officers to obtain a daily permit, called jeton, to cross to the other town. A jeton only allows an individual to move within the municipal limits. Those who want to travel onwards are required to buy a pass, a so-called laisser passer, which is also required for Congolese and Rwandans living outside Goma and Gisenyi. However, crossing the border is not so easy for many others. Especially on the Congolese side of Petite Barrière, people often spend hours discussing with border officials about the amount of a small bribe to be given before they can get a jeton. Besides these official movements, there are hundreds of smugglers and traders, as well as commuters who simply avoid the time-consuming official procedures, who negotiate their own way across the border, especially along the strip between the border posts.

On the Rwandan side, there are five services operating at the border: army, police, the Rwanda Revenue Authority, the Rwanda Immigration Service, and Magasins Généraux du Rwanda which is a kind of public warehouse. By contrast, the Congolese side is characterized by a multiplicity of services in addition to the five main services, the Congolese Revenue Authority, the border police, the Immigration Office, the Congolese Bureau of Control, and the health service, which are all involved in the lucrative customs practices.[34] What makes things even more confusing is that most of these services seem to have their own civilian 'subcontractors', approximately 250[35] in number, usually unemployed men, who have permission to search border crossers for a share of the gains.

Cross-border trade and tariffs

In order to shed light on the incentives for cross-border trade and smuggling, we will elaborate in what follows on the contradiction between officially high importation costs in the DRC, which are also due to the above-mentioned multiplicity of Congolese state services operating at the border, and comparatively low prices for many products on the markets of Goma.

Situated between the Congo Basin and the densely populated highlands of Uganda and Rwanda, the area around Lake Kivu has always been an important transit region for long-distance trade connecting the east and the west of Central Africa. At the Goma-Gisenyi border, minerals from the mines of North Kivu are exported overseas via Rwanda and East African ports. In return, and along the same routes, consumer goods in transit from Mombasa or Dar es Salaam,

---

34   To name only a few: Service d'Hygiène, Police Spéciale des Frontières, Bureau du Receveur, Direction Générale des Douanes et Accises, Bureau de la Brigade Douanière, la Police Economique, sécurité militaire, Office des renseignements, Direction générale des migrations, Agence National des Renseignements, Gouvernement de la Province, Mairie de Goma, Service de Transport et Communication, Garde Républicaine.

35   Interviews with the head of the Congolese border police (Goma, November 2007) and a former head of the immigration office at Petite Barrière (Bunagana, October 2008).

construction materials and petroleum products are imported (see Tegera/Johnson 2007). As local products, foodstuffs such as beans, maize and palm oil, but also tobacco, timber and charcoal, are taken to Rwanda for consumption, while meat, milk products and vegetables from Rwanda are sold at local markets in Goma.

A look at the customs regime for some of the most traded commodities at the Goma-Gisenyi border makes clear that despite the statements of Rwandan traders, who usually complain about high import taxes in their country compared to the DRC, customs duties for some valuable and highly demanded goods such as alcohol are lower in Rwanda (table 2).

Product	Customs duty in % of value of goods / DRC	Customs duty in % of value of goods / Rwanda
Mineral water	77	58
Alcohol (wine, spirits)	77	58
Woven fabrics	37	78
Fish	37	33
Powdered milk	22	58
Food products (e.g. potatoes, tomatoes)	27	33
Tinned tomatoes	29	58

Tab. 2: Total customs duties on imported goods in Rwanda and DR Congo (Source: RRA 2008; MiniFin 2007; various interviews with border officials in Rwanda and DRC.)

The cumulative taxation regime, with a multiplicity of customs duties and rates imposed by often competing services, ultimately ought to make imports costly for the traders. Yet instead, alcohol is much cheaper in Goma than in Gisenyi. A three-litre bag-in-box of South African red wine, for example, bought by Rwandan and Congolese traders at the same place (usually Dubai or Nairobi) and with more or less the same transportation expenses, is 20US$ in Goma, 26 in Gisenyi and even 33 in the Rwandan capital Kigali. These price differences can only be explained by a massive underestimation of the customs value by traders in alliance with Congolese border officials. The phenomenon of fiscal evasion and the associated problem of a low tax contribution to the GDP are recognized by the Congolese Ministry of Finance[36]. The possibility of underestimating customs value is also attractive for traders from Rwanda, where state services are much more rigid. Many of them prefer to clear their goods in the DRC and to re-

---

36   See http://www.minfinrdc.cd/poli_fiscale_probleme.htm (last access: 17.09.2010).

export them unofficially to Rwanda, from where they came in transit. As we will show in the following section, unofficial cross-border trade and smuggling particularly concerns those products whose customs value is underestimated.

5   Chora Chora, small-scale trade and the cross-border organization of everyday life: using the border to navigate uncertainty

In what follows we will analyse three main types of border-related activity as strategies for coping with risk and uncertainty linked to the respective shape of statehood, in order to gain insights into state-society relations and an understanding of the state's legitimacy: commuting, small-scale trade and smuggling.

Escaping disorder: Congolese in Gisenyi

Congolese traders buy goods at the Gisenyi markets that have become rare in Goma due to persisting violent conflict and insecurity spread by uncontrolled militias and government soldiers in the rural hinterland. In addition, there are two principal groups of Congolese that use the border to escape the risks and uncertainties linked to weak state institutions in their country.

The first group that uses the border in this way consists of carpenters, mechanics and other craftsmen who cross the border every morning to work in Gisenyi. Talking with these men, it quickly becomes apparent that it is not only the better pay they get for their work, but also the lack of legal certainty in Goma that makes Gisenyi so attractive for them.

"The Rwandans treat us very well. They pay directly after you have finished the work. Otherwise they will be punished by their own people... There is no problem as in Congo. People in Congo do not want to pay. And when you call the police your client will pay them in order to be in the right. And the police will make life difficult for you. Take my word for it!"[37]

Like the privatization of security which we will address below, the commodification of law, and the legal vacuum that has emerged due to protracted violent conflict and that has been filled gradually by a legal pluralism (for the example of land tenure in rural Eastern Congo, see Lecoutere et al. 2009), have led to a situation of pronounced legal uncertainty. For most Congolese the rule of law probably does not exist anymore, which makes some

---

37   Interview with a Congolese carpenter, September 2010, Gisenyi.

of them seek legal certainty in the neighbouring country, where law enforcement, even if sometimes politically manipulated, is strong.

The second group consists of young pragmatic Congolese with a regular income who have relocated their family's residence to Gisenyi, where living costs are lower and where they escape the prevalent insecurity in Goma. They navigate easily between the two orders that provide them security on the one side and business opportunities on the other. Just like many traders and street vendors, they cross the border on a daily basis, but I seldom saw them having problems with border officials.

> "I live here (in Gisenyi), I have rented a house. Here I'm studying but every day I go to Goma for business. My life is in Goma, the only thing I do here is sleep and I sleep well. … There is a lot of insecurity in Goma and once we were raided in my house. I feel safe now even if they want to control everything. But I don't care, I have nothing to hide, you know. I like them; they know how to rule a country. But on the other hand, I feel pity for them. They are always scared."[38]

This quote expresses the ambivalent attitude of the Congolese towards Rwanda: appreciation of apparently effective organization, while the omnipresence of control and surveillance is disconcerting. However, it also shows that the decisive thing for these people is that life in Rwanda, at least for them as Congolese, is more predictable than in Goma, where the logics of the functioning of the Congolese state heavily impact on the everyday life of the inhabitants. Raeymaekers and Vlassenroot (2009: 141) describe the Congolese form of statehood as 'mediated' in order to underline the analytical shortcomings of concepts such as 'state collapse' or 'failing state', and point to the fact that what is described as absence or weakness of the state is the result of competition between state and non-state spheres of regulation, composed of antagonistic institutions that often neutralize each other. However they may be described, the realities of how public authority is implemented and the everyday practices of state representatives complicate life for people in Goma. From the beginning of the 1990s, the political struggle for the control of different services and agencies at the local, regional and national level has accelerated the decline of the public sector, which already began in the Mobutu era. Today, the national electricity and water companies are largely unable to regularly supply at least ten percent of the population. People are forced to walk extremely long distances to get water from the Lake Kivu, which also poses serious health problems. And as soon as the sun goes down, the city turns into a romping ground for criminals who take advantage of the fact that due to insufficient power supply the major part of the city is unlit. Though there is no research on violent crime in the city, nor reliable

---

38   Interview with a Congolese student and shop owner, March 2007, Gisenyi.

official statistics, a report by the Pole Institute (2009) on the security situation in Eastern DRC gives a depressing insight into the issue, listing eighty-two homicides in Goma between January 2007 and April 2008, while raising no claim to completeness. People accuse the state, in the form of the national army, of being at the heart of the crime problem.

> "If the government would pay the army regularly and guide and supervise them as is right and proper, we wouldn't have this problem. It's the soldiers, they are unpaid and undisciplined. At least they cooperate with the robbers."[39]

Those who can afford it engage the services of one of the private security providers, which costs between 250 and 370 US$ per month. Since these companies are not allowed to carry weapons, they have to pay the police command to reinforce their teams with armed policemen. Other wealthy house owners hire an armed policeman directly from the next police station; protection from dusk till dawn costs about 80 US$. As a result of the detachment of policemen to protect private houses, banks and facilities of the international humanitarian organizations, we have small islands of purchased security while the rest of the city is totally unprotected by the police during the night. Thus, for more and more Congolese not able to afford private security and wanting to live in an affordable house with reliable power and water supply, living in Gisenyi while working in Goma is a real option.

The above analysis gives the impression that Rwanda is a haven of security and the rule of law. Even if there is some truth in this, these achievements seem to be superficial and dearly-bought for many Rwandans.

Escaping order: Rwandan female traders in Goma

Every morning a huge crowd of Rwandan women can be observed carrying baskets of agricultural produce and marching towards the border post known as Petite Barrière. Many of them live in the villages in Gisenyi's hilly rural hinterland, and have to walk for two hours or more. At the border, they have to negotiate with the Congolese authorities in order to reduce the sum they have to pay to enter with their goods, which is fixed arbitrarily by one or another service operating at the border. This small reduction is a great help in view of the modest profit they gain from selling their tomatoes or eggplants in the streets of Goma.

---

39   Interview, October 2008.

> "In Gisenyi we are starving. People in Congo are well off, there is a lot of money in Goma and they eat… There is no money in Rwanda and people are jobless. And the government controls what we are growing. Beans are forbidden now and they have destroyed our field with beans. I do not understand why… Selling tomatoes in Goma means 300 francs for me. With that money I buy some manioc flour."[40]

For these women, the border is a welcome opportunity to escape the economic restrictions of the authorities in Rwanda, where non-registered street sale is prohibited and a repressive developmental state even regulates what peasants are allowed to grow. Especially the ban on street selling, one of the few economic activities the rural poor and the urban unskilled labour force can practise, comes hard for these women. In order to reduce unofficial trade and to increase the fiscal revenue, all vendors nowadays have to rent a small stall in Gisenyi's two official markets, Bugangari and Murigari. However, the cheapest place in these markets costs 12US$ per month, not including the bribe traders usually have to pay to the management of the market to get a place[41], which is far too much for the majority of female traders who then have to go to Goma to ensure their livelihoods. Crossing the border to work as a street vendor in Goma can be considered as a temporary exit option, a strategy for coping with the very specific uncertainties that arise from the Rwandan model of development.

The ban on street sale and the strict regulation of what is mainly subsistence agriculture are only two among numerous measures contained in the Rwandan rulers' project for a 're-engineering' of rural society (see Ansoms 2009). Accompanying the female traders back to their homes in the hills around Gisenyi gives a good impression of the anti-rural bias in Rwandan policy-making that refers to "poverty as at least partially a problem of mentality" (ibid: 302). In sharp contrast to the 'tarted up' capital of Kigali, the rural areas of the densely populated Rwandan north-west are inhabited by peasants who for the most part fear the long arm of the state, as represented for instance by agricultural advisers. These state agents enforce regulations that often impede the peasants in their efforts to cope with harsh conditions and a degraded environment. Sometimes peasants are urged to plant their crops in rows and adopt monocropping, although mixed cropping has been proved to minimize risk; sometimes they have to replace their banana trees with flowers, and sometimes beans are forbidden. People also told us that they were obliged to wear shoes or sandals, which caused trouble for them, since they had to spend money reserves on buying shoes instead of food. Overall, these regulations are an expression of the Rwandan Government's doubtful aim of transforming agriculture from a survival sector to

---

40   Interview with a Rwandan street vendor, November 2007; Goma.
41   This goes up to 35 US$. Various informal conversations with traders in Bugangari and Murigari market, Gisenyi; October 2008, August and September 2010.

a productive sector with maximum productivity, while on the other hand they illustrate a wish to mask poverty instead of alleviating it. Like the street children and beggars in the streets of Kigali, who are regularly arrested, peasants walking barefoot or wearing tattered clothes do not fit the vision of the Rwandan modernization project, which promotes information technology and the ideal of a service society, and which is clearly focused on the urban centres (see GoR, 2000), thus widening the rural-urban gap and "by-passing the poor" (Ansoms 2008).

The strained state-society relations in Rwanda are further illustrated by the fact that the female traders easily accept the difficulties they face while selling in the streets of Goma: exclusion from the official market places and harassment from both Congolese civilians and officials (for a recent overview, see Kimanuka/Lange 2010). This starts at the border when the women have to negotiate afresh each day the sum they have to pay in order to enter with their goods. This amount is still below the official customs duty, and so it is no wonder that they are quite content with the Congolese authorities.

> "These Congolese are good children. They take whatever you can give them, even 50 francs. Ok, you might get in trouble at the border if you do not have something to give. But you can lie to them; you can hide what you really have. I prefer to quarrel with the Congolese than to do nothing in Rwanda."[42]

Since street sale is in competition with the markets of Goma, where most Congolese traders sell their products, including those they have imported from Gisenyi, the Rwandan women have to pay both the homeless people, the so-called Rasta, without whose authorization nobody is allowed to sell on the streets, and the police, in order to be protected against the arbitrary law of Congolese traders. However, nobody feels really safe and while escaping the uncertainty that emerges from a political order shaped by overregulation and strict law enforcement, these women expose themselves every day to a pronounced legal uncertainty, as described in the previous section.

> "We give 200 francs to the Rasta; for the police there is no fixed price. Sometimes we give them 100, 200, or even 500. It depends. And sometimes they take all the commodities and disappear with them. Once, they took all my tomatoes, saying that I have not respected them because they were calling me and I did not respond. But this was not true. I did not hear that they were calling me. They just wanted to take my products."[43]

Smuggling to survive: Of chora chora, Mavubi and APR

---

42   Interview with a Rwandan street vendor of smoked fish, August 2010; Goma.
43   Interview with a Rwandan street vendor, September 2010; Goma.

Similar to the Rwandan women selling on the streets in Goma, Rwandan smugglers refer to their activity as a means to survive in a political and economic environment shaped by a development vision which largely ignores the living conditions of the people. Comprehensive control, formalization of the entire economy, strict law enforcement and the massive tax liabilities pose a real threat to their livelihoods.

Borderlanders refer to smuggling as *chora chora*. *Chora* is a Swahili word and has multiple meanings: 'to flee', 'to avoid / to by-pass' and 'to hide'. *Chora chora* provides an income for many people in the two cities, particularly in Gisenyi, and is a part of everyday life, just as at many other borders. It is not so much the spectacular smuggling of minerals to Rwanda, or the petroleum import fraud (see Tegera/Johnson 2007; Mitchell/Garret 2009), that gives meaning to this border for the people who live with it, but their mundane efforts to make a living out of it by changing sides with undeclared goods. However, to enter the DRC with contraband, particularly bread and other convenience goods that are scarce on the Congolese side, can hardly be called smuggling, as it takes place more or less openly. It is more a matter of negotiation with the agents of the various services operating at the border. Hence, this border is a lucrative field, not only for contrabandists, but also for a multitude of Congolese border officials and semi-officials, the so-called 'collabo'. These are civilians recruited by higher-ranking border officials to collect money for them from traders and smugglers. Each 'collabo' is attached to one official who seldom appears in public asking for money himself. Even isolated initiatives to formalize the border regime, as during the visit of Rwanda's president Kagame to Gisenyi in October 2008, are perceived by these 'collabo' as a restriction of their income opportunities.

> "We are subcontractors, we work for the security of our nation but we are not paid. But my family must eat. I have six children and today for example I have absolutely nothing I can give to them. It's all because of Kagame's visit. He came with his soldiers from Darfur to secure the border. And now, nobody passes through the makoro[44]. Normally we make money from the smugglers and traders who come with petrol or meat, but now everybody is obliged to pass at Grande Barrière or at Petite Barrière where we are not allowed to work."[45]

A peculiarity is that of disabled people in Goma and Gisenyi, who use special wheelchairs with a luggage carrier to convey all sorts of goods across the border. Since they are unofficially exempt from taxes and customs, at least on the

---

44   Makoro means 'stony area' and describes the former buffer zone between the two states in the strip between the official border posts.

45   Interview with an unofficial agent of the Congolese intelligence service, October 2008.

Congolese side, it is very popular among businessmen from both sides to use them for smuggling[46].

However, smuggling is mainly from Goma to Gisenyi, and seems to be first and foremost a Rwandan phenomenon, as it is almost solely a matter of unofficial re-exports of those products whose customs value is underestimated by the alliances of traders and Congolese border officials. In a group discussion with Rwandan small-scale smugglers acquainted with our research assistant, it turned out that especially cosmetics, alcohol, woven fabrics, powdered milk, tinned tomatoes and second-hand clothes are brought to Gisenyi. Basically there are two groups of smugglers. The first is that of Rwandan small-scale traders who have a shop in Gisenyi and smuggle the goods themselves. By smuggling a box of tinned tomatoes, for instance, which costs 21 US\$ in Goma, they avoid paying 12 US\$ in customs duties. While this product ought to cost about 33 US\$ in the Gisenyi market, it is hard to find it for more than 30 US\$. To be protected from prosecution, traders clear a small amount of their goods and get an invoice from the Rwanda Revenue Authority (RRA). Only the quantity that has been cleared appears in the shops and is immediately replaced by the smuggled goods that are stored in the private home.

> "Listen, no one here in Gisenyi can say that he pays all the customs duties for products such as wine, Nido (powdered milk) or tinned tomatoes. None of us can afford to clear those products entirely."[47]

The second group consists of couriers. They smuggle for those traders in Gisenyi who either cannot do it themselves, because they are already known to the border authorities, or who can afford to hire a smuggler, thus avoiding the risk of being caught personally. While the traders claim a reduction of customs duties and taxes, the couriers depend on this strong regulation to survive. Among these couriers, two groups can be differentiated. The so-called *Mavubi*, which means bee in Kinyarwanda, carry great quantities and valuable goods, avoid the border posts, often work together, and are known to defend the contraband, even violently, against border officials. We once observed a *Mavubi* carrying seven boxes of tomatoes and beating an RRA agent who wanted to stop him. *Mavubi* is also the name of the national football team of Rwanda, which means that the name is also given to distinguish them from the smugglers called APR. APR is a football club in Kigali which is considered as being weaker than the national

---

46   The role of disabled traders in cross-border trade and smuggling is a fascinating question. The activities of these people require navigating between pity, agency and entrepreneurship, and instrumentalization by big traders. However given the scope and the aim of this paper, we cannot go into detail here.

47   Interview with a shop owner in Gisenyi, July 2010.

team. Accordingly the APR are the many smugglers who usually pass through the official border posts and carry small quantities of contraband.

Besides the large-scale smuggling of entire lorry loads, which is not the topic of this article, one can observe two principal practices of chora chora. The first one, mostly practised by the Mavubi, is to pass through the makoro. Here, the smugglers have to negotiate with the authorities. Whereas Congolese border officials are usually easy to bribe, the big challenge is to avoid controls by the RRA and to convince the Rwandan border guards. Contrary to the RRA agents, whose salary is ten times higher, soldiers and policemen seem to be generally open to negotiations but are much more aware of observation by their superiors; they only cooperate with people they already know. This practice has given rise to veritable networks, causing smugglers to wait, sometimes for hours, at the border, before they spot 'their' Rwandan soldier or policeman. Smugglers cannot contact a policeman or a soldier with whom they have never dealt with before since the risk of being arrested by the Rwandan border guards who always fear walking into a trap is high. Hence, smugglers mutually introduce themselves to policemen and soldiers and we observed how they carefully tried to obtain the border guards' confidence by giving small gifts and discussing other issues during the first contact before suggesting a smuggling deal next time. The second strategy is to hide the contraband in clothes and bags and to pass through the official border posts, especially *Petite Barrière*, by taking advantage of the confusion due to the great crowd.

In the following section, we will try to draw some conclusions from the analysis above.

6   Conclusions

In this article, we have tried to highlight some aspects of contemporary state-society relations in the borderland of Goma and Gisenyi by linking the concepts of risk and uncertainty to the study of cross-border agency. We have shown that people from either side employ a repertory of strategies with respect to using the border, which allows them to come to terms with the risks and uncertainties linked to the patterns of statehood on the respective side. It is not only the absence of the state, as in the DRC, that makes everyday life hard to predict, but also an exaggerated presence, as illustrated by the rigid developmental state in Rwanda. The border can therefore become a source of certainty, for some groups and to different degrees. Risk is selective and not everybody uses the border in the ways we have described. However, those who do so employ these strategies first and foremost to temporarily escape from their state and not necessarily to challenge it. It is true that the popular perceptions of the Rwandan state, which has to project itself in a distrustful and reluctant rural area, lead us to question the public image of a prosperous and developing country, and the more or less open alliances between smugglers and Congolese border authorities confirm to some degree the weak performance of the Congolese state. However our study confirms Roitman's observation (2005) that unofficial cross-border trade, smuggling and the involvement of state officials must not necessarily bring about alternative political models that challenge the legitimacy of the established one. Rather, it is a proliferation of statehood that can be observed, and what is remarkable is that this proliferation of statehood subverts the nation state and at the same time seems to continually reconfirm its territorial logic, as it depends on the border for its perpetuation. The contradictory meaning of borders for the people who live with them could not be better illustrated than through this very aspect: at the border, Congolese encounter their own state, otherwise often invisible, exerting a hybrid of real and symbolic control, as a rare expression of state territoriality. Rwandans use the border to escape, at least temporarily, from their state's omnipresence. In doing so, they simultaneously subvert and confirm the state through an outsourcing of problems and practices, which somehow stabilize the established order in the country. Congolese and Rwandan accounts of the border as a resource show that this navigating of uncertainty, and the mutual exchange embedded in everyday border practices at the local level, has the potential to deconstruct official versions of otherness, and to overcome the pronounced division between the inhabitants of the conurbation that is due to civil war, redefinition of citizenship and nationhood, and flight and expulsion.

From a methodological point of view we have chosen an approach in which the borderlanders' everyday experiences and understandings gain centre stage rather than contributing to a de-peopling of border studies by "reading and interpreting texts on boundaries instead of doing time-consuming fieldwork among border people" (Paasi, 2005: 668). However, gaining insights into the strategies of border crossers, their sometimes illicit activities and their encounters with the respective state is a difficult and, regarding the involvement of state officials in smuggling, sometimes also a risky task to undertake even in less complicated geopolitical settings. Hence our strategy was also one of navigating: that is to say a navigating between the entangled milieus of traders, commuters, smugglers and state (semi-) officials. Such an approach may inspire other scholars who also feel uncomfortable with the 'remote sensing' of borders.

References

Ansoms, A. (2008): "Striving for growth, bypassing the poor? A critical review of Rwanda's rural sector policies". In: Journal of Modern African Studies, 46, pp. 1-32.

Ansoms, A. (2009): "Re-engineering rural society: The visions and ambitions of the Rwandan elite". In: African Affairs, 108, pp. 289-309.

Beck, U. (1986): Die Risikogesellschaft. Auf dem Weg in eine andere Moderne. Frankfurt am Main: Suhrkamp.

Bhagwati, J. / Hansen, B. (1973): "A Theoretical Analysis of Smuggling". In: Quarterly Journal of Economics, 87, pp. 172–87.

Bonss, W. (1995): Vom Risiko: Unsicherheit und Ungewissheit in der Moderne. Hamburg: Hamburger Edition.

Donnan, H. / Wilson, T. M. (1999): Borders. Frontiers of Identity, Nation and State. Oxford, New York: Berg.

Flynn, D. K. (1997): "'We are the Border': Identity, Exchange, and the State along the Bénin-Nigeria Border". In: American Ethnologist, 24, 2, pp. 311-330.

Giddens, A. (1991): Modernity and Self-Identity. Stanford: Stanford University Press.

Girtler, R. (2006): Abenteuer Grenze. Von Schmugglern und Schmugglerinnen, Ritualen und "heiligen" Räumen. Münster: LIT.

Goloobo-Mutebi, F. (2008): Collapse, war and reconstruction in Rwanda: an analytical narrative on state-making. Crisis States Working Paper 2.28. London: Crisis States Research Centre.

Golub, S. S. / Mbaye, A. A. (2009): "National Trade Policies and Smuggling in Africa: The Case of The Gambia and Senegal". In: World Development, 37, 3, pp. 595–606.

GoR – Government of Rwanda (2000): Vision 2020. Kigali: Ministry of Finance and Economic Planning.

INICA – L'Initiative pour l'Afrique Centrale (2006): Les Dynamiques Transfrontalières dans la Région des Grands Lacs. Burundi, République Démocratique du Congo, Ouganda et Rwanda. n.p.

Kimanuka, C. / Lange, M. (2010): La Traversée. Petit commerce et amélioration des relations transfrontalières entre Goma (RD Congo) et Gisenyi (Rwanda). London: International Alert.

Kodi, M. (2008): "Corruption and Governance in the RDC during the Transition Period (2003-2006)". Monograph Series 148. Pretoria: Institute for Security Studies.

Kolossov, V. (2005): "Border Studies: Changing Perspectives and Theoretical Approaches". In: Geopolitics, 10, pp. 606-632.

Lecoutere, E. / Vlassenroot, K. / Raeymaekers, T. (2009): "Conflict, institutional changes and food insecurity in eastern D.R. Congo". In: afrika focus, 22, 2, pp. 41-63.

Lemarchand, R. (2009): The dynamics of violence in Central Africa. Philadelphia: University of Pennsylvania Press.

Luhmann, N. (1993): Risk – A Sociological Theory. New York: De Gruyter.

Lupton, D. (1999): Risk. London, New York: Routledge.

Macamo, E. (2008): The Taming of Fate: Approaching Risk from a Social Action Perspective – Case Studies from Southern Mozambique. Unpublished habilitation dissertation, University of Bayreuth, Germany.

Mamdani, M. (2001): When victims become killers: colonialism, nativism, and the genocide in Rwanda. Princeton: Princeton University Press.

MINIFIN – Ministère des Finances (2007) : Tarif douanier Congolais. Kinshasa.

Mitchell, H. / Garrett, N. (2009): Beyond Conflict: Reconfiguring approaches to the regional trade in minerals from Eastern DRC. London: Crisis States Research Centre.

Newman, D. (2006): "The lines that continue to separate us: borders in our borderless world". In: Progress in Human Geography, 30, pp. 143-161.

Nugent, P. (2002): Smugglers, secessionists and loyal citizens on the Ghana-Togo frontier: the lie of the borderlands since 1914. Oxford: James Currey.

O'Malley, P. (2004): Risk, uncertainty and government. London: Glashouse Press.

O'Malley, P: (2008): "Governmentality and Risk". In: J. O. Zinn (Ed.): Social Theories Of Risk And Uncertainty. An Introduction. Malden, Oxford, Carlton: Blackwell, pp. 52-75.

Paasi, A.(2005): "Generations and the 'Development' of Border Studies". In: Geopolitics, 10, pp. 663-671.

Painter, J. (2006): "Prosaic geographies of stateness". In: Political Geography, 25, pp. 752-774.

Pole Institute (2009) : "Est de la RDC: le crime banalisé!". In : Regards croisés 23, Goma.

Prunier, G. (2009): Africa's world war: Congo, the Rwandan genocide, and the making of a continental catastrophe. Oxford: Oxford University Press.

Raeymaekers, T. (2009): "The silent encroachment of the frontier: A politics of transborder trade in the Semliki Valley (Congo–Uganda)". In: Political Geography, 28, pp. 55-65.

Raeymaekers, T. / Vlassenroot, K. (2009): "Reshaping Congolese Statehood in the Midst of Crisis and Transition". In: U. Engel and P. Nugent (eds.): Respacing Africa. Leiden, Boston: Brill, pp. 139 – 167.

Roitman, J. (2004): "Productivity in the Margins: The Reconstitution of State Power in the Chad Basin". In: V. Das and D. Poole (eds.): Anthropology in the Margins of the State. Santa Fe: School of American Research Press, pp. 191-224.

Roitman, J. (2005): Fiscal disobedience. An anthropology of economic regulation in Central Africa. Princeton, Oxford: Princeton University Press.

RRA – Rwanda Revenue Authority (2008): Customs tarifs of Rwanda. Kigali.

Sheikh, M. A. (1989): "A Theory of Risk, Smuggling and Welfare". In: World Development, 17, pp. 1931-1944.

Slemrod, J. / Yitzhaki, S. (2002): "Tax Avoidance, Evasion, and Administration". In: A.J. Auerbach and M. Feldstein (eds.): Handbook of Public Economics, Vol. 3. Amsterdam: North-Holland, pp. 1423-1470.

Stearns, J. K. (2008): "Laurent Nkunda and the National Congress for the Defence of the People (CNDP)". In: S. Maryse, F. Reyntjens and S. Vandeginste (eds.): L'Afrique des Grands Lacs: Annuaire 2007-2008. Paris: L'Harmattan, pp. 245-267.

Tegera, A. / Johnson, D. (2007): Rules For Sale: Formal and informal cross-border trade in Eastern DRC, Pole Institute, Regards Croisés 19, Goma.

Thuen, T. (1999): "The Significance of Borders in the East European Transition". In: International Journal of Urban and Regional Research, 23, 4, pp. 738–750.

Tull, D. (2005): The Reconfiguration of Political Order in Africa: A Case Study of North Kivu (DR Congo). Hamburg: Institut für Afrika-Kunde.

Vlassenroot, K. / Büscher, K. (2010): "Humanitarian presence and urban development: new opportunities and contrasts in Goma, DRC". In: Disasters, 34, S2, pp. 256-273.

Zinn, J. O. (ed.) (2008): Social Theories Of Risk And Uncertainty: An Introduction. Malden, Oxford, Carlton: Blackwell.

Transborder trade on the Russian-Chinese border: Problems of interethnic communication[48]

Kapitolina Fedorova

1   Introduction

State borders can be seen as both physical and symbolic barriers, prohibiting any uncontrolled transition between neighbouring countries. They function as sites for implementing state's power (see Pickering/Weber 2006). At the same time requirements of national boundaries collide with requirements of people living in the bordering areas (see Horsman/Marshall 1994), and the very fact of the existence of borders inevitably provokes various types of economic activity on adjacent territories such as small-scale trade, tourist services etc. These economic activities, in turn, make people from the bordering states communicate with each other both literally, in their everyday interaction, and symbolically, in constructing images and perceptions. People separated by the state borders usually see each other as totally different: they speak different languages, have different traditions and practices, and collision of these differences influences habitual ways of living and thinking in various aspects. Mutual attitudes on the border are shaped by many factors, and state policy and propaganda can play a rather serious role (see Wilson/Donnan 1998). What is more, any serious changes in the state policy towards the border regulations can dramatically influence the socioeconomic situation in the border region and promote or put an end to the interethnic communication. Political, sociological, cultural, historical and linguistic aspects are equally important in the study of international borders; the study of this type demands interdisciplinarity and "the convergence in method and theory" (Donnan/Wilson 1999: 61).

Economic contacts therefore provoke linguistic and cultural contacts which may induce serious changes in local communities' social and verbal behaviour

48   This research is supported by the German Research Foundation grant 'Russian-Chinese Language Contacts and Border Trade: the Past and the Present' (GZ: 436 RUS 113/960/0-1). I would like to acknowledge the contribution of other researchers involved in the project, my German colleagues, Christian Voss (Humboldt University, Berlin) and Dieter Stern (University of Bonn); my colleagues from Chita State University, Dina Sundueva and Nadezhda Likhanova, helped me enormously during my fieldwork in the Zabaikalskii territory.

due to the necessity of somehow adjusting to their 'neighbours'. Linguistic strategies used by native speakers of a given language when communicating with non-native speakers are usually described as a part of foreigner talk register specific to this language.[49] The mutual adjustment of linguistic systems by native and non-native speakers sometimes even results in the appearance of new hybrid linguistic systems like pidgin and Creole languages.[50] Another important aspect of interethnic communication is speakers' attitudes towards accented and grammatically incorrect language forms used by non-native speakers and cultural conventions about foreigners and their speech. From linguists' point of view, non-native speakers' verbal behaviour reflects their interlanguage, the linguistic system created during the second-language acquisition process (see Selinker 1972). But for native speakers these language variants can be 'socially loaded', and their attitudes towards someone depends on the ways he or she uses the language (see Garrett 2010). According to their tolerance towards non-standard speech people can be more or less inclined to cooperate in interethnic communication and use certain features of foreigner talk, especially those demanding serious speech modifications such as ungrammatical utterances.

Mutual adjustment affects people's life and surrounding social space but one should bear in mind that different ethnic and social groups tend to differ in their reactions to a change of their habitual world. Sometimes we can discover with some surprise that these reactions tend to be considerably stable in the course of many years – if we compare modern data with historical ones similar interethnic attitudes and social interaction practices can be found in the same border region nowadays and in the remote past. My article deals with this type of situation. Historically, the Russian-Chinese border was a place of intensive economic, cultural and linguistic contacts not only between the Russians and the Chinese; several ethnic groups (Manchu, Mongolians, Koreans, Tungus, Udege and others) were involved in the process. The modern situation in the border area is by no means less complicated; and comparing field data with that from historical sources it is possible to reveal similar patterns. In my article I attempt to utilize both a sociolinguistic and anthropological approach to study the contacts

---

49   The term 'foreigner talk' was first suggested in 1968 by Charles Ferguson as analogous with baby talk, speech addressed to infants (see Ferguson 1981).

50   The term 'pidgin' is used in language contacts studies to refer to the linguistic system created as a restricted communicative tool in the process of regular contacts between two or more groups of different languages speakers. Unlike Creoles (created by new generations of speakers in the process of acquiring a given pidgin as their first language) pidgins 'belong to no one' (i.e. they are not anyone's native tongue), have rather limited functions, and therefore tend to be lexically and grammatically simple compared with natural languages. For more information on contact languages see e.g. Mühlhäusler 1986; Romaine 1988.

between Russian and Chinese speakers in the border area where their everyday lives are strongly shaped by the border and border crossing activities.

Fig. 13: The map of Chita region and bordering territories (Source: http://www.chitaobl.ru/)

First I will give a short overview of the history of contacts on the Russian-Chinese border; then I will briefly describe the present socio-economical situation in the region on the basis of both sociologists' publications and my own field work. Finally I will turn to different aspects of interethnic communication, both linguistic (usage of different language variants) and cultural (mutual attitudes and changes in urban spaces). The present situation therefore is in the focus of my study whereas historical data is used as background information important for a deeper understanding of the processes we can currently witness. The field work was conducted in the Zabaikalskii territory of Russia (in fig. 13 named as *Забайкальск*) and the Chinese city of Manzhouli (in fig. 13 named as *Маньчжурия*), the province Inner Mongolia (see fig. 13), in 2008, 2009 and 2010. Several methods of obtaining data were used: observation (including participant observation), audio recording of spontaneous interaction between Russian and Chinese speakers, interviews with Russian and Chinese speakers from different ethnic (Russians, Buryats, Mongolians, Han Chinese) and socio-professional groups (salespersons, businessmen, students, school teachers, workers, taxi-drivers etc.) with different levels of involvement in the interethnic contacts, gathering data on linguistic landscape (advertisements, signs etc.; see Landry/Bourhis 1997) and gathering data from websites and forums dedicated to the border area and related border-crossing practices

2   History of contacts on the Russian-Chinese border: An overview

Undoubtedly some trade contacts in the Russian-Chinese border area existed long before official documentation and regulations were introduced. Goods exchange between Chinese and Mongolians, on the one hand, and Russians, on the other hand, was conducted through caravan trade. However since 1727, when the treaty of Kyakhta was concluded, this small frontier town (actually founded for this purpose) became the main and then, in 1757, the only place where Russian and Chinese merchants could carry out trade deals. This centralization of contacts resulted in a constantly growing number of Chinese merchants residing in Kyakhta and trying to speak Russian. There is even some evidence, although rather dubious (see Stern 2005), that the Chinese authorities made these merchants take an examination in the Russian language. Chinese speakers' 'imperfect' Russian (an 'interlanguage' in the terms of second language acquisition theory) and oversimplified and ungrammatical forms of foreigner talk used by Russian native speakers eventually gave birth to a new pidgin, first called the Kyakhta language, or the Russian-Chinese language. It was documented by several travellers and amateur linguists amused by this 'broken' and extremely 'funny' language (see Cherepanov 1853; Maksimov 1864).

Strict regulations on trade continued for 133 years, and in 1860 the treaty of Peking was ratified, in which the restrictions on trade between Russia and China were finally abolished. As a result mass Chinese migration to the Russian Empire started. The exact number of Chinese living or regularly travelling to Russia at the beginning of the twentieth century is unknown, and different scholars estimate it differently, from 100,000 to 200,000 or even 250,000 people (see Nesterova 2008: 48ff.). According to some data (see Anikhovskij et al. 2005: 170), the Chinese (including the Manchu people[51]) amounted to around 10 percent of the whole population of the Russian Far East and were the second (after the Russian majority) ethnic group in the region. Evidently they played an important role in the regional economy and gradually became virtually indispensable for the everyday activities of the local population. Chinese migrants were engaged in several economic niches: trade and small-scale business, providing domestic services, manual labour, and agriculture. Although it should be noted that their positions in urban and in rural areas were rather different. In villages Chinese farms often were the richest and the most economically efficient, and their owners were respected by locals, especially from non-Russian ethnic groups (such as Udege or Tungus). There are evidences that speaking Chinese was considered prestigious in rural areas, and in some aboriginal languages some traces of the Chinese influence can be found, such as tone differences in some Udege dialects (see Perekhvalskaya 2007). At the same time the social prestige of Chinese migrants and their language in towns was rather low.

Chinese quarters (usually called 'Kitajskie slobodki' by locals) began to appear in Siberian and Far Eastern cities in the second half of the nineteenth century. This process was spontaneous: first Chinese 'slobodki' formed around markets where Chinese merchants were selling their goods. In Vladivostok, e.g., the first 'manzovskij bazar' (Manchu market) appeared in the 1860s, and was almost immediately surrounded by Chinese residential houses, so called 'fanzas'. These settlements created serious problems for the authorities since Russian citizens made constant complaints against Chinese quarters' insanitation and the possible threat of epidemic diseases. The Chinese presence in the region was evident both for locals and for travellers from European Russia: 'Chinese, Koreans and Japanese are scurrying all over the city [Vladivostok] streets.

---

51   The region of Manchuria, on the Chinese side of the border, was originally populated by Manchu people, aboriginal ethnic group, but it was experiencing growing Chinese influence in the time. According to a contemporary observer, 'Manchuria Chineseation is going so successfully that now even experienced people can hardly tell Manchu from Chinese. Starting with their clothes, lodging organization, way of living and finishing with the language – everything is Chinese' (cited from: S. E Anikhovskij et al. 2005: 186; my translation). Local citizens of Siberia and the Far East, therefore, did not usually draw a distinction between Manchu and Chinese people. The word 'manza' (from distorted 'Manzhou' (Manchu)) was used to refer both to Manchu and Chinese.

Chinese are especially numerous, Russians are almost invisible, and there are few of them here anyway in comparison with the sons of Celestial Empire'.[52]
This visible presence of Chinese (often felt as dominance) influenced natives' attitudes towards migrants from China. For Russian speakers Chinese people were aliens, their behaviour, habits, personal traits, and language were considered strange and sometimes even threatening. Chinese quarters were seen as criminal dirty spaces, marginal despite their closeness to the city centre, labyrinths where one could get lost forever − there were rumours that Chinese made soap from killed Russians (see Nesterova 2008: 54f.). Even positive qualities attributed to the Chinese people were treated at the same time as a threat to Russian dominance in the region. Thus, A. A. Kaufman lists these qualities described by his interlocutors: honesty, thoroughness, accuracy, diligence, and natural talent for business and agriculture, and adds: "And among these enthusiastic words one can obviously see people's fear of 'the peaceful invasion of the yellow race' which local people do not expect to fight off as easily as they fought off the military invasion in the nine-hundredth year" (Kaufman 1905: 18; my translation). The so-called 'yellow peril' became an important part of the official discourse in the Russian Empire (see Siegelbaum 1978).

In their contacts with Chinese and aboriginal people Russians never tried to learn the languages of their interlocutors; instead they relied on their knowledge of Russian-Chinese pidgin. After 1860 this language was spreading fast along the border all the way to Russia's Far East, and gradually became the main tool for interethnic communication in the region, with a great number (around one million by some calculations − Belikov manuscript) of speakers belonging to at least eight ethnic and linguistic groups (see Belikov 1994: 297f.).[53] Vast evidence of this interethnic communication can be found in written sources; the pidgin was also used in fiction to depict the way Chinese and aboriginal people of the Far East spoke Russian. The most famous examples are the books by Vladimir Arsenjev (see Arsenjev 1978) 'Po Ussurijskomu krayu' and 'Dersu Uzala' (later made into a movie by Akira Kurosawa). For most Russian native speakers, this language was no more than just 'broken Russian', a grammatically incorrect version of the 'true language'. It lacked social prestige and was used by Russians to communicate with underprivileged social groups − aboriginal people (Tungus, Udege), Chinese seasonal workers and street vendors. The attitudes

---

52 From D. I. Shrejder, Nash Dal'nij Vostok, St. Petersburg, 1897. Cited from: Nesterova 2008: 55; my translation.
53 There are different theoretical approaches to these variants among linguists. Some of them consider the Kyakhta language and the Far East pidgin to be the same language; others believe them to be separate (see Perekhvalskaya 2008).

towards both 'Chinese Russian' and its speakers were condescending: it and they were not liked, but had to be tolerated.

Long-term Russian-Chinese contacts in the border area were put to an end in the late 1930s with repression in the Soviet Union and a cooling in relations with China. The border between two countries was closed,[54] the Chinese were deported, and any communication across the border was forbidden. Gradually, a strong Russification policy was put in place, and most aboriginal people shifted from 'broken' to normative Russian. As a result, the Russian-Chinese pidgin was no longer used and was soon forgotten. For the next fifty years all economic and cultural exchange between China and the Soviet Union could be implemented exclusively through official authorities, no informal relations on the border were possible. Militarization of the border and state propaganda transformed the image of Chinese people in the eyes of Russians from 'close strangers' to 'mysterious enemies', not real people from the neighbouring country.

3   Modern situation on the Russian-Chinese border: Economic exchange and urban space transformation

Sometimes history repeats itself, and now the Russian-Chinese border again turns into a scene of trade contacts and interethnic communication. At the very end of the 1980s, serious changes in the Soviet Union resulted in the loosening of border regulations. It became possible for the people from the Russian-Chinese border area (Amur and Chita regions[55], the Khabarovsk Territory, the Jewish Autonomous Region, and Primorye) to cross the border without pre-arranged visas, instead obtaining entry permits at the check-points themselves. At the beginning of the 1990s, cross-border trade became the main source of income for many Russians, and cheap Chinese goods invaded the region. The opening of the Russian market for the Chinese stimulated substantial migration between the two countries and transformed Chinese settlements near the border (e.g., Heihe and Manzhouli). In less than ten years, small frontier posts changed into cities populated by hundreds of thousands of people. The urban landscape of the cities and towns on the Russian side of the border underwent serious changes as well: Chinese markets became an indispensable part of these cities' everyday

---

54   Since the late thirties the borders of the USSR have become physically impenetrable for anyone due to the construction of heavy fortifications: barbed wire fences, ploughed up fields and armed guards patrolling the forbidden frontier zone (up to several kilometers wide) are still reality in border areas of Russia.

55   The Chita region was (in 2008) consolidated with the Aginskii Buryat autonomous district into the Zabaikalskii territory.

life in a sense resembling Chinatowns in many European and American cities (see Ryzhova 2008: 24–25). Therefore since Perestroika unofficial transborder trade (so called 'shuttle trade') has been developing very fast affecting life-styles and everyday activities of most people from the border region.

There is common belief among Russians (especially those in the European part of the country) that Siberia and the Far East are literally flooded by millions of Chinese immigrants, mostly illegal. The so-called 'yellow peril' phenomenon has a long history in Russian society (see, e.g., Siegelbaum 1978), and modern mass media actively depict the Chinese as a serious threat for Russia and its cultural values (see Lukin 1998; Diatlov 2008). At the same time, sociological studies show that in fact Chinese immigration is kept under strict control and legislation continues to become tougher all the time (see Gelbras 2004; Larin 2001). There are very few illegal migrants from China in Chita or Blagoveschensk, and the total number of immigrants tends to be stable because of the seasonal character of these migrations (see Sharmashkeeva 2007). Most immigrants do not aim to stay in Russia, and their cultural and linguistic adaptation, therefore, can be minimal. As is common practice with Chinese immigration all over the world (see Skeldon 1995), Chinese immigrants to Russia form close-knit communities and occupy several business niches. Chinese migrants in the border regions of Russia are employed in construction, market trade, small repair enterprises and agriculture. There are many joint Russian-Chinese enterprises and business relations are often based on family ties. Mixed marriages between Russian women and Chinese men are not uncommon – according to the stereotype Chinese (unlike Russian men) work hard, earn money and do not drink.

In fact it is Russian citizens who can be called illegal migrants: apart from those officially working in China many Russians go to China as tourists but in fact carry out trade business there. Even more participate in transborder trade from time to time as so called 'camels', persons transporting goods[56] through the border for someone else. For many years Russian authorities have constantly decreased the amount of goods which can be taken by one person into the country for personal use. In 2009 it was allowed to bring 35 kg and only once a month, and small-scale trade almost yielded to 'big' smuggling schemes involving corruption on high levels of custom officials. In July 2010 however the amount of untaxed import was increased again to 50 kg per person and the 'per month rule' was also abolished. It is possible that this lenience will stimulate

---

56   The goods are mostly clothes, footwear, cosmetics, household chemicals, crockery etc. – the same things people buy for themselves but in greater quantities. The smuggling practices (involving medicine and ethyl alcohol) are, according to my informants, rare now.

shuttle trade and provide more possibilities for informal economic exchange in the coming years.

As a whole transborder trade plays an extremely important role in the region's economy. Most of the goods one can buy in Chita, Blagoveshchensk or Khabarovsk are not only imported from China (it is almost impossible to buy shoes or clothes manufactured in Europe or 'mainland' Russia) but are imported unofficially through shuttle trade or smuggling. What is more, China has become the main tourist destination in the region: doing business in China means not only business but fun; it is a possibility to dine out, have spa treatments, visit night clubs etc., i.e. to do many things most of the people cannot afford at home:

> "There were people in my [tourist] group who had never been abroad at all: just ordinary middle class people worn out by their work, children, fields. When coming to Manzhouli their chins dropped because of the extent of low cost goods, low prices in cafes, for them it was all right abroad. Surely they cannot afford to dine at a café every day at home, where they have to count their money from salary to salary. And here they could have a rest and buy something for the family."[57]

Russian citizens involved in the transborder trade therefore act both as transmitters of Chinese goods to their fellow countrymen and as consumers of Chinese goods and services. It should be mentioned as well that although official tourism to Southern Chinese resorts is popular most Russians never go to 'mainland' China but only to Chinese border cities, and for them the cities of Manzhouli or Heihe symbolize China as a whole. This fact is evident, e.g., in the following discussion between Russian frequent travellers to China taken from the same Internet forum:

> Nick: "I prefer Italian clothes. And in China there are only three shops where you can buy cool clothing. It is Jack and Jones, Giordano, and in 'Druzhba' [lit. 'Friendship', the name of the popular shopping mall in Manzhouli] there are some cool ones but the prices there are dreadful. <...>"
> Iraki: "Write Manzhouli, not China!"
> Nick: "What is the difference? Anybody can understand me here."[58]

'Manzhouli' therefore means 'China' for Russian 'shopping tourists' (see Wachowiak 2006: 176–179 for the description of shopping tourism phenomenon), and experience gained in trips to this city and interactions with its dwellers is projected on the image of China and Chinese people which in due course creates and supports popular stereotypes. However, border cities by no

---

57   See internet forum www.manchzhuriya.ru, March 2009, my translation.
58   See Internet forum www.manchzhuriya.ru, September 2008, my translation.

means are typical for the whole country,[59] and for the Chinese themselves they mean something totally different.

Fig. 14: Manzhoulis city centre

Manzhouli positions itself as a modern tourist-oriented city, a crossroads of different cultures and styles. The official Internet site of the city's administration states in its unforgettable Russian:

> "On coming to the Manzhouli city you can enjoy special constructions and streets with a European style, the city constructions of Manzhouli look like classical European constructions, have Gothic architecture, classical Russian-style constructions, classical French-style constructions, Baroque constructions, Renaissance architecture and many other, tourists have given it the name 'Museum city'." [60]

---

59   It was demonstrated, e.g., by the example of Mexican cities not far from the US-Mexican border (see Alvares 1995; Arreola 1996; Griffin/Ford 1976).
60   See http://www.bigport.com.cn/zwmdcs.htm?ChannelID=755 (last access: 25.06.2011); my translation.

Eclectic architecture dominates in the city centre: Hotels and shopping malls are quartered in pompous many-storied buildings with high towers, sculptures, modelling etc. (fig. 14). What is more, some buildings and sculpture compositions are built exclusively to represent Russian architectural history: There are copies of famous monuments and buildings along the road leading to the checkpoint at the Russian-Chinese border (fig. 15). In addition the monumental 'Matryoshka square' (fig. 16) with its statues in the forms of matryoskas, Fabergé eggs and Chinese zodiac symbols serves as a visual representation of the multi-cultural self of the city. In other aspects of the city's life (e.g. cuisine and music in restaurants, assortment of goods in shops, advertisement etc.) adaptation to 'European tastes' (as Chinese perceive them) is no less important and also results in creating hybrid forms.

Fig. 15: Monuments representing Russian culture along the road to the check-point.

Manzhouli then is more European and Russian (and these attributes are interchangeable in the official discourse of city's authorities) than a Chinese city for its own citizens who unlike their Russian guests do not consider it a 'typical Chinese city'. This case of conflicting interpretations can serve as a brilliant metaphor for the different problems Russians and Chinese are confronted with when communicating with each other.

Fig. 16: The 'Matryoshka square'

4   Problems of intercultural communication in the border area

Transborder economic activity results in and is complicated by different problems of interethnic communication. The first logical question of course is the language of communication. Just like two hundred years ago it is the Chinese who make efforts to learn Russian and not vice verse – very few Russians, mostly young people, learn Chinese. Even women married to Chinese men do not usually speak Chinese at all or only know several words and phrases. The Russian language therefore serves as a main communicative tool. However the situation is much more complicated than that. First, actually it is not just

Russian-Chinese contacts. We should bear in mind that the border regions – and especially the Zabaikalskii territory and Inner Mongolia – are very ethnically heterogeneous. There are other ethnic and linguistic groups (Buryats, Mongolians, Chinese Buryats,[61] Cantonese etc.) and they are involved in trade and providing services as well. Some of them use different strategies for communication and business organization. Thus as my interview with Buryat merchants show when coming to China they prefer to buy goods not directly (like Russians) but through the help of Chinese Buryats with whom they communicate in the Buryat language. Russians also use so-called 'pomogaj's or 'pomogajka's ('helper'; from the Russian verb 'help' in the form of imperative) and can sometimes maintain rather friendly and close relationships with them but their 'helpers' are mostly Chinese speaking well or at least some Russian so there is no need for Russians to use any other language than their native one. Bilingual Buryats (even those who mostly speak Russian and for whom the Buryat language is more like a hereditary tongue, a symbol of their ethnic identity and not the tool of everyday communication), have additional linguistic resources. Their relations with their 'helpers' are not only based on personal liking and trust but on the common ethnicity and feelings of belonging to minority groups. At the same time they tend to express more negative attitudes towards the 'real' Chinese and their communication when in China it is rather restricted.

The second important aspect we need to consider when speaking about the interethnic communication on the Russian-Chinese border is the language itself. First, the Russian language spoken by the Chinese is not 'ordinary' Russian. Very few Chinese immigrants, especially those employed in manual labour, get any formal language instruction; the overwhelming majority of them learn Russian during their communication with Russians in everyday situations or pick up some words from their linguistically more competent fellow countrymen. One of my informants, a Chinese businessman who owns a construction firm, teaches his employees some Russian words and expressions essential to communicate with their Russian clients (e.g., brick, water, spade, where, when, how much etc.). To do this he writes down the words in Chinese hieroglyphs, trying to reflect the pronunciation with similar syllables. As a result, his 'pupils' from the start learn these words in the form adapted to the Chinese phonological system: [ka-ga-da] instead of [ka-gda] (*kogda*, 'when') or [zy-de-si] instead of [z'des'] (*zdes'* 'here') (fig. 17). Acquired in this form, words become conventionalised. Considering that most Chinese do not aim to learn the 'full version' of Russian and are content with the restricted form of the language, the gradual emergence

---

61   So-called Shanhens – Buryats who moved to China in 1920–1930s not willing to submit to the
      communist rule in the Soviet Union.

of a conventionalised ethnolect of Russian is possible such as, e.g., Gastarbeiterdeutsch in Germany (see Gilbert/Pavlou 1994) or Moroccan Dutch in the Netherlands (see Cornips 2008).

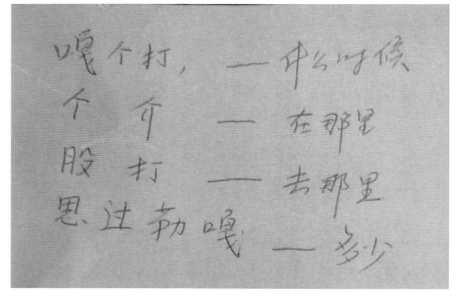

Fig. 17: Russian words and expressions adapted in the Chinese phonological system

'Broken' Russian is also used in written communication. Signs, advertisements, instructions on goods packing etc. demonstrate numerous mistakes in Russian grammar and spelling (fig. 18). Ungrammatical forms and phonetic transformations typical for 'Chinese Russian' are perceived as erroneous and extremely funny by native speakers of Russian, and in native to native communication the same features are widely used for imitating and parodying the way 'silly Chinese' butcher the Russian language.

At the same time some words used by the Chinese trying to speak Russian have become popular with Russian native speakers, turning into a local jargon, the restricted set of lexemes used in interethnic communication or, metaphorically, to refer to the contact situation. Words of this type are called 'Shuttles language' or 'Shuttles jargon' by Russian speakers in the region. The most frequently used elements of this jargon are:

- kapitana – chief, master or anyone in a higher position than the speaker [from Russian *kapitan* 'captain' as pronounced by Chinese speakers]
- druga – address to a man [from Russian *drug* 'friend' as pronounced by Chinese speakers]
- kunia – address to a woman [from Chinese word meaning 'girl', but normally not used as address (see Tsze 2007)]
- kemel – person going to China to bring goods for someone and get paid for it [from English *camel*]
- super-mimimum – best price
- pamagaj(ka) – person helping a Russian tourist or *kemel* with buying goods, packing, transporting etc. [from Russian *pomogaj* – imperative form of 'to help']

Fig. 18: Signs, advertisements, instructions on goods packing etc. demonstrate numerous mistakes in Russian grammar and spelling

These words are used by both Russian and Chinese speakers as in the following dialogue:

R: "Druga, chego stoit? (Friend, what does it cost?)"
Ch: "Pisiat. (Fifty)"
R: "A super-minimum dash? Ustupi, a? (And will you give me super-minimum? Please, go a bit lower)"
Ch: "Sorok piat'. (Forty five)"
R: "Davaj sorok! (Let it be forty)"
Ch: "Ne. Sorok piat' super-minimum. (No. forty five is super-minimum)"[62]

Using these words in their communication with Chinese speakers Russian native speakers make a sort of linguistic compromise with their interlocutors: they demonstrate some minimal convergence towards the Chinese variant of Russian. Linguistic strategies used by Russian native speakers in communication with Chinese speakers are interesting because they demonstrate their attitudes towards the Chinese people. Unlike the Chinese speaking the only form of Russian available to them due to their restricted knowledge of the language, Russian speakers using their native tongue for intercultural communication can choose from several types of verbal behaviour according to the communicative norms and stereotypes of their own. They can either retain their habitual behaviour speaking with non-native speakers the same way as with a native one or use different variants of foreigner talk. Various studies based on several European languages (see an overview in Long 1981) showed that, while talking to foreigners, native speakers try to simplify their utterances to make them easier to perceive and understand. Various means of grammar simplification and sense clarification are employed, some of which are universal while others are unique to a particular language. Universal means include slower and louder speech, frequent repetitions, and grammar simplification. The use of ungrammatical utterances (e.g., 'I not see men you speak' instead of 'I haven't seen the man you are talking about') occurs more often when the speaker feels s/he is 'talking down', and considers the interlocutor socially inferior (see Long 1981). As my previous study on Russian foreigner talk in St. Petersburg shows (see Fedorova 2006) there is a strong ban in Russian culture against using ungrammatical utterances (so-called 'broken language') in real communication with non-native speakers (although these forms are numerous in stereotypes of this communication). Furthermore the hypercorrect form of speech with longer and more complicated sentences can prevail. On the contrary, when communicating with Chinese speakers in the border regions at least some Russian native speakers felt free to employ directly opposed linguistic strategies: they can use

---

62   Here and henceforth I use the abbreviation 'R' for the speakers with Russian as a dominant language and 'Ch' for the speakers of Chinese. It should be underlined that this does not always indicate the ethnic origin of the informants, e.g., some 'R's (as well as some 'Ch's) are Buryats.
      Field records 2008, Chita.

ungrammatical utterances and 'jargon' words justifying themselves by the linguistic incompetence of their interlocutors: "Well, here with them we forget Russian ourselves. They don't understand otherwise, so we have to break the language. It's terrible, of course".[63]

Interestingly, this 'broken' form of Russian used as a foreigner talk has certain linguistic features (e.g. the imperative serving as a main verb form) which resemble that of the Russian-Chinese pidgin of the past:

> R: "[talking about a mobile phone that is not working] Novyi, megafon. Ne mogu, antenna ne rabotaj, meniaj. (New, Megafon [name of mobile company], can not, antenna not work-Imperative, change)"
> Ch: "A-a, davaj ia delaj. (Aha, let's I do-Imperative)"[64]

> Ch: "[talking about long-distance calls bill] Eto chio? (What's this?)"
> R: "A, eto ia, ia Oksana pozvoni. (that's me, I call-Imperative Oksana-Nominative)"[65]

Cf.: "A schasa toka kartoshka sadi, sio magazina kupi, a lan'she ne. ('Now people plant only potatoes and buy everything in the shop; this was not the case before')."[66]

At the same time this type of behaviour − using of ungrammatical utterances − is typical for those informants, who are closely involved in communication with the Chinese on a constant basis, as business partners, spouses, or bosses for Chinese employees. The same people tend to express more positive attitudes towards the Chinese: they underline such 'typical Chinese' qualities as diligence or thrift. Yet at the same time they can speak of their partners (or even spouses) as some sort of aliens with a different language, culture and way of life: "Of course, we are so different, our cultures, the way we think, I mean, sometimes he just can't understand why I take offence. It is difficult of course, one has to adjust in a way... They do not think like us".[67]

They also depict Chinese people as kind, loyal, hardworking, and 'unspoiled by civilization' (meaning they are simple-minded people who can make do with just basic food, goods and facilities). Other people for whom communication with the Chinese is not part of their everyday experience demonstrate more overt negative attitudes. Usually they describe the Chinese in such terms as dirty, uneducated, uncultured, primitive, etc. Even positive qualities usually attached to 'typical' Chinese are often perceived as 'unnatural' for Russian culture − in one of my informant's words 'No normal person would work that hard'. And any

---

63   Field records 2008, Aginskoe.
64   Field records 2006, Chita.
65   Field records 2008, Chita
66   Belikov, Perekhvalskaia manuscript.
67   Field records 2009, Aginskoe.

usage of 'broken Russian' to adjust to communicative needs of Chinese speakers is extremely untypical among those people who are not disposed to the Chinese.

5   Interaction on the Russian-Chinese border: Nowadays and in the past

Communication between Russian and Chinese speakers is therefore asymmetrical: Chinese people try to learn the Russian language and adapt themselves to fast changing border conditions both economically (by organizing different business enterprises) and culturally (by creating hybrid cultural (e.g. architectural or culinary) and linguistic forms). Russian citizens, on the other hand, are not so keen on adaptation and merely tolerate their partners in trade and communication. Thus, unlike Manzhouli, in Chita one could hardly find many signs or advertisements in Chinese, and any changes in urban landscape (e.g. Chinese shops and restaurants with their bright signs) are produced by Chinese migrants and not by Russian businessmen or city authorities.[68] Another interesting example of differences between communicative strategies employed by these two groups is the fact that in their contacts with Russians Chinese prefer to name themselves by Russian names (usually in the shortened form, e.g. 'Volodya' or 'Sasha') and use them in the advertisement of their business ('Fruits and vegetables Lena', 'Money exchange Vika' etc.) rather than try to teach Russians to pronounce their Chinese names. Russians, from their part, use these names in their communication with Chinese and do not try to obtain 'true' names. At the same time addressing someone (especially an older person) just by the shortened form of the name can conflict with the rules of politeness typical for the Russian culture. However this fact does not affect the actual behaviour of Russian speakers in the border regions; what is more, the Chinese are usually addressed by the 'ty' (in singular) not 'Vy' (in plural; polite form like 'Sie' in German) pronoun regardless of their age and relations with the Russian speaker. Such forms of address would hardly be appropriate for communication with Westerners.

Attitudes towards the Chinese on the part of the Russians are condescending, they are treated as inferior people, and communication with them is of a 'talking down' kind − by imitating their 'broken' language one can demonstrate his or her (and actually it is 'her' in most cases − according to my field data women use the 'ungrammatical' form of communication more often) tolerance towards the Chinese. If we compare this situation with those of the nineteenth century considerable similarities may be found. Just as nowadays no special efforts are

---

68   Similar unenthusiastic attitudes towards foreign visitors can be found in other border regions of Russia as well, e.g. on the Russian-Finnish border (see Fedorova/Gavrilova forthcoming).

made by the Russian authorities to adapt urban space to the needs of the Chinese newcomers and international trade activity. They were keener on regulating and suppressing Chinese migrants, and the 'yellow peril' was an important part both of official and informal discourse.[69] Linguistic accommodation of Russian and Chinese speakers was again asymmetrical: the Chinese tried to learn Russian (in fact Russian-Chinese pidgin in most cases; the same way Chinese ethnolect of Russian is acquired by contemporary migrants from China and citizens of Chinese border cities) and Russians tolerated their 'broken language' sometimes using Russian-Chinese pidgin and sometimes avoiding it.[70] In other words, the Chinese were treated both socially and culturally as the Russians' inferior. And the same situation existed not only in pre-revolutionary Russia; after the revolution and defeat of the White Army in the Far East many Russians emigrated to China and especially to Harbin. As a result the so-called 'Russian Manchuria' sprang up and for the next 30 years existed as a Russian community in China, very different from Russian diasporas in the Western countries. Usually emigration conduces to the sharp changes in the sociolinguistic situation: a given group which used to be a majority in the country of their own turns into a minority group and has to adjust to the new conditions by changing its verbal behaviour. The same was true for the Russian emigration to the West – Germany, France and the USA. Yet if we consider linguistic practices of Russians in Manchuria in the first half of the twentieth century we will see the difference: "Russians spoke a foreign language on Parisian streets, but the language of their own on Harbin's ones" (Bobin 1994: 7). As every observer confirms, most Russian emigrants were not in the least interested in learning Chinese. Just as in pre-revolutionary cities, native speakers of Russian did not consider Chinese (or aboriginal languages) 'worth' studying sticking to monolingual verbal behaviour.[71] Russian speakers kept their language functioning not only as a vernacular in everyday communication but also as a language of official communication, mass-media, literature, and education, i.e. in all public spheres. Therefore, despite technically being a minority, Russian emigrants behave as a majority retaining their cultural habits and social infrastructure and virtually ignoring their hosts' language and culture. The same social asymmetry typical for pre-revolutionary Russia was preserved despite the

---

69 Even the Chinese Eastern Railway construction in the beginning of the century aimed, among other purposes, to recover Russian government power in the region and 'save' Siberia and the Far East from Chinese influence. For more information on the Chinese Eastern Railway see Urbansky 2008.

70 E. A. Oglezneva states that using the pidgin was untypical for Russian speakers (see Oglezneva 2007: 55).

71 Chinese was taught as a subject in most Russian schools in Harbin but this fact had very little influence on the linguistic situation in the city (see Oglezneva 2007: 94, 100f.).

change in political conditions of Russian-Chinese interaction. Two groups –
Russians and Chinese – living separately, restricting their communication to the
necessary minimum and using a special restricted language form for this
communication. In most cases Russian speakers could rely upon the Chinese's
ability to speak pidgin and did not intend to make special efforts to learn
Chinese.

6   Conclusions

Attitudes and stereotypes are stable and difficult to change. As the case of the
Russian-Chinese border area shows the same linguistic patterns and sets of
attitudes can be discovered in the same region in different epochs. Both now and
a hundred years ago one can witness a similar social asymmetry between the
contacting sides. The same way as in pre-revolutionary Russia and in 'Russian
Manchuria' in the middle of the twentieth century modern Russian speakers tend
to consider Chinese being socially inferior and anthropologically alien: even
positive attitudes reveal some level of estrangement. On a linguistic level
asymmetry is also apparent: it is the Chinese who try to learn and use Russian
and not vice versa (as again was typical for the situation in the past) but due to
their imperfect knowledge of the Russian language they are not regarded as
equals. Native speakers of Russian can either tolerate their interlocutors' 'broken
language' or use similar speech themselves to match what they believe to be the
Chinese's inability to understand proper Russian. A simplified and
ungrammatical hybrid version of Russian – be it a stable pidgin or just a set of
typical contact strategies – functions at the same time as a means of interethnic
communication and as an instrument of building and supporting group
boundaries since it supports existing negative stereotypes. The same is true of
images of bordering groups in the eyes of each other: the same things, e.g.
buildings and monuments or cuisine, are perceived differently by Chinese and
Russians. Whereas the former consider hybrid forms one can find in border cities
as an attempt to adjust to Russians' needs the latter tend to see them as 'pure
Chinese' and base on them their impressions about Chinese culture. This
discrepancy in mutual images creates tension in interethnic relations and can
provoke conflicts between contacting ethnic groups despite the fact that their
economic activity demands closer cooperation. That's why paying attention to
attitudes and behavioural strategies is so important to understand the ways of
intercultural contacts on the borders.

References

Alvares, R. R. (1995): "The Mexican-US Border: The Making of an Anthropology of Borderlands". In: Annual Review of Anthropology, 24, pp. 447-470.

Anikhovskij, S. E. / Bolotin, D. P. / Zabiyako, A. P. / Pan, T. A. (2005): 'Man'chzhurskij klin': istoriya, narody, religiya. Blagoveshchensk: Amurskij gosudarstvennyj universitet.

Arreola, D. D. (1996): "Border-city idee fixe". In: Geographical review, 86, 3, pp. 356-369.

Arsenjev, V. K. (1978): Po Ussurijskomu krayu: Dersu Uzala. Leningrad: Lenizdat.

Belikov, V. I. (1994): "Russko-kitajskii pidzhin". In: V. M. Pan'kin (ed.): Kontaktologicheskii entsiklopedicheskii slovar-spravochnik. Moscow: Nauka, pp. 294-298.

Belikov, V. I. (n.d.): Kratkaya sotsiolingvisticheskaya kharakteristika russko-kitajskogo pidzhina. Unpublished manuscript.

Belikov, V.I. / Perekhvalskaia, E.V. (n.d.): Polevye materialy 1990 goda. Unpublished manuscript.

Bobin, O. B. (1994): Proschanie s russkim Kharbinom. Moscow: Progress-akademia.

Cherepanov, S. I. (1853): „Kiakhtinskoe kitajskoe narechie russkogo iazyka". In: Izvestiia imperatorskoj Akademii Nauk po otdeleniiu russkogo iazyka i slovesnosti, 2, pp. 370-377.

Cornips, L. (2008): "Losing grammatical gender in Dutch: The result of bilingual acquisition and/or an act of identity?". In: International Journal of Bilingualism, 12, 1/2, pp. 105-124.

Diatlov, V. (2008): "Rossiia: v predchuvstvii chainataunov". In: Etnograficheskoe obozrenie, 4, pp. 6-16.

Donnan, H. / Wilson, T. M. (1999): Borders: Frontiers of Identity, Nation and State. Oxford: Berg Publishers.

Fedorova, K. (2006): "Russian foreigner talk: stereotype and reality". In: D. Stern and C. Voss (eds.): Marginal linguistic identities. Studies in Slavic contact and borderland varieties. Wiesbaden: Harrassowitz Publ., pp. 177-190.

Fedorova, K. / Gavrilova, T. (forthcoming): "Native speakers of Russian in interethnic communication: sociolinguistic situations and linguistic strategies". In: Slavica Helsingiensia, 40.

Ferguson, C. A. (1981): "'Foreigner Talk' as the Name of a Simplified Register". In: International Journal of the Sociology of Language, 28, pp. 9-18.

Garrett, P. (2010): Attitudes to language. Cambridge: Cambridge University Press.

Gelbras, V. (2004): Perspektivy kitajskoj migratsii na Dal'nem Vostoke, In: Otechestvennye zapiski, 4, URL: http://www.strana-oz.ru/?numid=19&article=905 (last access: 18.07.2011).

Gilbert, G. G. / Pavlou, P. (1994): "Gastarbeiterdeutsch, 'Foreign Workers German': An Industrial Pidgin". In: C. Blackshire-Belay (ed.): The Germanic mosaic: Cultural and Linguistic Diversity in Society. Westport/Conn.: Greenwood Press, pp. 147-154.

Griffin, E. C. / Ford, L. R. (1976): "Tijuana: landscape of a culture hybrid". In: Geographical Eeview, 66, 4, pp. 435-447.

Horsman, M. / Marshall, A. (1994): After the Nation State: Citizens, Tribalism and the New World Order. London: Harper Collins.

Kaufman, A. A. (1905): Po novym mestam. Ocherki i putevye zametki: 1901−1903. St. Petersburg: Izdanie tovarischestva 'Obschestvennaya pol'za'.

Landry, R. / Bourhis, R. (1997): "Linguistic landscape and ethnolinguistic vitality: an empirical study". In: Journal of Language and Social Psychology, 16, pp. 23-49.

Larin, V. (2001): "Poslantsy Podnebesnoi na Dal'nem Vostoke: otvet alarmistam". In: Diaspory, 1/2, pp. 76-112.

Long, M. H. (1981): "Input, interaction and second language acquisition". In: H. Winitz (ed.): Native language and foreign language acquisition. New York: New York Academy of Sciences, pp. 259-78.

128   Kapitolina Fedorova

Lukin, A. (1998): "The image of China in Russian border regions". In: Asian Survey, 38, 9, pp. 821-35.
Maksimov, S. V. (1864): Na vostoke. St. Petersburg.
Mühlhäusler, P. (1986): Pidgin and Creole linguistics. Oxford: Basil Blackwell.
Nesterova, E. I. (2008): "Atlantida gorodskogo masshtaba: kitajskie kvartaly v dal'nevostochnykh gorodakh (konets XIX − nachalo XX veka)". In: Etnograficheskoe obozrenie, 4, pp. 44-58.
Oglezneva, E. A. (2007): Russko-kitajskij pidzhin: opyt sotsiolingvisticheskogo opisaniya. Blagoveshchensk: Amurskij gosudarstvennyj universitet.
Oglezneva, E. A. (2009): Russkij yazyk v vostochnom zarubezhje (na materiale russkoj rechi v Kharbine). Avtoreferat diss. doktora filol. nauk. Tomsk.
Perekhvalskaia, E. V. (2007): "Dialektnye razlichiia kak rezultat yazykovogo sdviga (bikinskii dilaekt udegejskogo yazyka)". In: N. B. Vakhtin (ed.): Yazykovye izmeneniia v usloviiakh yazykovogo sdviga. St. Petersburg: Nestor, pp. 252-281.
Perekhvalskaya, E. V. (2008): Russkie pidzhiny. St. Petersburg: Aleteia.
Pickering, S. / Weber, L. (eds.) (2006): Borders, Mobility and Technologies of Control. Dordrecht: Springer Netherland.
Romaine, S. (1989): Pidgin and Creole languages. London: Longman.
Ryzhova, N. P. (2008): "Blagoveshchensk: v poiskakh 'chajnatauna'". In: obozrenie, 4, pp. 17-31.
Selinker, L. (1972): "Interlanguage". In: International Review of Applied Linguistics, 10, pp. 209-231.
Siegelbaum, L. H. (1978): "Another 'Yellow Peril': Chinese Migrants in the Russian Far East and the Russian Reaction before 1917". In: Modern Asian Studies, 12, 2, pp. 307-330.
Sharmashkeeva, N. Z. (2007): Sotsiokulturnaia adaptatsiia kitajskikh migrantov v Buriatii. Avtoreferat diss. kand. filol. Nauk, Moscow.
Skeldon, R. (1995): "The Last Half Century of Chinese Overseas (1945−1994): Comparative Perspectives". In: International Migration Review, 29, 2, pp. 576-579.
Stern, D. (2005): "Myths and Facts about the Kyakhta Trade Pidgin". In: Journal of Pidgin and Creole Languages, 20, 1, pp. 175-187.
Tsze, I. (2007): "Zabaikalsko-manchzhurskii prepidzhin. Opyt sotsiolingvisticheskogo issledovaniia". In: Voprosy iazykoznaniia, 2, pp. 67-74.
Urbansky, S. (2008): Kolonialer Wettstreit: Russland, China, Japan und die Ostchinesische Eisenbahn. Frankfurt, New York: Campus Publishers.
Wachowiak, H. (ed.) (2006): Tourism and Borders. Contemporary Issues, Policies and International Research. Aldershot: Ashgate Publishing Company.
Wilson, T. M. / Donnan, H. (1998): Border Identities. Nation and State at International Frontiers. Cambridge: Cambridge University Press.

An economy of survival and reinventing the way of life: The case of oil commerce in Southeast Turkey

Gulcan Kolay

1 Introduction

"With rare exceptions, borders have always been fairly porous", says Andreas (2000: 22). Appadurai explains this phenomenon very clearly: "The mobility of people has always been an essential characteristic of the world" (1991, cited in Monsutti 2004: 43). Therefore, since the early 19th century with the foundation of nation-states, governments have wanted to control their political and economic spaces. So with the creation, construction, or reconstruction of borders, they have tried to persuade the population of the frontier regions that the borders are impassable using modern practices (for instance, passport controls, immigration laws, walls). However most of the people who live in the border regions know that they are 'virtual'. Furthermore in spite of the well-controlled borders, the social and economic relationships between the inhabitants of border regions have quite often continued in a legal or illegal way. Consequently, smuggling (or *petit trade*) is a product of the border construction and it will exist as long as the borders do. This is because the border zone is also an economic region with generally two more or less different economic systems, such as the border regions of Iraq and Turkey, which is my study subject.

On the other hand, we have to underline that cross-border trade continues rather differently in new political constructions today, such as the European Union, by invalidating the borders of nation-states. For example, there are practices at present, called 'cross-border shopping'. The English can go to the French city of Calais, make purchases there and then return to their country. In addition, due to the evolving relationships between the countries of Western and Eastern Europe, especially after the destruction of the Berlin Wall in 1989, Russian markets emerged in Poland and Polish markets in Berlin and Vienna. The citizens of the ex-East bloc countries (some of them now members of the EU) began to exchange all that they could put in their suitcases by making round trips between the neighbouring villages of the borders. This transformed into the important form of business that has since spread, in particular between certain countries, as Mirjana Moroksavic suggests in reiterating a slogan that had been circulating then in Berlin: "To be English it is to have a nationality, to be French is to have a nationality, to be Polish is a profession" (Wenden 1999: 73).

While we see cross-border trade as extraordinarily diverse, it should in fact be called suitcase trade, as we demonstrated in the example of Poles and Russians above. The very subject of this paper also provides an example: The truck drivers who buy oil in Iraq and sell it in Turkey, which is considered smuggling.

Although *my* main topic is small-scale trade and smuggling, this study can be considered part of a more general corpus on borders because the so-called 'cross-border small-scale trade/smuggling' phenomenon treated here, as the name suggests, has evolved between the borders of countries. As mentioned, there is a strong correlation between borders and smuggling, in other words, "border law evasion dates as far back as border law enforcement" (Andreas 2000: 3). Thus, while writing on a relevant subject (smuggling, border trade) scholars cannot avoid stressing the borders themselves. Therefore, smuggling as a topic is primarily carried out in the field of international relations, geography, and sociology. Nevertheless, border issues, especially "the clandestine cross-border economies have been marginalized subjects" (ibid: 5).

Even though 'border-trade/smuggling' affects every region in the world, most of the studies on smuggling cover human smuggling and migration. Since transnational migration has been a major concern in politics, a wide range of studies on smuggling has been carried out in the two last decades. Researchers agree that illegal migration and human smuggling have recently become a mass phenomenon.[72]

Moreover, in today's global economy, attention is mostly focused on global questions such as organised crime and the flow of people across international borders.

In my case, I will focus on another phenomenon. In fact, this type of smuggling (illegal oil commerce between two countries) might be explained from an economic perspective, as part of a strategy for coping with poverty as any border of the world. With regards to my example here, there is also a political dimension as well because of the conflict between the PKK (Kurdish Workers Party) – a separatist militant group – and the Turkish army. Hence, my theoretical perspective will not be of the globalisation process and its results, but rather that of economies in conflict. This is due to the fact that this kind of smuggling or illegal commerce was in response to the state's 'predatory politics', described by Jean-Christophe Rufin as destructive methods of appropriation that result in the deprivation of most possible resources from the population, as well

---

72   See www.paraplyprojektet.se/upload/Human%2520smuggling.pdf (last access: 20.06.2011).

as the lack of concern about the economic consequences of this despoliation (see 1996: 36). Additionally, it is important to emphasize that there is a strong relationship between conflict, violence, and economics. In several regions of the world where there are conflicts – such as in Latin America, Afghanistan, or many African countries –, violence is done in the name of politics while everyone knows that there are almost always economic objectives. It is obvious that cross-border smuggling, illicit and clandestine commerce, arms and drug trafficking, and organized crime flourish in conflict and resistance regions. As Michel Wieviorka clearly describes: "The passage from political violence to economic criminality could take place in economically dynamic zones, but it could also operate in the devastated territories" (Wieviorka 2004: 59).

2   Methodology

For the elaboration of this work, numerous sources have been used: Literature on the social and economic history of the region, reports by public institutions, regional reports established by the cities' chambers of commerce and industry, French, English and Turkish newspapers, reviews and websites. Nevertheless, the most important sources are the interviews obtained on the field, the privileged place for better knowledge on this subject. Reading newspapers was insufficient, however the conversations opened up new perspectives. These interviews were conducted with members of the region's population concerned by the study topic. Interviews were carried out in Habur, Diyarbakir, Gaziantep, and Silopi – Silopi and Habur in particular – with truck drivers, storekeepers, businessmen, etc. At the beginning, in Habur, I let people speak without any intervention on my part. That is, the interviews had no leading questions. Then, when they stopped talking, I began to ask them some questions. Generally, these were open-ended questions, although sometimes I asked closed questions as well. On the other hand, conducting a good interview requires a trusting relationship. So, I told them the truth: As a PhD student in a French university, I wished to know how cross-border business took place. In spite of their disappointment not being in front of a journalist, they spoke without fear. At first, some people did not want to speak, but after the intervention of others, they were able to express themselves. In Habur, I conducted interviews with about 40 men who were all truck drivers, apart from one former truck driver who had become a drink and sandwich vendor.

For my first visit, I was only able to stay in Habur for 10 hours because of accommodation problems. As there were no vacancies in Silopi, the city closest to the customs gate, I had to stay in Diyarbakir, one of the major cities in southeast Turkey that is considered by some Kurds as the capital of Great Kurdistan. In the beginning, the only concern I had was a possible confrontation with the Habur police, as I had been told by some journalists that one had to have permission to work in Habur, and unfortunately I did not have any. However, I was lucky and did not see or meet any police at the border gate. I did encounter the police on the road between Diyarbakir and Habur, yet they did not interrogate me. It would have been quite different if I had met them in Habur: In spite of the levying of the state of emergency, the policemen could have asked what I was doing there and then could have demanded that I show them authorization for these types of interviews. Ultimately, I had no difficulty and nobody asked me what I was doing, apart from certain truck drivers who would not participate in the interviews until they understood what it was for. I did not limit the interviews to only the truck drivers. I also met some businessmen in Silopi, the last city between Iraq and Turkey. The city is of particular importance for cross-border business, as people who come from or go to Iraq take a break here, which explains the abundant number of restaurants in former times. However when I visited Silopi within the timeframe of my fieldwork (27 May 2003), there were very few restaurants. Like the truck drivers, I went to a restaurant and became acquainted with the restaurant owner, with whom I spoke about the situation. Afterwards, he said to me that he had friends – storekeepers, restaurant owners, and businessmen – inclined to speak with me. I sometimes completed the conversations by asking questions. Being the main actors concerned by the situation, they supplied me with a great amount of information on the consequences of the economic situation. Aside from this, I conducted other interviews in larger cities like Diyarbakir and Gaziantep with the leaders of the storekeepers' association and the industrialists of the region.

3   Smuggling was (is) always a mechanism to help survive

The country borders of Turkey, Iraq, Syria, and Iran divide unofficial Great Kurdistan. These borders – coinciding with the mountainous regions of Kurdistan (fig. 19) – sometimes escaped border controls, thus smuggling developed there. Most of the people with whom I met said that either they themselves or a member of their family had done some smuggling at least once in their life. Their motive was to live, to survive, and to not let their children and their families starve.

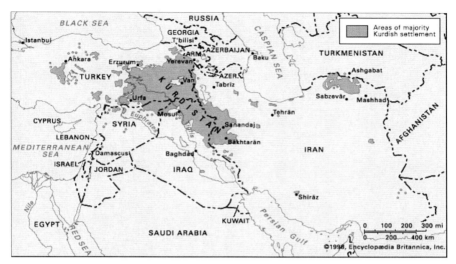

Fig. 19: Areas of Kurdish settlement

According to S. Diken, who was an adviser to the mayor of Diyarbakir city, which is situated in southeast Turkey but relatively far from the border, smuggling was one of the main activities bringing sustenance to the regional population. He said:

"Here, the inhabitants of several prefectures and sub-prefectures lived on the illicit border business, which the local population calls smuggling. I know it from my own family. My father was also a smuggler. There were nearly brand-new clothes, which were sent from Europe to Syria and Iraq through the international charity bodies. These clothes were sold at a reasonable price. My father went to buy them in Syria and sold them here after having cleaned and ironed them. Now, there are people who do the same work in Urfa, but on a larger scale. I am from one of the sub-prefectures of Diyarbakir, which has dedicated itself to this work (smuggling). I am a native of the city of Lice. The sub-prefecture is mountainous, which means agriculture is not possible there. Therefore for many years the inhabitants of Lice practiced this illicit business on the backs of mules in the territory that extends from Iraq and Syria towards the Iranian border, Agri and Dogubeyazit. At present, you know there are lots of companies in Turkey who transport via trucks and boats. But if the inhabitants of Lice own a good mule and a good weapon, there is no better carrier or smuggler than them. They've lived and led things in this way for years. But, it is not something unique to the city of Lice; in this region, there are several places that lived and continue to live in this way. The living conditions, the natural circumstances, and the system did not provide them with other means to sustain themselves. The poverty, the discordance with the system, and, even more so, the conditions offered by nature and despair caused by economic concerns (marigolds), drove these people towards this domain. They first began smuggling (contraband) by selling some tea, then fabrics, and then the world of drugs in Afghanistan and Iran offered them new products."[73]

Moreover, in his book entitled *The city that murmurs its secret to its walls*, Sehmuz Diken tells to which point mules are important for the smugglers:

"It is necessary to speak about mules, about the mules which transport 50-kilogram loads to either side. In Lice, even the architectural structure of the house doors was conceived with regard to mules; the dimensions of the doors were planned in a way that their mules could easily pass through" (Diken 2002: 212).

It is evident that the mule is an important animal for the smugglers, not only in this region, but also for those in other places and borders of the world.

In his book entitled *Globalization through the bottom*, Alain Tarrius says that

"people who smuggle – an activity taking place from the subterranean economy between Morocco, Algeria, and Europe – consider themselves "mules" or say that they are employed through mules. Some succeed finally in fitting into the subterranean economy, sometimes becoming, according to their expression, mules, meaning smugglers" (Tarrius 2002: 150).

Although mules and horses have been used for smuggling for many years at the border region between Iraq, Turkey, and Iran, they have been gradually abandoned and replaced by cars.

"There was some smuggling until 1991, 1992. People had brought many boxes of cigarettes from Iraq or Syria and sold them in Turkey, in the village. Naturally, at that time those who controlled the border turned a blind eye to such smuggling. I am going to give you an example: I myself smuggled. Normally the identity check is done one by one at the control point. I filled up the car with tea and cigarettes, and at that time the servicemen turned a blind eye. Sometimes we gave nearly half of the box to them. They also took advantage of the village. For example, we were told that the army post in the village needed to be restocked, that they needed some items worth 2 billion Turkish lira (approximately 1,000 Euro), we were asked to send this money to them and we sent it, thus they turned a blind eye. We made roundtrips rather freely. On the other hand, people had had enough of poverty, so instead of starving they preferred to take the risk."[74] (a truck driver)

---

73   Interviewed in Diyarbakir (25.05.2003).
74   Interviewed in Habur (27.05.2003).

4   Habur border gate and the birth of oil commerce

As it is known, in spite of the well-controlled borders in the Middle East, economic and cultural exchanges continued and these borders simultaneously became a zone of separation and contact.

Since it was the only crossing point at the Turkey-Iraq border, the Habur gate became this kind of contact and separation zone. Habur is situated in Silopi (see fig. 20), a district of the Sirnak province in southeast Turkey. This border post first began to operate in 1973.

Fig. 20: Location of the Haber river crossing (Source: Google Maps)

After the opening of this customs gate, it became a point of 'reunification' for north and south Kurdistan. Under these ideal conditions, both parts of the border began to provide for their economic needs; for them, there was only one obstacle: The state's border between them. We can say that it is not the same case for other borders of the world, where we can also see, for example, language as an obstacle. For instance, "the lack of common language and learning mutual languages on the border between China and Russia becomes a major handicap for the implementation of border business between both communities" (Larin/Rubtsova 2001: 252)

Before the application of the embargo on Iraq by the UN in 1990, this road and customs post acted as the door for the passage of trucks from Europe and Russia to the Middle East. Cities such as Cizre, Silopi, Gaziantep, and Sirnak benefited considerably from this trade route through the customs post in Habur. The dynamism stemming from this business not only contributed to the development of Turkey, but also regional cities, which in turn benefited the neighbouring population. This is why a regional economy decline is seen after the closing of the customs post at Habur because of the embargo on Iraq. We can understand the importance of the Habur customs post for the local population in this significant expression: 'No customs, no life'. This population perceives Habur as a 'means of production'. If the customs is open then the survival of the population is assured, on the other hand, if it is closed, we then see a sudden impoverishment of the region.

Ahmet, a truck driver, describes this situation as the following: "Habur is our factory; it is the factory of southeast Turkey. There is no factory in the region of Sirnak, Siirt, and Batman until Urfa. There is no work. If there is no cross-border business, there is no more work in our region."[75]

He also answers the question concerning the existence (or rather the lack thereof) of agriculture and herding: "There are no more cattle in the region because of the ban on herding. We sold everything, animals, lands (...) and we invested in this old car. We began to make some cross-border business".

We can also study the impact of economic activity and the Habur customs' capacity of creating jobs via the data of the Institution of State Statistics (DIE). According to the studies of this institute, in particular the 'Industrial Inventory of the East Regions and the Southwest in 2006', 220 firms (industrial plants) were found in Diyarbakir, one of the largest cities of the region with a population exceeding one million inhabitants today. As for the other cities of the region, there were 49 firms in Mardin and 290 in Urfa (see table 3). With regard to employment, the number of people employed in both the eastern regions and southeastern Anatolia reached 69,638 in 2004. According to the information that I collected from regional drivers' associations, there were 52,000 registered trucks in the regions of Sirnak, Silopi, and Cizre in 2003. If we suppose that every truck provides a job for five people, we can easily understand the importance of Habur to the regional population.

The local population, who, before the embargo, took advantage of the jobs created by the Habur customs, were constantly comparing the period before and

---

75   Interviewed in Habur (27.05.2003).

after the embargo. One of the truck drivers, Kemal from Silopi, explains the period before the embargo:

"Previously, we did not have a lot of money or many possessions, but we were not so miserable. For example, some worked in auto garages and in the evening, they received 10 million (6 dollars with the current exchange rate). They could then buy tomatoes and some bread. That was before 1991: everybody had a normal situation. There were people who sold some bread, water, or ice cubes on the road crossed by trucks, and the others sold their vegetables, tomatoes, or melons that they had harvested from their garden on the roadside. In fact, everybody managed as he could and assured his life."

Name of Province	Food industry	Tex-tile	Oil-chemistry	Stone-soil	Ma-chine	Wood-Forest	TOTAL
Adiyaman	33	47	6	6	6	1	99
Batman	11	15	8	10	11	1	56
Diyarbakir	37	58	33	60	18	11	220
G.Antep	161	509	78	18	61	21	839
Kilis	14	2	3	2	1	-	22
Mardin	21	9	10	5	3	1	49
Siirt	4	2	3	-	2	1	12
Sanliurfa	92	144	20	15	19	-	290
Sirnak	2	2	-	3	-	-	7

Tab. 3: Industrial Inventory of the East Regions and the Southwest in 2006 (Source: http://dergiler.ankara.edu.tr/dergiler/42/998/12142.pdf; last access: 04.07.2011)

Sezgin, an itinerant food salesman, sold meals to the truck drivers who waited in traffic jams in front of the Habur customs. He remembered days when he saw 1,000 even 1,500 vehicles a day crossing by this road:

"I also worked at this customs gate before the embargo. Before the embargo, the situation was different: Bulgarians, French, Russians, people from everywhere entered and went out through this customs point. Some people bought balls or bread, others Coke. Our work made good progress. 1000, 1500 vehicles, trucks-tanks, trucks passed a day."[76]

The other drivers who worked during this period enthusiastically approved of every word Sezgin said.

In 1990, the situation changed. With the UN's decision to implement an embargo on Iraq, the passage of goods via this customs gate towards Iraq and

---

76   Interviewed in Habur (27.05.2003).

other countries in the Middle East stopped. Hence, the local population lost its only source of livelihood and the regional economy collapsed.

After the loss of their main means of survival, the customs post, the local population had only one choice: It is obvious that the worse the economic crisis becomes, the more the underground economy flourishes. In such a situation, the local population started to search for ways to develop unofficial cross-border oil imports from Iraq. The practice violated the UN economic sanctions against Iraq, but almost everyone turned a blind eye: The Kurds, because they were making money and the Turks, because the income generated helped compensate Turkey for the billions of dollars it lost when it cut off legal trade with Iraq as a result of the Gulf War.

In 1996, with the UN program 'Oil for Food', the cross-border trade between Turkey and Iraq began its most fertile period. The purchase of the oil from Iraq at a very low price and the sale of it in Turkey appeared favourable, and the local population began buying several trucks. At that time, this was a real phenomenon. Suddenly, everyone in southeast Turkey seemed to be buying trucks and fibreglass tanks. Those who did not have enough money to purchase a vehicle sold the gold of their spouses, of their children, their houses, their livestock, or their lands.

These trucks were second-hand, old-fashioned vehicles. According to the truck driver Ahmet, "All the ruined Bedfords, the BMNs, the damaged MANs" had been bought. The most important characteristic was that these trucks had big fuel tanks. The condition of the old trucks did not really matter because they were only going a short distance, 60-70 km, between the place where they were going to buy the oil (south Kurdistan) and the place of sale (north Kurdistan, Silopi, Cizre). Afterwards, they made additional reservoirs under the trucks to transport even more oil.

From the beginning, this kind of cross-border commerce has been seen as smuggling. Therefore, sometimes the oil transported via Iraq began to raise problems between the state customs employees, the police, and the drivers. But after seeing how much income this trade provided to Turkish regions, the Turkish government attempted to regulate and tax this illicit trade. According to the legislation of 1996, the greatest amount of transported oil per small truck was limited to between four and, at the most, eight tons.

The oil commerce between these two borders was a "brilliant example of the power of the profit motive to transcend political strife" (Naylor 1999: 327). Turkey, not wanting to recognize the Kurds inside its territory and pretending not to see those outside it, began such an economic relationship with the Kurds, who established an administration in northern Iraq, because of the consequences of the embargo.

However, it is necessary to underline the fact it is not only the local population that took advantage of Habur, but also other regions of Turkey. Thus, we could make a comparison: If the border gate of Habur is a factory for the region, we could say that products supplying this 'factory' were coming, for example, from Adapazari, Izmit, Mersin, Kayseri, etc. – in other words, from the west of the country.

The businessman Hakan explains that:

> "Half the people who passed by this road came from Istanbul, from Ankara, or from Izmir. It is not only the inhabitants of southeast Anatolia that earned their living thanks to this commerce with the countries of the Gulf and Iraq, but also those who lived in the west of the country as well."[77]

This special commerce that we cannot easily see elsewhere in the world worked as follows: the truck drivers transported basic daily products, taking companies' goods to Iraq at no charge within the framework of the Oil for Food program. In counterpart, they would resell the oil that they bought cheaply in Iraq in Turkey. In this business, there was no place for banks, cheques, etc.

5   The multiple cross-border actors

In this section, I would like to identify the various actors in cross-border business. Through my fieldwork, I determined that the truck drivers were not the only major players. Customs officers, soldiers, the ruling elite, and politicians also played important roles in the extension and the eventual halting of this type of business.

5.1   The truck drivers

I observed that the proliferation of the cross-border business developed naturally as the final recourse for the local population whose possibilities of agriculture work and the exploitation of cattle had reached a very low point. When the closure of the customs gate could no longer assure their survival, these people, who had sold all their property to buy a truck to trade oil, had no other job options. The driver Ali explains the fact that they could not do anything else: "In this region, all these people are drivers. If we do not know how to do anything

---

77   Interviewed in Habur (27.05.2003).

else, then how can we change? We are all illiterate. We can only be a driver or a shepherd."[78]

The educational level of these impoverished drivers and their families is very low. Among the 30 drivers with whom I conducted interviews, the highest level of education achieved was at the primary school level. Their families, without any encouragement, have no desire to make their children study. Most of them have more than five children. Their only objective is that the male children can start working as quickly as possible to earn money. In this region, the male child is perceived as being a source of power, work, and money...

"Those who have five, seven, or ten boys are rich. The family situation of those who only have one son is a little bit different. Some of these children have to carry burdens, and little by little they arrive at something."

Other truck drivers and storekeepers echoed these comments made by the truck driver Murat concerning the importance of male children.

The role played by truck drivers in the cross-border business was capital. Within the framework of the Oil for Food program, the drivers transported goods – salt, sugar, oil, and flour – free of charge or sometimes even offered the storekeeper some money to give them a pretence to go to Iraq (except those who worked for the UN, who were paid for the transportation of the organisation's goods). After having delivered the goods to Iraq, the truck drivers would transport the oil bought in northern Iraq back to Turkey, where they would sell it and make a profit. It was a win-win situation for everybody: The storekeeper benefited from the free transportation of his goods and the truck driver, thanks to the transportation of these goods, managed to enter Iraq and buy some oil to sell in Turkey.

5.2 The customs officers

Other important actors in the cross-border business were the customs officers, who worked with custom regulations that changed almost every day. These ever-changing regulations made life difficult for the truck drivers and businessmen.

"Go wherever you want, and you will never meet such problems. When we go out in the morning, we return in the evening with new customs laws. For example, when we leave in the morning, the transportation of 300 litres of oil from Iraq was authorized, and later when we arrive in the evening the customs officer says to us that we cannot bring more than 200 litres. There are numerous customs in Turkey, but you will not see as much going on as here. What did we do, what do they want from us? It has been years since we've done this work, we do not have other working possibilities here",

---

78   Interviewed in Gaziantep (29.05.2003).

the truck driver Hasan moans.[79]

> "The cross-border customs depend on the customs head office. Such daily changes in the regulations should not take place, but the Khabur customs gate is a particular case: it is the meeting point with northern Iraq, in other words Kurdistan of Iraq. All the events taking place in this country influence the situation in Turkey. That is why this customs gate is sometimes closed or open",

says Arif, manager of a café in Silopi.[80]

As Arif says, Habur has been one of the most problematic subjects in Ankara concerning the Kurdish issue. The decisions that Turkey made concerning Habur were security and sanction-based. The Turkish central administration in Ankara did not see the problem of this region as a whole, but only as a part, which was sometimes reflected in its security or economic dimensions. They saw the problem from the perspective of the people with whom they had had discussions. For instance, when there was a crisis between Turkey and the Kurdish administration in northern Iraq, Turkey decided to close down the Habur border gate after discussing the issue with the Turkish armed forces. However when the Turkish government discussed this issue with local business firms, they decided to reopen the border gate. It is obvious that the army's decision is more important than others for Turkey. *Hence, Turkey sometimes did not openly close down the Habur gate, but in practice the Habur gate did not work efficiently.* Habur was repeatedly closed and reopened after the embargo. The local population describes this fact as a kind of children's game because, for instance, the Habur gate was closed in the morning and reopened in the evening. There were several reasons for the decision to close the gate and afterwards ban the oil trade, which will be revisited in more detail below.

5.3 Ruling elite and politicians

Income obtained via the Habur customs drew the attention of some pro-state regional politicians. In 1995, the district of Sirnak created the SIR-GEV foundation. It gained enormous profits by taxing truck drivers for their crossing. The SIR-GEV decreed 80 Turkish lira for large trucks and 40 for small trucks. The truck drivers did not dispute these taxes – taken legally or illegally – because they were earning a good deal of money at this time.

---

79   Interviewed in Habur (27.05.2003).
80   Interviewed in Habur (27.05.2003).

"For example, there was an oil tax. There was also an excise transport stamp and a standard of life tax. We paid it without any problem because we worked and earned well. Now that the cross-border commerce has been banned, thousands of people like me can no longer pay these taxes. These are valid for the tax of the vehicle and the tax of transport",

says a shopkeeper.[81]

Following the rumours about this illicit commerce and the incapacity of the control of the oil brought from Iraq by the State, the TPIC (Turkish Petroleum International Company) – a collectively 'typical' conscript by people of the region – was established in 1999. Thus, the oil coming in from Iraq was limited. The most important problem was that the TPIC had become the only buyer of oil, contrary to free market laws, as truck drivers were forced to sell their oil to this company.

Ahmet Yildirim, brother of Salih Yildirim, deputy of Sirnak of Anap, a coalition party of that time, and Suayip Okten, brother of Neset Okten, ex-mayor of Silopi, were among the partners of the TPIC. This is proof that the politicians and policies were involved in this business. They too tried to find the means to earn some easy money in the oil commerce.

"Some spiteful people with ties to the State wanted to steal these 50 million TL of earnings from the people and decided to create the TPIC. This company said to us: 'You used to sell your oil for 350 Turkish lira in Silopi, but from now on you are going to sell it to TPIC for 280 Turkish lira. And it is the TPIC that is going to resell it'. Meanwhile, we are the ones who go to Iraq to take the goods and who have to negotiate in the free market in Turkey. Then we decided to no longer sell our oil to the TPIC. We transported the Iraqi oil with our own vehicles, therefore risking our lives. We bought it with cash, using our own capital, and we wanted to sell it for cash whereas the TPIC wanted us to sell the goods and after a week we would receive our cheques from the bank. We refused and we protested. Then the servicemen arrived and ended the demonstration. They told us that we absolutely had to sell our oil to the TPIC. As far as I know, nobody could sell more than 400 litres of oil to the TPIC. The TPIC made enormous profits",

says café manager Arif.[82]

Before the creation of the TPIC, those who had capital in the region opened agencies to buy the oil transported from Iraq to Turkey. They deposited invoices and sent the oil to the western regions. After the creation of the TPIC, many companies that were only specialized in buying and selling oil had to close. Thus, 450 companies in Silopi, 400 in Cizre and 450 in Nusyabin, in Kiziltepe, and in Viransehir filed for bankruptcy and thousands of people were laid off.

On the other hand, the fact that the TPIC did not pay for the oil upfront, but rather sent a cashable cheque one week later shook the truck drivers' confidence

81   Interviewed in Silopi (27.05.2003).
82   Interviewed in Silopi (27.05.2003).

in this institution, which they perceived as "the State mafia". The situation before the TPIC was totally different: they could ask for money upfront for the oil, which they had not yet brought, from people with whom they were familiar and used to dealing with. It was mutual confidence, which played a role in this type of commerce that functioned without banks or formal institutions.

> "These people we sold our oil to acted as a bank. Whether we had money or not, we could quietly use some money as if we had it. For example, if I wanted to buy a car and I didn't have enough money, I could just ask these people to loan me some money and they would. In turn, when we went and came back from Iraq and when we unloaded the goods, they first took the money that they had given us, and then gave us the surplus",

explains Sezgin, an itinerant salesman.[83]

However, these difficulties and tense relations with TPIC went on until the prohibition of oil commerce in 2002.

6   Prohibition of oil commerce by Turkey

In spite of the embargo, the cross-border oil commerce was able to bring a serious dynamism to the local economy. Therefore, truck drivers, storekeepers, carriers, tyre salesmen, producers and sellers of foodstuffs, gas stations, sectors of transport, restaurant owners, etc. took advantage – directly or indirectly – of this commerce. The customs of Habur and the oil commerce, which saw its most beneficial period between 1995 and 1997, contributed enormously to the regional economy. For example, the number of vehicles that passed by the Khabur customs gate in 1994 was 90,685 and in 1997, this number rose to 249,600. The amount of transported oil was 234,000 tons in 1994 and increased to 945,142 tons in 1997.

Nevertheless Turkey decided to forbid the oil commerce on 1 September 2002 due to growing problems with the Kurdish groups in Iraq. Actually, Turkey had already attempted to limit this commerce for numerous reasons, which will be mentioned later on. However in order to understand the situation better, a brief explanation of the political and economic status of the southeast part of Turkey, in other words Turkish Kurdistan, is necessary.

There is a clear difference between the economic development in the western and eastern parts of Turkey. Many have debated on whether or not Turkey has deliberately left this region in poverty (see Jafar 1976: 96; Bozarslan 1996: 129). In any case, it is true to say that there are many factors that undermine economic development in the region. In that sense, the first factor is Kurdish separatism

---

83   Interviewed in Habur (27.05.2003).

and its consequential conflict between Kurdish separatists and the Turkish state has played a significant role in the economic situation of the area. Briefly, from the establishment of the Turkish Republic in 1923 to nowadays there have been numerous Kurdish rebellions against the Turkish Republic. As a result, Turkey has seen the Kurdish minority that lives in the southeast as threat to Turkey's territorial unity. The Turkish Republic clearly did not know which approach to take *vis-à-vis* this question. Turkey generally preferred to control the region through security methods that rely on the military. Ultimately, the methods used by security forces were predation policies that "destroy the economic resources necessary for the survival of the population; but these policies essentially motivated a military logic that is hardly stimulated by the concern to get itself economic resources" (Bozarslan 1996: 131).

However, one thing is sure: Turkey's anxieties concerning the region have caused an obstacle to its development. Similar fears played an essential role in banning cross-border oil commerce as well. We can see this sentiment plays an essential role in the Turkish policy regarding the Habur gate, located at the heart of the small-scale cross-border commerce or smuggling. The Turkish military and civil bureaucracy thought that this commerce was being done in the name of the PKK and that the PKK was gaining from this commerce. Another reason is that Turkey realized that the Kurdish Democratic Party [KDP], one of the main parties in northern Iraq, was profiting from the oil proceeds and helping to pave the way for the *de facto* Kurdish in Iraq. At that time, the greatest portion of the regional income was coming from the custom duties in Habur (or the Ibrahim Halil border gate; the Turkish side calls its border gate Habur while the Kurds call it Ibrahim Halil). The fear of an independent unified Kurdish state still plays a major role in the decisions about the Habur gate. This fear can be seen in recent media coverage like 'Could Northern Iraq Be the Attractive Centre for Turkey's Kurds?' This question greatly occupies Turkey's state institutions. For example, an official secret report (dating from 2000), which was signed by the Turkish intelligence agency (MIT) and a National Security Committee's representative, reveals an analysis on the subject. It is said in the report:

> "In the near future, the business capacity between Turkey and Iraq is going to increase and thus simultaneously effect northern Iraq's income as well…the KDP (Kurdish Democratic Party) will receive a considerable income from the trade between Turkey and Iraq."

Therefore, Turkey from time to time has put another border gate project on the agenda and has discussed it with the Americans, but it has not yet been accepted. This border gate project does not pass through the Kurdish area in Iraq, but rather through the Turkoman region in Iraq.

7 Conclusion

Following the ban on oil commerce in 2002, the region once again appeared to have lost its means of survival. A traveller to this region would have been able to note the number of abandoned trucks that spanned across the kilometres of road that connect numerous cities to the southeast. Nevertheless, this desperate situation did not last too long. This time many of the drivers started to transport American Army supplies from the Turkish harbour Mersin to Iraq.

As my fieldwork has shown, these communities who live on both sides of the national border between Turkey and Iraq could not be isolated from each other, even under the very extreme conditions, such as conflict or under the pressure from the State. The presence of the same ethnics on both sides of the border encourages the relationship between them. Furthermore, the interviews I conducted in the Habur region on the Turkish side show that Habur and the border are not seen as the end of the fatherland. Quite on the contrary, the border is perceived in this region as the starting point of freedom of their identity. Moreover, I can hypothesise that the State's or armed forces' predation practices on the local population cannot be achieved one hundred percent, especially in the border regions because of collaboration between border communities, as we see through this study. Consequently, border communities know how to manage their difficulties *vis-à-vis* national legislation and local administrators.

Today, there is a sort of smuggling or cross-border trade between the cities of Silopi, in Turkey and Zakho, and in Iraqi Kurdistan. There are about 300 individuals who make the daily journey between these two cities, bringing a couple of kilos of tea, some sugar, etc. These people are called 'ants' in Silopi. It is evident that it is poorer people who do this kind of business.

References

Andreas, A. (2000): Border games: policing the U.S.-Mexico divide. Ithaca, London: Cornell University Press.

Bozarslan, H. (1991): "Un Nationalism Kurde". In : E. Picard (ed.): *la question Kurde.* Bruxelles: Edition Complexe, pp. 97-113.

Bozarslan, H. (1996): "Kurdistan: Economie de Guerre,Economie dans la Guerre". In: F. Jean and J.C. Rufin (eds.): Economie des Guerres Civiles. Paris: Hachette, pp. 105-146.

Bozarslan, H. (2005): "Türkiye'de Kürt Milliyetçiliği: Zimni Sözleşmeden Ayaklanmaya 1919-1925". In : E.J. Zurcher (ed.): İmparatorluktan Cumhuriyete Türkeye'de Etnik Çatışma. İstanbul: İletişim.

Diken, S. (2002): sirrini surlarina fisildayan sehir: Diyarbakir. Istanbul: Iletisim.

Jafar, M. R. (1976): Under-underdevelopment a regional case study of the Kurdish area in Turkey. Helsinki: Painoprint oy.

Kolay, G. (2004): L'Iimpact de L'Embargo Applique par l'ONU en Irak sur Le Commerce Transfrontalier au Sud-est de la Turquie, (un-published master thesis). Paris: EHESS.

Larin, V. / Rubtsova, A. (2001): "At the Crossroads: Russian-Chinese Interactions". In: D. Papademetrios and D. W. Meyers (eds.): Caught in the Middle. Washington: Carnegie Endowment for International Peace, pp.228-259.

Monsutti, A. (2004): Guerres et Migrations: Réseaux Sociaux et Stratégies Économiques des Hazaras d'Afghanistan. Paris: éditions de la maison des Sciences de l'homme.

Naylor, R. T. (1999): Economic Warfare: Sanction, Embargo Busting and their Human Costs. Boston: Northeastern University Press.

Odgers, O. (2001): Identités Frontalières: Immigrés Mexicains aux Etats-Unis. Paris: L'Harmattan.

Rufin, J.-C. (1996): "Les Économies de Guerre dans les Conflits Internes". In: F. Jean and J.-C. Rufin (eds.): Économie des Guerres Civiles. Paris: Hachette,pp. 19-59.

Tarrius, A. (2002): La Mondialisation par le Bas. Paris: Editions Balland.

Wieviorka, M. (2004): La violence. Paris: éditions Balland.

Wihtol de Wenden, C. (1999): Faut-il Ouvrir Les Frontières. Paris: Presses de Sciences PO.

Shadow Triangle. Trans-border smuggling between Kosovo, Albania and Montenegro

Enza Roberta Petrillo

> "Geography is about power. Although often assumed to
> be innocent, the geography of the world is not a product
> of nature but a product of histories of struggle between competing
> authorities over the power to organize, occupy and
> administer the space."
> (Gearóid Ó Thuatail)

1   Introduction

There is a common view among West European scholars that, in Kosovo, Albania and Montenegro illegality and corruption are pervasive at all levels of society. In this context, the superficial perception of trans-border smuggling is that it is widely accepted as a form of substitute social welfare.

Starting from these summary elements, this article aims:

- to analyze the ways in which the economic and political transition is affecting changes in such a context, bringing about widespread illicit practices and
- to understand how these practices affect the regional dimension of trans-border relations in the 'territorial triangle' between Albania, Montenegro and Kosovo.

In this area, according to international and local sources, the Deçan-Plav route has become a channel for smuggling weapons and drugs as well as human trafficking. The same area, lake Vermica, bordering Kosovo and Albania, has been described as an open gate for cross-border criminality by law-enforcement authorities. International police suspects that criminal groups engaged in racketeering, smuggling and prostitution rely on close links to people in power. Studies on corruption in the Southeast European region, and in post-Yugoslavian states, indicate that the dominance of the shadow economy is a fairly pervasive problem. Corrupt practices such as bribery and nepotism still persist in the ethnical Albanian areas as well as in the former Yugoslavian countries. Instead, a significant part of the studies does not take into account that the overlapping of illicit and licit practices creates confusion in the concept of 'illicit' itself. Given

that premise, this 'grey' setting will be analyzed as a complex and problematic set of representations and practices, rather than as a coherent, neutral and objectivist field, using a 'critical geopolitical perspective'[84].
Consequently, several questions arise, here:

- Is trans-border smuggling a form of organized enterprise embedded in the local social context?
- Is it correct to speak about a symbiotic nexus between the licit and illicit sector that affects society, politics and the economy?

In 2003, a report published by USAID (see Spector/Winbourne/Beck 2003), suggested that corruption exists in Kosovo but that it, despite public opinion and media discussion perceiving the problem to be of high importance, is not as large a problem as elsewhere in the region. "In comparison to other countries in the region- the report observed- the survey results suggest that the corruption situation in Kosovo is more optimistic. Corruption does not appear to be as extensive among public officials, the demands of corrupt officials are lower, and the extent of citizen involvement in corrupt transactions is lower in Kosovo than in other countries of Southeast Europe. In addition, Kosovars seem to believe that they can cope with the problem. In terms of tolerance for corruption and susceptibility to corruption, Kosovo seems to be at the same level as other former republics of Yugoslavia" (Spector/Winbourne/Beck 2003: 2). On the other side, more recently, 'Corruption Perceptions Index' published by Transparency International (2009)[85], an international NGO devoted to fighting corruption, gives Kosovo the grade 3.4 from the maximum 5 for the worst cases. Several studies highlight that corruption remains endemic at the borders of

---

84   Critical Geopolitics is an ongoing theoretical project which started when the French geographer Yves Lacoste founded the journal Hérodote. The subject entered the Anglo-Saxon Geography literature in the 1990s thanks to a special 'Critical Geopolitics' issue of the Political Geography journal in 1996 (vol. 15/6-7), and the publication in the same year of Gearóid Ó Tuathail's seminal Critical Geopolitics book. Currently, critical geopolitics is most commonly associated with a group of 'dissident' academics including John Agnew, Simon Dalby and Ó Tuathail . In 1996, the book Critical Geopolitics written by Ó Tuathail defined the state of critical geography at the time, and codified its methodological and intellectual underpinnings. Subsequently, the definition of Critical Geopolitics has been broadened such that the project is no longer associated solely with the works of a small number of scholars. Overall, critical geopolitics has opened up new research agendas and contributed to debates across the social sciences and the humanities on globalization, identity politics and sovereignty.
85   See   Transparency   International   in   Corruption   Perception   Index,   URL: http://www.transparency.org/policy_research/surveys_indices/cpi/2009   (last   access 29.06.2011).

former Yugoslavia, and that the wars and post-war years have reinforced corrupt and criminal networks. Corruption is particularly likely to be a problem in relation to customs services and any privatisation process. However, the problem exists in all sectors and has spread to areas previously not heavily affected.

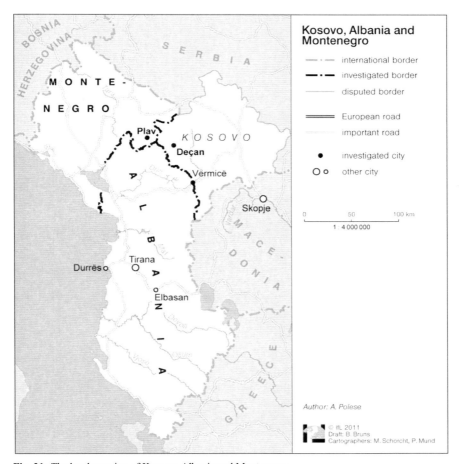

Fig. 21: The border region of Kosovo, Albania and Montenegro

The breakdown of the legal system, the fast economic and social transformation, the social fragmentation, and the lack of security must not be underestimated as important factors for social behaviour. As in many countries in transition, in the analyzed area, some sectors of the political and civil élite believe that the control of the illegal economy may help to consolidate their power and therefore speed up economic transition and the democratic process. Since the 1999 war, criminal activities have prospered and, as noted (see Strazzari 2008a) the war itself provided an opportunity for criminal groups to take advantage of favourable political conditions for smuggling and trafficking. Illicit investments, black market transactions, obscure dealings are reported daily by local investigative newspapers.

In conclusion, the dark side of the post-war transition seems to be in sharp contrast with EU accession parameters. Organized crime in south-east Europe is regularly listed by the EU in its assessments on security. The European Security Strategy published by the EU in 2003, for example, said Europe was a prime target for organized crime which was "often associated with weak or failing states" (European Council 2003: 4). "This internal threat to our security", it stressed,

> "has an important external dimension: cross-border trafficking in drugs, women, illegal migrants and weapons accounts for a large part of the activities of criminal gangs. All these activities undermine both the rule of law and social order itself. In extreme cases, organized crime can come to dominate the state" (ibid.).

On these bases, finally, the paper will focus the attention on the role of the international community in facing smuggling and trying to review the law enforcement strategies that the international agencies have made to address the question.

2   Methods

A cautionary note is due at this point. The rise of the 'shadow triangle' in the social sciences debate is a very recent fact. For that matter, describing and analyzing the trans-border smuggling between Kosovo, Albania and Montenegro was not an easy task, especially regarding the collection of empirical findings and quantitative data such as statistics and analytical figures. In this case – as observed in an anthropological perspective (see Pardo 2004)[86] – an up-to-date approach should be employed, as far as the significance of corrupt behaviours that are not strictly illegal and individual moralities underlying such behaviours

---

86   Based on descriptive analysis of corrupt practices at and beyond the local level, this volume "stands as demonstration that empirical investigation, can, and indeed should, be carried out, drawing on long-term research based on a combination of traditional anthropological methods, background knowledge and the study of the documentary sources" (Pardo 2004: 3).

are concerned. In other terms, in the considered case-study we have to take into account the multiplicity and the complexity of this phenomenon at the levels of official and unofficial practices.

Following critical geopolitics' approach, this article will base its analysis on:

– investigative journalism articles[87],
– specialized literature[88]
– 'grey' sources[89]

utilized with the aim to understand the connection between illicit practices and socio-political context and the role of the international community in facing trans-border smuggling. With these premises, the selected methodological approach will analyze smuggling, 'territorializing' it in its specific historical, social and spatial meanings. Even if the spatial element is central, territory has, in fact, a double nature: it is at the same time material, as a geographic space, and symbolic, as the representation of a social system. 'Space' implies thinking about the territories' limits, continuities and reconstructions, while 'territory' mixes spaces, culture and networks. Discussions about territory appeared rather late in the geographical debate, and more widespread in the social sciences.

From the 1980s the uses and meanings of the word 'territory' increased, amplifying the different theoretical perspectives. In 2004, the Dictionary of Geography (see Levy/Ferras/Thery 2003) dedicated ten pages to this word, whereas Les Mots de lagéographie (see Brunet/Ferras/Thery 1992), published in 1993, only dedicated one page to it. If Roger Brunet (1990: 70) describes territory firstly as a geographical space in which there is a belonging and appropriation feeling; Guy Di Meo (1998) – one of the main noticeable scholars of social geography in France – describes territory as an economic, ideological and political appropriation of space by some groups. This approach introduces

---

87   In particular, this paper takes into account the investigative articles on illicit practices in the shadow triangle, published by Balkan Insight and Balkan Investigative Reporting Network. "The Balkan Investigative Reporting Network, BIRN, is a close-knit group of editors and trainers that enables journalists in the region to produce in-depth analytical and investigative journalism on complex political, economic and social themes. BIRN emerged from the Balkan programme of the London-based Institute for War & Peace Reporting, IWPR, in 2005. As part of that process, IWPR's original Balkan team was entrusted with the task of taking local ownership for that programme and making it sustainable, in the light of the changing realities in the region" (see http://birn.eu.com/en/1; last access: 23.05.2011).

88   Scientific grey literature comprises newsletters, reports, working papers, theses, government documents, bulletins, fact sheets, conference proceedings and other publications.

89   Here, consider the remarkable inputs offered by Klaus Dodds, according to whom critical studies of newspapers, films and magazines are useful to understand the ways in which 'lay' understandings of geopolitical issues are produced and reproduced through societies.

the tools of historical materialism to geography, including a "nonlinear and evolving concept of time, and an awareness of spatial or territorial contradictions that partly give meaning to and explain social life" (Jeremy/Crampton/Stuart 2007: 122). Thus, it lays either on the existence of a social space and of a lived space, or on an arranged geographical space. As a result, the territory is linked to the life of the societies that live in it, in an abstracted wide meaning when we study the representations the people have[90]. This thought space is conceived as the result of the societies' practices. It is the subject of mental representations systems on the basis of historical and cultural facts. Lastly, appropriation is as important as the local action of the societies who live in the territory and transform it. In this perspective, each territory has its own actors and its encased power levels. According to Etienne Balibar,

"This can be understood, of course, only if one uses a generalized concept of 'territory', which includes not only the division and articulation of spatial units, but their institutional counterparts, whereby *power structures* shape spaces, languages, moralities, symbols, labour distribution, productive activities, etc. To 'territorialize' means to assign 'identities' for collective subjects within structures of power, therefore to categorialise and individualize human beings (and the figure of the 'citizen', with its statutory conditions of birth and place, its different sub-categories, spheres of activity, processes of formation, is exactly a way of categorizing individuals)" (Balibar 2004: 4).

3   Results

The theoretical dimension of the territorialization has offered the opportunity to analyze the specific features of the case-study referring it to a particular socio-spatial context. As Strazzari indicates in relation to the analyzed case-study,

"Kosovo's illicit sector is molded by a history of resilient survival and resistance along informal channels and transnational illicit trade. The peculiarity of this history radically diverted the concept of social legitimacy from the notion of legality" (Strazzari 2008: 161).

This point was also stressed by Michael Pugh. He observed that the social legitimacy granted to criminal activities is linked with the social protection granted by clans.

"Throughout south-east Europe the heads of clans traditionally offered social stability through the distribution of land, revenues and welfare. Ottoman and subsequently Habsburg efforts to establish property rights in law failed to eradicate the robust clientist and patrimonial systems. Moreover, shadow economies of barter and black markets thrived in the Tito period and permitted the avoidance of socially-discriminating and time-consuming bureaucratic obstacles

---

90   See the theoretical propose of Badie (1995).

to exchange. Shadow economies, local predation, and reversion to clientist and patrimonial protection of the exposed populations accompanied the economic fragmentation of Yugoslavia" (Pugh 2005: 2).

After the 1990s wars, the increase in the smuggling channels between Kosovo, Albania and Montenegro[91] was influenced by specific elements, less evident in other former Yugoslavian Republics and even less so in other transitional countries: the revival of ethno-national linkages and sharing the experience of the difficult transition to the post-socialist phase. In this perspective, smuggling came to be regarded as essential for survival.

The disintegration of Yugoslavia which started in the late 1980s and led to the break-up of the country and to the first war in 1991 was a fundamental event for Kosovo. By far the most under-developed part of the former country, Kosovo, depended heavily on 'funds for under-developed regions' contributed by the other Yugoslav republics. With the collapse of Yugoslavia in 1991, the Kosovo Albanians were left on their own. All outside financial help was cut off. Kosovo's industry, mismanaged for decades and by 1991 completely deprived of investment, was virtually brought to a halt. Subsistence agriculture, the remittances from the members of the large and well-organized diaspora, living and working in Western Europe, and the shadow economy were the only sources of revenue available to Kosovo Albanians in the 1990s. More generally, in the former Yugoslavia the self-management based economy maintained a central role in each state of the Federation with the exception of Slovenia. This system did not discourage the consolidation of local ethnical elites and their clientelistic relations which also affected the 1990s' conflict and post-conflict scenarios.

The shadow economy that characterized the transition in Kosovo, Albania and Montenegro has caused the rise of stereotypes such as 'smuggling-states' and 'narco-states'. This fact is well-described by a report published by the Center for the Study of Democracy:

"Kosovo Albanians have been associated with the European drug trade for decades. Their presence has especially been felt on the heroin markets in Germany, Austria and Switzerland. Being able to travel freely between Istanbul and Western Europe, they have developed elaborate drug smuggling channels. Besides remittances from abroad, the drug money was the most important pillar of the Kosovo Albanian organized social and health care as well as education system after 1991. By 1994 and especially after the Dayton Agreement of November 1995, which completely ignored the Kosovo issue, the majority of Kosovo

---

91   An indicator of the strength of the relation between Albanians in Kosovo and the Albanian state is the Albanian common language convention, referred to as 'GjuhaLetrare', a common grammar based on the "Tosk" dialect of Southern Albania. After the war in Kosovo, Letrare was introduced as a first language in all the media networks based in Pristina replacing the Kosovo Albanian 'Gheg' grammar.

Albanians became disillusioned by the peaceful resistance policy, led by Ibrahim Rugova, Kosovo's unofficial 'president', and started to turn towards armed resistance. Again, remittances from the Kosovo Albanians working abroad (they supplied roughly one third of the funding, setting aside three percent of their monthly income for that purpose) and the drug money were the primary sources for funding the arming of the newly-created Kosovo Liberation Army (KLA)" (Hajdinjak 2002: 9).

Ethno-State survival, *de facto*, legitimated smuggling and corruption as legal instruments. To understand the complexity of the problem, some of its aspects need to be approached in detail.

The first feature to focus on is the specific social structure present in the observed area. In Kosovo, Albania and Montenegro the Albanians' social structures are organized according to the strict rules of ethno-national community and kinship. Consequently, the main characteristic of the crime structures is that they are based on the respect for territorial divides, which reflect the spheres of influence of clans. Overall, traditional clan hierarchy, closed and impermeable relations among members as well as the strict discipline of the family members outline the main characterizing aspects of this social structure. This characterization is particularly evident in the ethnical Albanian context. As observed:

"If we look at the Albanian house from the perspective of the medieval code *LekeDukadjinija*, in its ethnologic and socio-cultural aspects, then it becomes a very important institution. And in the case that there is no state, it has the key role in maintaining national identity and autochthon culture. In a sense such a house can be seen as a 'microstate' where the chief of government is the master of the house, the head of the family, the host. There are also other important people, who play the role of ministers and who accomplish important tasks assigned by the head of the family. Everyday life is sanctioned by the legal norms of the LekeDukadjinija code and the religious norms" (Rusche 2006: 3).

Till 1990, a clan's internal relations were very strong, and accession or penetration by external elements was difficult. External elements from other communities, especially national communities, were connected only as contractors to carry out defined, initial and secondary tasks. Today this social structure faces the novelties raised by the institutional and social transition as well as by the globalization of organized crime. In the last twenty years, the role played by clans has gradually changed, transforming the customary social norms and existing regulations. Increasingly, individual clans are engaging in inter-ethnical competition for the control of the territory and its criminal sphere. Nevertheless, nowadays, it is not correct to define organized crime in the Balkans as a mono-ethnical phenomenon. While a degree of pan-Albanian sentiment exists, based on common language and ethno-national affiliation, a range of cleavages are also present. Also, evidence suggests that in the Balkans, smuggling and organised crime have inter-ethnic, as well as intra-ethnic, dimensions. The regions in question are not mono-ethnic, nor are the societies in question necessarily ethnically segregated, the same applies for organised crime. On this point the analysis of Tom Gallagher seems seminal. He observes that during the 1990s, when UN economic sanctions were imposed on Serbia and Serbia in its turn closely watched what went in and out of Kosovo, old smuggling routes were reopened. According to Gallagher, in this context the relevant element was that clandestine economies that sprang up were controlled by men who owed no allegiance to any state and never paid their taxes.

"The smuggling of cigarettes, hard drugs and weapons coupled with the trafficking of illegal migrants and women sold into sexual slavery, created fiefdoms which conventional states and transnational agencies found it difficult to subdue. Albanians were to the fore in developing this underground political of economy of crime. For elaborate explanation, it is necessary to look at the fact that they were the biggest loser in the state formation process that ensued between 1878 and 1945. Accordingly they had less cause to give loyalty to the states, which they felt treated them badly" (Gallagher 2005: 189).

In a similar perspective, it is presumable that the rise of informal economic activities in the last decade is the product of two distinct analytical dimensions: The provisions of illegal goods and services on the one hand, and criminal organizations on the other hand. According to Strazzari, in the considered case-study, the illicit practices do not necessarily reflect the existence of organized crime groups like the 'Mafia' or other organized structures. In the shadow triangle the small forms of smuggling and illicit trades are perceived as licit forms of enterprises embedded in the local social context. This perception can be ascribed to the social and economic de-structuration experienced in this area during and after the 1990s. In the general collapse of economic and political structures, transborder smuggling, thanks to its informal and uncodified modalities of action, created markets, alimenting economic flows. As observed: "Transborder crime also claimed a central role, because in time of evanescent institutions and collapse of tax-capacity, borders became the largest mechanism for redistributing national wealth" (Strazzari 2008: 157). After the 1999 war, the establishment of new ethno-territorial borders combined with the passivity of the population in accepting the clientelistic system confirmed the illicit practices as fundamental elements of this system. Today, going beyond the intra-ethnic dimension of smuggling, evidence suggests that in this area trafficking and organized crime also affect the inter-ethnic illicit relations. News reports outlined by the national and international newspapers demonstrate the contiguity between smuggling and new structured forms of organized crime. An evolution well-described by the specific sector of cigarette smuggling:

"Using mules and horses for smuggling cigarettes through mountain paths along the border between Montenegro and Kosovo are not the truckloads of cigarettes swarming Peja after the end of the 1999 war. But smuggling continues with the animals or vans, and a local prosecutor says that a 2007 bust of 15 tons of cigarettes in the region shows it is the work of organized crime. Cigarettes are smuggled from Albania into the southern Kosovo region of Prizren, again with mules. Kosovo and Albania police say they have failed to arrest smugglers in this area, though they had found carriage animals with cigarettes, and several operations have failed. One policeman is quoted saying that he suspects that smugglers and some policemen work together. Smuggling also happens along Albania's border with Montenegro, both along the Skadar Lake, and the mountains that Albania shares with that country, police admit" (Shala 2009).

3.1 The overlapping between the licit and illicit sector

In the Western Balkans several elements confirm that borders are often a source of cooperation between neighbours. States frontiers often coincide with rocky and inhospitable terrain that is ideal for smuggling. On the other side, flows of people, goods and capital pose problems for the neighbouring countries especially when border crossing is fluid and contested as in the case of the Kosovo, Albania and Montenegro border. Kosovo's border with Albania is 113.55km in length. Its border with Montenegro is smaller: 78.6 km-long. To the north-west, Albania shares a 172 km border with Montenegro. The mountainous region of this area is perhaps the best example of "recalcitrant regions that have tried to go their own way over a long historical period" (Gallagher 2005: 189). In this context, states have found it difficult to impose their authority on refractory regions. Clandestine economies have sprung up transforming the shadow economic activities into an income for survival. Here, the general insight is that the clientelistic ties are sustained because they perform a social function. In this perspective, as observed by Pugh 'the black market may also be considered a kind of 'free' market, or at least 'managed' in a sense not dissimilar from the management of capitalism. For example, as with free markets, successful entrepreneurship depends as much on social networks of assistance, protection and marketing as much as competitive pricing. In this sense, too, the black market provides a social function in underpinning networks of clientism and allegiance: "'Self-help groups' par excellence" (Pugh 2005: 9). However, more than a few local newspapers describe this area as an extremely important hub of organized crime. Articles, analysis and reports[92] have shown how pervasive the connection is between the licit and illicit sector. A pacesetter, in this investigative field, was the enquiry published by Balkan Insight in May 2009

---

92   See, the video documentary on http://wn.com/Arms_smuggling,_Waffenschmuggel_nach_ Kosovo_1998wmv (last access: 31.05.2011).

(see Musliu/Marzouk 2009). For the first time, the attention was focused on the strategic role played by Lake Vermica, bordering Kosovo and Albania. This investigation proved that the lake in south-eastern Kosovo is being used to smuggle arms, counterfeit documents including visas, drugs and stolen car parts. Several witnesses said that small boats frequently enter from the Albanian side and anchor on the north shore of the lake, opposite, and inaccessible from, the border point, according to documents published by the European Commission Liaison Office in Kosovo, ECLO[93]. The journalists' sources have been supported by a senior border police official and by a police officer with in-depth knowledge of smuggling in Kosovo. In their perspective, intercepting the smugglers is a hard task. Border police at Vermica declared that they must travel two hours by road to Prizren and then back west to reach the target area. At the end of 2009 a tender process was launched to secure patrol boats, as well as snowmobiles, quad bikes and 4x4 vehicles, to bolster border policing in Kosovo. These logistical weaknesses are analyzed in details in the article:

'Documents supplied as part of the tender process, which is being led by the ECLO, report: 'Vermica Lake is an area regarded by law enforcement authorities as an open gate for cross-border criminality of all types between Kosovo and Albania'[94]. Speaking on condition of anonymity, one border official at Vermica told Balkan Insight: "All we can properly control is smuggling during the day, but we lack the equipment which would enable us to control the situation during the night, which is the time when all the smuggling happens. We have a single static camera which is not enough to ensure safety and to tackle smuggling".

"We have asked EULEX to bring us a moving camera for night control but that machine costs around a million Euro. It would also be good if we had helicopters because we can also not

---

93   In December 2009, the European Commission chaired a public meeting where the findings of the Study of Corruption in Kosovo 2009 were presented to give a focus on future anti-corruption activities in Kosovo. The study reveals that the main manifestations of corruption in Kosovo fall within three distinct patterns of behaviour that are firmly embedded across all sectors of society:
- Opportunity: As well as being recognised as a wrong-doing, corruption is widely accepted as being an opportunity for financial gain. As a consequence, individual and collective resistance to corruption pressure is low.
- Social networks: Close family ties and clan loyalties provide protection and wrong-doing is not exposed. As a consequence, corrupt behaviour is copied and repeated.
- Professional networks: Lack of transparency in the relationships between politicians, civil servants, civic leaders, their families and businesses creates a closed environment where opportunity exists and corruption pressure is high
(ECLO 2009b).

94   See ECLO Report, URL: http://www.delprn.ec.europa.eu/?cid=2,49,690 (last access: 25.06.2011).

control what is happening with the smuggling through the mountains just along the lake" (Musliu/Marzouk 2009).

On the other side, Paul Acda, head of EULEX Customs, said he was aware of only one serious smuggling attempt at the lake in his eight years in Kosovo. He added that he suspected increased patrols would significantly reduce levels of smuggling. Anything that attempts to reduce cross-border smuggling is to be welcomed. He added: "Kosovo Customs already has two patrol boats. These were procured by UNMIK Customs to patrol the Gazivoda Lake" (ibid.). Qamil Kroni, captain of Kosovo border police at Vermica, told Balkan Insight that the border police were committed to fighting smuggling on the border. "We still lack equipment to tackle smuggling properly but if EULEX provided boats and other equipment that would translate into a more efficient border policing" (ibid.). An investigative police officer, with in-depth knowledge of smuggling in Kosovo, told Balkan Insight: "Cars stolen in Kosovo are chopped up and then sent to Albania or vice-versa. We all know that smuggling is freely happening, but this is happening all over Kosovo. This is not just the fault of the police, but the courts and prosecutors too" (ibid.). Meanwhile the scenario is evolving. The Kosovo government has announced plans for an important highway that will run from Prizren to the Albanian border. Negotiations involve the American-Turkish Company, Bechtel-Enka Joint Venture. Illicit interests on competitive tenders are foreseeable. South East Times reported:

> "'Kosovo will have easier access to the world markets; the movement of people will be easier, as well as the access to the harbours,' said Kosovo Prime Minister HashimThaci. 'Kosovo will have access to the sea, via Durres, Albania, via this highway.' Specifics about the highway — cost, length and exact route – will not be known until negotiations with Bechtel-Enka are completed, though it is estimated to run some 118km and include exits at Pristina International Airport. It will also give Kosovo access to the Adriatic Sea. (...) To reduce costs and avoid unnecessary problems, the highway route has been changed to avoid heavily mountainous areas. It will run from Pristina to Vermica, at the border with Albania, and from Pristina to Merdare, a crossing point on the border with Serbia" (Karadaku 2010).

Thaci told local media that Kosovo would greatly benefit from the project because it will open a variety of European corridors and create construction jobs. If these corridors are used as the new infrastructures of the illicit sector remains an open question. The same open question that concerns the new strategy plans by the EU to face trans-border smuggling (see Karadaku 2010).

On this basis, conceptualizing what is smuggling in the 'shadow triangle' is quite an intricate task. Nonetheless some structural elements can be fixed. First, the illicit sector has various *nuances*. If on the one side crimes such as the trafficking of human beings, especially women and children, produce social blame, on the other side crimes like drug or arms smuggling are perceived as a usual form of enterprise. The Western approach to what the term 'criminal' implies is not useful in this case. In this sense this work fully accepts the distinction proposed by Michael Pugh:

> "Economic 'crime' can be deconstructed into at least three varieties of 'shadow economy': organized mafia rackets and trafficking; corruption, fraud and nepotism in business and public life; and the coping or survival shadow economies of the population at large. To some degree these varieties can overlap. And they probably all draw on traditions of economic organization that resisted the pressures of modern, centralized and audited economic exchange well before the disintegration of Yugoslavia" (Pugh 2009: 9).

Secondly, illicit practices managed by informal actors take advantage of political and territorial fragmentation. As observed:

> "Illicit actors know the terrain quite well, and besides having long experience of collaboration along informal, adaptative networks, they have a stronger stake in the process: nothing would convince a conscript or a bad policeman to risk his life by going out at night to stand in the way of organized smugglers" (Strazzari 2007: 203).

Thirdly, in the considered case-study, smuggling does not act on a pre-existing market but is the market itself. In this sense the criminal chain's actors do not alter the market rules. In fact, smuggling concerns deeply taxed commodities such as fuel, cars, alcohol, cigarettes; or forbidden and limited commodities like weapons, drugs, goods violating intellectual property rights.

The last consideration, here, is linked to the point described above and affects the relationship between smuggling and the socio-political system. In the considered case-study, the illicit sector acts as provider of services, jobs and in *latusensu* of welfare. In this context smugglers have a new, more professionalised profile. Smuggling drugs, tobacco, fuel, weapons guarantees the actual step up in class. In the considered case-study several notorious smugglers hold public positions having taken advantage of this. As argued by Fabio Armao (see 2000), transborder smuggling activities is a typical business by which the illicit sector emancipates itself from the marginal role of a provider, acting and intervening directly in political life.

3.2 (Il)licit for whom? The gap between international and local actors

The institutionalization of corruption in the South Eastern European countries cannot be explained by national circumstances alone. Although illicit practices are visible at the local level, several region-wide causes need to be considered.

The Yugoslav conflicts and the interweaving of political-ethnic and criminal interests analyzed above are not the only causes for the rise in the criminal sector, based on enduring smuggling channels and multi-level corruption. As observed by the Bulgarian Centre for the Study of Democracy (see CSD 2003), there are at least two important factors, which have contributed to the criminalization of trans-border traffic and the resulting endemic corruption.

The first concerns the liberalization of the movement of goods and people and the lifting of visa and other restrictions in the regional post-Communist countries. In this context, the removal of the state from strict controls over the movement of people and goods across the borders encouraged the processes of privatization of old and newly-born smuggling channels. Concerning the considered case-study, these channels were managed by the illicit and semi-illicit groups in close cooperation with former agents of security services. State officers, employed in key institutions like welfare, police and other services involved in border control, also became included in the illicit system through the expansion of corruption networks. If during the years before the 1990s wars, border control was gradually passed from the hands of the state into the private domain of illegitimate actors, during the first decennium of post-conflict transition the succession of armed conflicts and ethnic cleansing campaigns in the former Yugoslavia led to the creation of quasi-states and weak states, basically unable to control their borders.

The second factor contributing to the development of trans-border crime and corruption during the last two decades has to be ascribed to the main features of the Balkan economies: the national borders in this period represented the largest redistributing mechanism of national wealth. Due to the small capacity of regional economies, the value of goods transported to and from the Balkan countries reached up to 85% of GDP in some cases.

Regarding the functioning of smuggling on the local scale, the CSD analysis is truly incisive.

"The smuggling of goods - the report stresses - is often accompanied by trafficking in banned or controlled substances and items; criminal acts; competition between the organized smuggling groups, and between traffickers and lawful importers. Moreover, in order to stay in the market, lawful importers are forced to resort to violations of the established foreign-trade regulations" (CSD 2003: 17).

Trans-border organized crime has a destructive effect not only on the economy, but also on the institutions and the rule of law in a country. The huge resources accumulated in this manner allow engaging in covert financing and refinancing of various types of legal and illegal undertakings. This is largely due to the fact that the revenues from smuggling do not enter official government statistics; they are never declared and thus never registered with the official authorities. Several cases have showed that all too often proceeds from illegal trafficking serve to finance political parties, labour unions and other organizations. Illegal import adversely affects domestic production and harms sectors of strategic importance to the country. In its various forms it is in fact one of the means companies employ to enter a given market. It is also used to monopolize a certain economic or other sector of activity - for instance the trade in cigarettes, sugar, alcohol, grain, video and audio equipment. The goods most frequently subject to smuggling are those with high import tax rates (cigarettes, alcohol, motor vehicles); goods subject to national bans and restrictions such as arms, narcotic substances and precursors, pornographic materials, subsidized goods, protected animal species and plants, goods and technologies of civil and military use, works of art and objects of cultural and historical value, strategic raw materials, forged goods and products violating intellectual property rights, goods subject to international control, nuclear and radioactive materials, hazardous and toxic substances and wastes, hi-tech products, etc. Illegal imports can be carried out at anytime and anywhere along the border, with the actual places of occurrence falling in two main zones - points where customs control is executed (ports, airports, border checkpoints, free trade zones, and others) and points outside customs control - a remote location along the coastline, a minor port or airport. Depending on the nature of smuggled goods, as well as on the initial and end buyer (destination), citizens of different states are engaged as perpetrators. In a number of cases the citizenship of the person used for smuggling is of great significance insofar as there are visa restrictions on the movement of persons and goods like in the Schengen Area.

According to the analyzed data, smuggling also affects the control of imports and exports, the racketeering on the goods smuggled, and in establishing monopolies in a number of the most profitable economic activities. The entire chain of the illicit is implicated, in particular regarding the redistribution of profits and the control of the black economy activities like car theft, drug trafficking and drug distribution, prostitution, counterfeiting of money etc.). From the local perspective the strategic projection aims at creating long-lasting corruption networks through redistribution of dirty money among the lobbies of organized crime in government structures.

The activities analyzed in this case-study plan the outline of the shadow economy as a 'quasi' economic system, which combines legal with illegal and criminal methods and licit forms of business, and which is to a great extent protected from law enforcement. The danger posed by this penetration is amplified by the fact that often regional societies and governments in one way or another tolerate the economy of crime as it is deemed different from traditional criminal activity. In accordance with the European Commission, the delivery of results in the fight against corruption on the part of the Kosovo authorities needs to be improved considerably.

> "The major concerns still revolve around the work of the public sector, procurement, the judiciary and law enforcement, with the number of final convictions in corruption cases remaining very low. There is no mechanism for tracking investigations, indictments, prosecutions and convictions that would ensure transparency on the status of corruption cases. The inter-agency cooperation on corruption is insufficient and results in inconsistent implementation of legislation, strategies and action plans as well as information to the public. The inter-ministerial working group on anti-corruption measures has failed to deliver tangible results. The Directorate against economic crime and corruption in the Kosovo Police lacks proper equipment and needs strengthening. Law enforcement agencies need to considerably step up their efforts in fighting internal corruption, free of political interference" (European Commission 2010).

In the considered context, state institutions and law enforcement continue to show a high degree of tolerance to the big players in the shadow and criminal business. The inefficiency of the judicial system has an especially destructive effect on the efforts to counteract the economy of crime, which is only partly due to imperfect legislation. In practice, not only does organized crime remain unpunished, but it also uses the judiciary to eliminate competitors through corruption. On the administrative side, despite the declared co-operation, there are no detailed regulated ways and procedures for co-operation, which in some cases creates a possibility for delaying and overlapping competencies on a municipal, district and regional level. What is claimed on the local level is the improvement of co-operation between all ministerial organizational units, to prepare internal standing orders, and to regulate common forms of co-operation, exchange of information, mutual work and training and lastly a common use of equipment and infrastructure on all levels.

However, in Kosovo, according to a recent Eulex report (see Eulex 2010), there were in the last months some positive steps, on the national level in tackling economic crime, financial crime and corruption.

The first was the establishment of the Directorate of Economic Crime and Corruption Investigations by the Kosovo Police Director General in December 2009. The Directorate has jurisdiction Kosovo-wide and coordinates investigations on the central level and regional level (Regional Economic and Corruption Crimes Investigation Units).

The second is related to the NGO's commitment in the fight against corruption and smuggling. These actions remain a high priority for many non-governmental organizations. Their analyses, reports and policy recommendations demonstrated a significant capacity in identifying strengths and weaknesses in the rule of law mechanisms.

The third step forward was the institution in February 2010 of the 'Anti Corruption Task Force' whose objective it is to investigate and fight high profile corruption-related crimes. During the process of establishing this body, EULEX cooperated closely with the Government to make this new body operational and effective as soon as possible.

The good news on the side of smuggling collides with the important sphere of the effective prosecution. Currently, the Kosovo criminal justice system capacity to move forward with the reform agenda remains very fragile and inconsistent. The lack of progress in establishing the basic mechanisms of co-operation and co-ordination between prosecutors and the Kosovo Police, as well as between prosecution offices and courts, remains a problematic factor. Furthermore, prosecution efforts are undermined by poor management and a lack of support staff. In this sense – Eulex stresses – the establishment of an anti-corruption task force in the Office of the Special Prosecutor of Kosovo (SPRK) could be considered as a positive step forward.

3.3 (The International) Fight against the illicit

As concerns international action, in practical terms, smuggling was not well managed by the international actors. As opposed to the local public actors and their collusion, they explicitly condemn the corrupted practices and the smuggling present in the region. In their case, the problem is that these politically offensive matters are not connected with specific plans about social development or work inclusion. This political inability is a key aspect to understand the failure on the international community's behalf to comprehend the social functions of 'crime'. For example, according to data collected by Pugh, in Kosovo UNMIK Customs was the first public body to be set up, and together with EU Customs Assistance Mission (CAM-K) reformed the collection system, tripling revenues between 1999 and 2003. Yet the shortage of staff has made the control mechanisms seriously deficient. Furthermore the data are also not hopeful on the side of the EU. It also took two years for the EU to establish a Kosovo Anti-Economic Crime Unit to counter crime and promote intolerance of criminality. Moreover, special processes were introduced for illegal activity by key political figures, which fostered a widely-held view that Kosovar leaders benefited from a degree of immunity. Overall the general feeling in the field is that criminality is not perceived as a high priority. Western security agencies are extremely active in monitoring organized crime on the international level. On the local level, de facto, anti-crime activities have been unable to expose the existence of links with politics. This aspect is confirmed by recent facts. If one looks at the seizures of goods smuggling in the considered case study, it is impossible to count any considerable confiscation. The following fact is clearly linked with the general failure of Kosovo in the anti-smuggling action:

"Data emerging from a project that EU and European Council of Europe funded to strengthen police capacities in South-East Europe are quite clear in this regard: for the period 2004-2006 Albania reported a confiscation of heroin amounting to 317 kg, Serbia 1,508 kg and Kosovo 74 kg. Out of some 5,000 cases of economic crime reported in Kosovo in 2004, only three revealed a link to organized crime groups: virtually no figures were available for 2005 and 2006" (Strazzari 2006: 163).

These data show first of all that in this context it is not feasible demarking what is legal and what not. Practices perceived as legitimate on the local scale do not stand to the legal standards on the international level. As analyzed by Charles Tilly (1985) in his pioneering studies based on a comparative historical sociological perspective, here, it could be useful to focus the analysis on the concept of 'state making as organized crime'. His theoretical proposal looks at the symbiotic nexus between war-making and state-making. In the case of the Balkans the protagonist of this relationship was organized crime and its consociated illegal and criminal enterprises. As Strazzari argued

"contrary to widespread perception, Balkan organized crime groups, not unlike other mafias, do not come into existence where the market and the state are absent, but they rather accompany (or guide) the unfolding of market and state structures. While they can be regarded -as external actors often are- as resisting economic modernization, they also represent a modality of relatively stable integration with the world economy" (Strazzari 2006: 166).

Recently, at the end of July 2009, the European Commission Liaison Office to Kosovo officially launched the *Strengthening the Rule of Law–Border and Boundary Police Twinning* Project (see ECLO 2009a). The project aims to improve the rule of law in Kosovo, by enhancing the professional capacities and capabilities of the Kosovo Police and in particular the border and boundaries police. European police experts will work together with their Kosovo counterparts in order to exchange experiences and best practices and, as a result of this mutual commitment, Kosovo should improve its ability to intercept and seize contraband and prevent illegal border crossings. Part of a larger EU strategy directed at dealing with the challenges of securing Kosovo borders and boundaries, this 18-month twinning project aims also to improve the legal framework, management and operational capacity of the Kosovo border and boundary police, implementing the coordination with other agencies and neighbouring countries on Integrated Border Management and identifying which are the necessary investments to better secure borders and boundaries from illegal trafficking. The project has been running for thirteen months since then but at this stage there are no partial data on the territorial outputs of the project. Overall structural weaknesses, logistical malfunctions as well as a shortage of resources complicate and slow down the fight against smuggling, also alimenting potential connections between smuggling and terrorism. In 2008, the United States Department of State published the Country Report on Terrorism. This report stressed the role of smuggling in affecting security:

> "Porous boundaries that were easily crossed by individuals trafficking in persons, weapons, and narcotics hampered Kosovo's counterterrorism efforts. Traffickers took advantage of numerous roads and trails leading into Kosovo that lacked border controls. Poorly paid border and customs officials were susceptible to corruption" (United States Department of State 2008).

An analogue evaluation was made by the report 'Kosovo National Integrated Border Management Strategy' (see Integrated Border Management 2006): Kosovo suffers like other countries within the region from its geographical location. It is at the crossroads of ancient trading routes leading from Persia, Eastern Europe and the Caucasus. These trading routes still exist and given the economic differential between the states in these regions and those of Western Europe, the trade in drugs, cigarettes, human beings, weapons and contraband goods is prolific in the southern Balkans. Organized criminal groups with international connections are able to bribe public servants and members of the government. They have access to relatively sophisticated, yet light, weaponry.

4   What does this means in terms of territorialisation?

Looking at the supranational scale, the resulting fact here is that the European Union is undergoing a process of enlightening its role in the western Balkans, which manifests itself, firstly, in its contrast to smuggling. In this context, the related geopolitical developments have impacts on cross-border, trans-regional, and supranational cooperation. There is some accord among scholars that a process of 're-scaling' and connected 're-territorialisation' of procedures and powers from supranational down to the national level, is now underway, resulting in the EU strengthening of fighting against criminality and trans-border smuggling. However, as previously claimed, cooperation between the EU and Albania, Montenegro and Kosovo, in the action against smuggling, takes place within an ambiguous interface that includes both external and internal elements of re-territorialisation. In fact, much of the external dimensions of smuggling's territorialisation, particularly on the trans-border/regional level, remains influenced by social and economic local aspects, like the persistence of institutional and political crises and the weakness of economic growth. At the same time, one can observe an initial re-territorialisation of EU anti-smuggling policies, a process visible for functional and political reasons:

On the functional level, the entrance of the EU is gradually scratching the historical predominance of the illicit flows in the analysed area. It is a fact that smuggling is becoming territorially differentiated as well as that there is significant positive feedback (such as the rise in seizures and the surfacing of local NGOs expressly dedicated to corruption and illicit acts) that have followed the EU's contrast strategies.

On the political ground, local territory, with its specific socio-economic features and its actors, remains the principal subject entitled to effect the growth or the breakdown of trans-border smuggling.

To sum up this consideration: The analysis of the social, political and economic re-territorialisation that has followed the came on stage of the EU in the anti-smuggling strategies implies a consideration on the de-territorialisation that will follow the resizing of the illicit economic industry that has worked as a substitutive welfare. As Deleuze and Guattari (1987) have explained in their volume, any process of 'territorialisation' is also the opposite of 'de-territorialisation', which takes place before, or after, or simultaneously. In the considered case-study, the de-territorialisation process takes place simultaneously to the re-territorialisation. This development is an effect of the deteriorated ties between society and place. Drawing on Deleuze and Guattari, de-territorialisation processes in the shadow triangle have consequently to be understood as combined processes of a re-territorialisation, producing new spatial formations. In this view, spatial arrangements and connections are not given and static structures, but contentious and unstable – nevertheless they are powerful.

5   Conclusion

This case study has been monitored and discussed since 2009, when the earliest goods seizures took place. Considering the absence of scientific research conducted on this specific issue, this analysis has chosen to focus the attention on journalist inquiries, combining it with the scientific and grey literature on smuggling. The construction of scripts that pattern common perceptions of political and social events was the key to a full understanding of the smuggling dynamics between national and international levels. The analysis of this case study remains a work in progress. Scarcity of statistical data on goods smuggled, and the absence of updated scientific literature led to choosing an analysis based on a combination of journalistic and grey literature findings. As well known, qualitative methodology includes a variety of methods, procedures, and research designs. Consequently, they are no standardized tools that can be adapted to every kind of research object, which can better be called research subjects because qualitative methods do not evaluate them objectively but interact with them. In this approach the selection of the investigative reports and articles was not a neutral tool useful to gain knowledge about researched subjects, but was an integral part of the social and political facts investigated.

This work has moved, in fact, from a consideration concerning the specific socio-political features of the case study. In this perspective smuggling has been understood as an ongoing process of performing and maintaining territorial practices and ideologies (see Vagaggini/Dematteis 1976; Corbetta 2009). In this sense, contrary to the general perception, we have read the recent processes of state-making in the former Yugoslavian countries as deeply colluded with illicit practices. Taking into account the lesson of critical geopolitics, the article has tried to show the symbiotic nexus between licit and illicit sectors affecting society, politics and the economy. In other words, a geopolitical act, smuggling, has been interpreted using and analyzing the acts and the facts described by local newspapers actively engaged in the fight against corruption. A final insight has been given into the role of the international community in facing the smuggling. The steps forward in the direction of effectively fighting smuggling are recent and far from having an effective territorial spin-off. In this sense, the general feeling is that illicit practices will continue because they also affect part of the international contingent displaced in Kosovo. On September 21, 2010 there were several arrests among soldiers from the NATO mission in Kosovo-KFOR, suspected of selling fuel intended for military purposes from one of their bases to petrol stations. KFOR admitted in a statement that soldiers were suspected of having "been involved in the case of fuel smuggling, tax evasion, and misuse of economic authorization" (Kosovo Compromise Staff 2010), officially condemned as criminal acts. However, despite the acknowledgement, no troops have been arrested to date. During 2008 and 2009, three million litres of contraband fuel were suspected of being sold to three private petrol stations: AS Graniti in Stime owned by Agim and SaliBeqaj, Alb Petrol in Podujevo owned by IdrizEjupi and Onazis in Pristina owned by brothers Nazmi and Nexhmi Kastrati. Again, it has been reported that soldiers from the Ukrainian contingent, based in the southern Kosovo town of Strpce, are suspected of involvement in the alleged smuggling operation.

Paradoxically, KFOR soldiers are protected by diplomatic immunity which would have to be lifted if any of them were to face trial in Kosovo.

References

ATRC – Advocacy Training and Resource Centre (2009): Kosovo Country Strategy Paper.
Armao, F. (2000): Il sistema mafia. Dall'economia-mondo al dominio locale. Torino: Bollati e Boringhieri.
Badie, B. (1995): La fine des territories. Paris: Fayard.
Balibar, E. (2004): Europe as Borderland, The Alexander von Humboldt Lecture in Human Geography, University of Nijmegen, 10 November 2004, URL: http://socgeo.ruhosting.nl/colloquium/Europe%20as%20Borderland.pdf (last access: 23.05.2011).
Bideleux, R. / Jeffries, I. (2007): "Kosova". In: idem.: The Balkans. A post communist history. Oxon: Routledge.
Brunet, R. / Ferras, R. / Thery, H. (1992): Les mots de la géographie. Paris: Reclus-La Documentation française.
Brunet, R., (1990) : Le territoire dans les turbulences, Paris: Géographiques reclus.
Corbetta P. (1999) : Metodologia e tecnica della ricerca sociale. Bologna: Il Mulino.
CSD – Centre for the Study of Democracy (2003): Corruption, Contraband and Organized Crime in South East Europe. Sofia: Centre for the Study of Democracy.
Deda, I. (2009): Kosovo Final Report: A Nation in Transit 2009. New York: Freedom House.
Deimel, J. / Van Meus, W. (eds.) (2007): The Balkan Prism: A Retrospective by Policy-Makers and Analysts. München: Otto Sagner.
Deleuze, G. / Guattari, F. (1987): A Thousand Plateaus: Capitalism and Schizophrenia. Minneapolis: University of Minnesota Press.
Di Meo, G. (1998): Géographiesociale et Territories. Paris: Nathan Université.
Džihić, V. / Kramer, H. (2009): Kosovo After Independence. Is the EU's EULEX Mission Delivering on its Promises?, URL: http://library.fes.de/pdf-files/id/ipa/06571.pdf (last access: 23.05.2011).
ECLO – The European Commission Liaison Office to Kosovo (2009a): European Commission Liaison Office launches new twinning project on border and boundary police. URL: http://www.delprn.ec.europa.eu/?cid=2,103,530 (last access: 05.06.2011).
ECLO – The European Commission Liaison Office to Kosovo (2009b): European Commission presents findings of the ,Study of Corruption in Kosovo 2009. URL: http://www.delprn.ec.europa.eu/?cid=2,49,690 (last access: 05.06.2011).
Eriksen, T. H. (1993): Ethnicity and Nationalism. London: Pluto Press.
Eulex (2010): Programme Report. Building Sustainable Change Together. Pristina: Eulex, URL: http://www.eulex-kosovo.eu/docs/tracking/EULEX%20Programme%20Report%202010%20.pdf (last access: 23.05.2011).
European Commission (2010): Kosovo 2010 Progress Report. Brussels.
European Council (2003): A Secure Europe in a Better World. European Security Strategy. Bruxelles, URL: http://www.consilium.europa.eu/uedocs/cmsUpload/78367.pdf (last access: 23.05.2011).
Gallagher, T. (2005): The Balkans in the New Millenium in the shadow of war and peace. Routledge: London.
Gambino, M. / Grimaldi, L. (1995): Traffico d'armi. Il crocevia Jugoslavo. Roma: Editori Riuniti.

Hajdinjak, M. (2002): Smuggling in Southeast Europe: The Yugoslav Wars and the Development of Regional Criminal Networks in The Balkans. Sofia: Center for the Study of the Democracy.

IKS   –   Iniciativa   Kosovare   për   Stabilitet   (2008):   Who   is   the   Boss?.   URL: http://www.esiweb.org/pdf/kosovo_Who%27s_the_Boss.pdf.

Independent International Commission on Kosovo (2003): The Kosovo Report. Oxford Scholarship Online.

Integrated Border Management (2006): Kosovo National Integrated Border Management Strategy. URL: http://www.eulex-kosovo.eu/training/police/PoliceTraining/BORDER_BOUNDARY/ DOCUMENTS/4.pdf?page=agreements (last access: 05.06.2011).

International Crisis Group (2004): "Pan-Albanism. How Big a Threat to Balkan Stability?". In: Central and Eastern European Series, 10, pp.1-34.

Crampton, J. W. / Stuart, E. (2007): Space, Knowledge and Power: Foucault and Geography. London: Ashgate .

Karadaku, L. (2010): "New Kosovo highway exits to world markets". In: South East Times, URL: http://www.setimes.com/cocoon/setimes/xhtml/en_GB/features/setimes/articles/2010/02/01/re portage-01Kosovo (last access: 05.06.2011).

Kosovo Compromise Staff (2010): "EU continues 'KFOR' fuel smuggling people". In: Kosovo Compromise, 21 September 2010, URL: http://www.kosovocompromise.com/cms/item/ topic/en.html?view=story&id=3055&sectionId=1 (last access: 05.06.2011).

Kostovicova, D. / Bojicic-Dzelilovic, V. (2008): Transnationalism in the Balkans. London, New York: Routledge.

Kostovicova, D. (2008): "Albanian Diasporas and their Political Roles". In: Batt, J. (ed.): Is there an Albanian question?. European Union Institute for Security Studies. Paris: France, pp. 73-86.

Le Berre, M. (1992): "Territoires". In: A. Bailly, R. Ferras and D. Pumain (eds.): Encyclopédie de Géographie, Paris: Economica, pp. 601-622.

Levy, J. / Lussault, M. (2003): Dictionnaire de la géographie et de l'espace des sociétés. Paris: Belin.

Lovell, D.W. (1999): "Nationalism, Civil Society and the Prospects for Freedom in Eastern Europe". In: The Australian Journal of Politics and History, 45, 1, pp. 65-77.

Malcolm, N. (1998): Kosovo: A short history. London: Macmillan.

Musliu, V. / Marzouk, L. (2009): Kosovo Lake is 'Open Gate for Criminality'. URL: http://www.balkaninsight.com/en/article/kosovo-lake-is-open-gate-for-criminality (last access 29.06.2011).

Naim, M. (2005): Illicit: How smugglers, traffickers and copycats are hijacking the global economy. London: William Heineman.

Pardo, I. (2004): Between Morality and the Law: Corruption, Anthropology and Comparative Society. London: Ashgate.

Pugh, M. (2005): Crime and Capitalism in Kosovo Transformation. Paper at ISA conference, Hawaii.

Raffestin, C. (1986): Espaces, jeuxetenjeux. Paris: Fayard.

Rusche, R. (2006): Activities of the Criminal Groups in Kosovo & Metochia and Independence of the Province. Warsaw: Center for International Relations, 10.

Shala, B. (2009): Smuggling continues in Albania – Now as Organized Crime. URL: http://i-scoop.org/index.php?id=24&tx_ttnews[tt_news]=866&tx_ttnews[backPid]=20&cHash=8d56e ddbf1&MP=24-50 (last access 29.06.2011).

Spector, B. / Winbourne, S. / Beck, L. (2003): Corruption in Kosovo: Observations and Implications for USAID. Pristina: USAID.

Strazzari, F. (2007): "The Decade Horribilis: Organized Violence and Crime along Balkans Peripheries". In: Mediterranean Politics, 12, pp. 185-209.

Strazzari, F. (2008a): Notte Balcanica. Il Mulino: Bologna.

Strazzari, F. (2008b): "L'oeuvre au noir: The Shadow Economy of Kosovo's Independence". In: International Peacekeeping, 15, pp. 155-170.

Tilly, C. (1985): "War Making and State Making as Organized Crime". In: P. Evans, D. Ruescemeyer and T. Skocpol (eds.): Bringing the State Back. New York, Cambridge: Cambridge University Press, pp. 169-191.

Transparency International (2009): Corruption Perceptions Index 2009. URL: http://www.transparency.org/policy_research/surveys_indices/cpi/2009/ (last access: 23.05.2011).

United States Department of State (2008): Country Reports on Terrorism 2008 – Kosovo. URL: http://www.unhcr.org/refworld/docid/49fac6931e.html (last access: 05.06.2011).

Vagaggini, V. / Dematteis, G. (1976): I metodi analitici della geografia. Firenze: La Nuova Italia.

From the Pamir frontier to international borders: Exchange relations of the borderland population

Tobias Kraudzun

1 Introduction

This paper deals with a population dependent on interregional goods exchange for their basic needs, and will discuss the opportunities and restrictions that have arisen from past delimitations of the frontier region and present reconfigurations of the borders enclosing the post-Soviet Pamirs.

After the end of the cold war the iron curtain was lifted and the developments seemed to wipe out the prototype of a sealed border, the big dividing line between East and West. The predominant discourse of globalisation and deterritorialisation promised a borderless world and tremendous advantages resulting from free trade (see Caney 2005; Ohmae 1990).

However, not all borders became permeable after the ideological or political differences disappeared. On one hand, the borderlands in the converging European Union became the arena of trans-border cooperation and were frequently the subject of borderland studies (see Anderson/Wever 2003; Perkamnn 1999; Perkmann/Sum 2002; Scott 2000). At the same time the administrational boundaries between the republics of the Soviet Union were transformed into international borders. This upgrading in many cases did not correspond with the integrity of its demarcation. Tensions arose from the enforcement of boundaries that were ignored by the infrastructure development and economic integration of the Soviet time. Although disputes arose along most of the 20 new international boundaries after the Soviet dissolution (see Kolossov/Gleser/Petrov 1992), comparably few studies have been published on post-Soviet border conflicts. Disputes that led to open conflicts, such as the cases of Nagorno-Karabakh, South Ossetia and Abkhazia seem to be studied most. Among the numerous disputes over boundaries within Soviet Central Asia the Tajik-Afghan boundary received a special focus because frequent penetrations took place due to the Civil War in Tajikistan (see Borcke 1994a, b; Halbach 1993; 1997). Especially this boundary has remained in focus because of the surge of Afghan drug production and trafficking through Central Asia (see Djalili et al. 1998; Gerstle 2006; Iskandarov/Lewington 2009).

Yet the majority of these borderland studies put a focus either on the inventarisation of border conflicts or on the international politics in the context of (critical) geopolitics (see Kolossov 1999; Kolossov/O'Loughlin 1998; Megoran 2004; Polat 2002).

However, the people that live in borderlands along unsettled boundaries are mentioned in most studies as passive victims of international politics. Although the new boundaries now trench the spaces of the everyday activities of these people, constraining their mobility and resulting insecurities, many of them can use the economic differences that have emerged from the different policies in the post-Soviet republics. For example differing market prices between both sides of the border are used through trans-border petty trade as an economic resource. Likewise, every borderland context comprises potentials and restrictions to the local population. They are perceived as options that translate into concrete actions. Only a few regional studies deal with the effects on the micro level (see Bichsel 2009; Gerstle 2006; Reeves 2005). Yet the outcome of individuals' activities in the borderland would deserve more attention in order to understand the effects of boundaries and bordering processes for the population.

Hence, the case study chosen for this paper will serve as an example for the consequences of border-making processes for the people in a post-Soviet setting. In this case a diachronic approach is helpful to show how emerging boundaries and reconfigured borders had positive and negative effects for the livelihoods of Kyrgyz mobile pastoralists who have lived in the eastern Pamirs for centuries. It is necessary to include the historical perspective in order to understand how the people, being exposed to the present-day borders, perceive their options to use their borderland status for securing their livelihoods. In order to reach these objectives, the paper has to deal with three questions. The first asks how geopolitical interests have shaped the opportunities and restrictions for the livelihoods of the local population, thus dealing with the structural preconditions' effects for the agency. The second one looks at the interplay between perceptions of structures and agency and calls for the mechanisms enabling the local population to use regional borders as a resource. Finally, it is necessary to find out how these mechanisms need to be differentiated for various social groups.

In a first step the developments of border conceptualisations are traced and actors in the social space of borders are introduced, followed by an outline of the case study area. In the methodological section the analytical framework is discussed and a short insight in the fieldwork is given. Now, the legacies of the colonial Russian boundary-making and the border enforcements as part of the Soviet modernisation project are outlined. Subsequently the current time period is depicted and viewed from the perspective of local livelihoods. Finally, in the conclusions the initial questions will be discussed.

2 Conceptualisations of the borders and their actors

Focussing on boundaries and arguing with power and politics, the discipline of geopolitics is concerned with nation states, its territories, and the dividing mechanisms between them. In the geopolitical discourse starting with Ratzel's *Politische Geographie* (1897), the boundary is primarily an object for the investigation of the spatial development of states.

Other geopolitically informed geographers continued to develop deterministic argumentations. In 1904, during the 'Great Game', the geographer Halford Mackinder held a lecture at the British Royal Geographical Society with an unambiguous argumentation: he identified the Eurasian territories ranging from Central and Inner Asia to Siberia as the 'pivot of history', where in his account "the expansive force of mobile power [was] originating in the steppe" (Mackinder 1904: 430). With an imperialistic argumentation he assessed the natural resources as sufficient for supporting an "empire of the world" (Mackinder 1904: 436). Other scholars followed him centring the 'Pivot of Asia' in Urumchi such as Owen Lattimore (1950) or Kabul like Milan Hauner (1989; cited after Kreutzmann 2005). The Russian school of centrography made similar attempts to define 'centres of gravity' that have to be moved by planning processes to geopolitically desired locations (see Poulsen 1959). These accounts seem to be rather interesting for the case of the Pamirs, as they might have informed not only political decisions on boundaries but also economic resources for borderlands.

A large part of the border studies literature in the middle of the 20th century was concerned with static classifications of boundaries, whereat definitions of the terminology of geographical separation lines were developed (see Boggs 1940; Hartsthorne 1936; Jones 1943; Kristof 1959). These categorisations generated the impression that the socio-cultural perceptions and practices can be explained by the political history that lead to the creation of boundaries.

Functionalist viewpoints widened the view to different roles that constitute a border. In these accounts the border is used by the state to fulfil several functions beneficial to the nation-state. They state five different functions: Legal, fiscal, control, military and ideological (see Raffestin et al. 1975, listed in Leimgruber 2005: 240).

As the paper deals with delimitation processes, it is necessary to distinguish the meanings of identifiers for different lines and spaces of antagonism or transition.

The term frontier linguistically originates from the French *frontière* that was originally connoted with the military front. Different disciplines have adopted it and use it in a different way. In geography, two meanings prevail. The first became popular with Frederick Jackson Turner. He used the term in his work dealing with the role of the frontier for American society (see Turner 1928[1920]) as a dividing line between settled, respective colonised, and 'unsettled', respective Native Americans' territory. The second meaning refers to the limits of a state, where it borders the neighbouring one. Historically, frontiers were rather areas than lines, where the ruler could not exercise absolute power. Significant levels of autonomy were granted to the *marcher lords* governing the frontier provinces (see Ellis 1995; Teschke 2003). Although in contemporary nation states sovereignty is considered to reach continuously to the edges, the borderland respective the frontier is often an arena of (military) conflict (see Kristof 1959; Prescott 1978; White 2004). Since the characteristics of classical frontier provinces are evident in this case study, I will use frontier for referring to a governed, but contested territory at the margin of a political entity.

The boundary, the next term in the vocabulary, denominates an imaginary or marked line on a map or the surface of the earth. When geographers became concerned with borders, they tried to understand its location and course. Subsequently, theories for natural respective 'scientific' justification of boundaries were developed. Some pretended that courses of boundaries could be settled 'scientifically'. The advocates of this account named the segregation of ethnic groups and land that is hard to settle or cross as a prerequisite for optimal boundaries (see Curzon 1888; 1908; Holdich 1916). In subsequent geographical discourses the meaning of boundary can be summarised as the "physical and geographical outcome of the political and historical process" (Newman 2006: 145). Although it was used increasingly metaphorically in the last two decades, in this paper the term boundary refers to the above mentioned line that is sanctioned by the state and confines its territory.

Finally, the use of the term border has to be defined. In this contribution, border will be regarded first and foremost as an institution of the modern nation state, which is related to the state boundary. The boundary is created, legally sanctioned, and maintained by the state (see Kristof 1959). In everyday social reality it is represented by the state border as a structural precondition, that poses as the arena for social and cultural practices (see Albert 1998). Although state borders are sustained and enforced by state structures, its functioning depends on the behaviour of the people interacting with this institution.

Accordingly, the research paradigms were broadened from the narrative of individuals exposed to the effects of borders to the acknowledgement of the interplay of structural state power and individual agency in the borderlands (see Newman/Paasi 1998). Research of the post-socialist transitions such as the post-Soviet republics during the past two decades has shown that the explanatory power of the politico-economic structures alone is very limited for the understanding of socio-economic realities of the population and the ongoing transition processes of the societies. Instead, the way Giddens understood the mutual interdependencies of structure and agency in his structuration theory (1984) can be helpful. The agency is grasped as performed within the context of a pre-existing social structure governed by both informal and formal rules, such as norms and laws. However, these structures are not imperishable and external, but sustained and modified by actions of individuals.

In this vein, empirical fieldwork on the micro level is necessary to understand the realities of different actors at the border. This knowledge needs to be regarded within the complex contexts of politico-economic structures such as legal regulations, power, finances etc. Combining both components makes it possible to understand how structural preconditions of the border are perceived by individuals and translated into particular agency. The way border officials, border crossers and the individuals of the borderland act towards the border, permanently forms this institution.

3   Introduction to the Case Study: The District Murghab in the Eastern Pamirs

The borders examined in this paper delimit the Tajik part of the eastern Pamir, a predominantly high mountain desert of Central Asia, located in the easternmost part of Tajikistan. This area is today bound in the north by Kyrgyzstan, in the east by the autonomous province of Xinjiang in China, and in the south by the narrow Wakhan corridor of Afghanistan, through which Pakistan can be reached. The eastern Pamirs is more or less congruent with the Murghab district and is located within the autonomous province of Gorno-Badakhshan in Tajikistan (fig. 22).

The high mountain plateaus are used by two different groups. Mountain farmers from the deep-cut Western Pamir valleys, where they cultivate irrigated terraces and drive their cattle to the eastern Pamir pastures during summers. The second group are Kyrgyz pastoralists. Some fled conflicts with emperors in the oases and came to live in the Pamirs all year round; others migrated seasonally over long distances from the fringes of the Pamirs and use the vast pastures of the Pamir plateaus in summer.

Some words may explain the natural resource base for local livelihoods. The altitude ranges from around 3500 m.a.s.l. in the valleys and reaches more than 7000 m.a.s.l in the northern and western mountain ranges. This orographic situation causes low temperatures throughout the whole year, reaching annual means of only -1 to -3°C in the villages. Additionally, the climatological situation is marked by extreme aridity with precipitation below 100 mm/a.

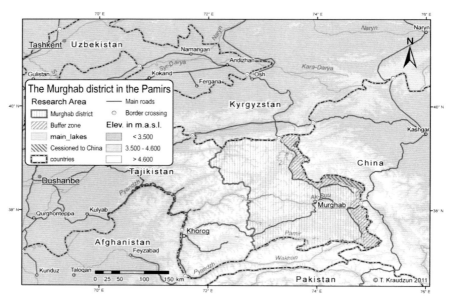

Fig. 22: Map of the case study area (own design)

These natural preconditions favour extensive livestock herding of yaks, sheep and goats as agricultural options. The population density today is still low in this district with an area of 38,300 km² but only 14,000 inhabitants, consisting of 77 % Kyrgyz and 23 % Pamiri. Half of the population lives in the district capital and economic centre Murghab, the other in remote villages (see GosKomStat 2007).

   These poor preconditions of the physical environment would be less grave if the regional population could rely on substantial economic alternatives to the subsistence-based livestock economy, which relies solely on pasture resources. Even more negatively the current status quo is assessed by the local population when compared to the historical situation: The high degree of economic and social integration of this region into the Soviet Union is well remembered. Most of the installed infrastructure is now dysfunctional without permanent funding, with only a few exceptions. For example, the Pamir Highway, the first infrastructural project of the Soviet Union here, is still a reliable transport connection despite long and heavy winters.

4   Methodology and fieldwork

To answer the above mentioned questions, some topics related to boundaries are especially important that follow out of the characteristics of mobile pastoralism. First, pastoralists need to move their herds to different pastures in order to use the meagre pastures. Second, the pastoralists are in the need of foods and goods that cannot be produced out of animal products. The full subsistence of nomads is a myth; the surplus of livestock breeding has to be exchanged for needed goods in the Central Asian oases where cultivation and trade connections make them available. Third, economic alternatives are helpful to absorb risks for the livelihoods relying solely on the income of animal breeding. These three preconditions shape the analytical framework to examine opportunities and restrictions in the border district. Accordingly, the analysis of how the borders impact on the livelihoods will focus on herd mobility, trade exchange and livelihood security.

Although the current situation may be most relevant for the local population, the institutions of the current borders must be seen as the result of the geopolitical confrontation of external powers. Hence, it is necessary to include a historical perspective in order to demonstrate how the differentiation of the Pamir frontier to diverse borders affects people's livelihoods. To do so, the above mentioned focus topics will be highlighted in a diachronic manner.

The access to information depends on the considered time period. During and after their acquisition of the Pamirs, the Tsarist Russian administration documented the social and economic life of the frontier region quite well. Yet the disturbances of the October Revolution did not leave much in the regional archives, instead the British intelligence could assist with the documentation. The administration and economic life of the Soviet era were documented exemplarily, all information concerning the external borders of the Soviet Union is still hard to obtain. However, the supposed distortion of official data to fit state plans and ideology suggest complementing information with alternative data, for instance oral history.

Since independence, official data has not gained in reliability. The informal economy constitutes a large share of border operations, giving benefits to most administrational, security and border officials. Therefore the hardest task is to assess the aggregated amount of the trans-border trade as the administration presents unrealistically low figures. Additionally, in the eastern Pamirs as a border district, all state authorities have special policies concerning confidentiality hampering access to all kinds of information originating from these sources. Even foreign researchers are often met with suspicion and mistrust. Accordingly, information on individual household livelihoods can be the best data source to understand individual differences in the border-related agency. As in other contexts, where people are dependent on informal arrangements for their economic activities, trust is the key to reliable information. Hence only general data was gathered in standardised surveys. Sensitive information on the informal arrangements during the border crossings were only asked for during repeated meetings with confiding informants.

The findings are based on extensive fieldwork conducted since 2003, and mainly between 2007 and 2009 (14 months) in the eastern Pamir. Information is derived from topic-specific interviews with key and knowledgeable informants about pastoral strategies, livestock economy and political frame conditions. Enquiries about historical contexts are based on regional archives and provided helpful insight into the current situation.

5   The historical legacy: Boundary-making, economic integration, external delimitation

5.1   Russian Colonisation: Restructuring the Pamirs through boundaries

In the 19th century, the territory of Central Asia was under the command of different principalities and China. The Pamirs were still shown as a blank spot on the map (see Boulger 2004[1878]: map). Prior to the encroachment of Tsarist Russian forces the khanate of Kokand claimed the Pamirs as its territory. Although the rulers took no efforts towards a permanent presence, they tried to levy taxes through the commitment of local leaders as representatives. The Chinese-ruled region of Xinjiang in the east claimed these mountains as well and intensified attempts to dominate the Pamirs, when the Russian forces were approaching this area after capturing Kokand in 1875. The western Pamirs were claimed by the Bukharan Emirate, but in the inaccessible valleys different local principalities resided, were comparably isolated and free from obligations. In 1883, however, these principalities came under Afghan rule and were subject to taxation. Furthermore, Afghan forces even tried to extend their rule to the plateaus of the eastern Pamirs.

Groups of Kyrgyz pastoralists used the pastures of the eastern Pamir; borders were unknown and even boundaries were unclear at this time. This situation presented them with some opportunities but also constraints. The Pamirs have long been a major transport route between adjacent markets. With their vast knowledge about routes and related risks of the vast high mountains, Kyrgyz pastoralists often served as experienced guides and guards for trade caravans, some of them acted as caravan robbers. On the other hand, they took unpredictable risks when operating with their own belongings. The pastoralists depend on the exchange of their livestock surplus against foodstuffs and other goods in agricultural markets like Kashgar. En route they risked being deprived of the flocks, in the market towns they tried to avoid being charged with extraordinary taxes by negotiating special arrangements for market access in Kashgar (see Di Cosmo 1993).

With Tsarist Russia's advance into the Pamirs during the crucial phase of the 'Great Game' the situation changed significantly. Pamirskiy Post was erected in 1893 as an outpost to show the military presence of the Russian empire and to control the activities of other powers in the vast territory (see Serebrennikov 1899: 235). Russian and British envoys agreed on the boundary between the Russian Empire and Afghanistan in 1895. When the Russian empire was entitled to exercise territorial sovereignty, the Pamirs were incorporated into the Governorate-General of Turkestan and control over the population was developed in a classical colonial way. At the same time, the Russian troops started to prohibit crossings of the new boundary.

Kyrgyz pastoralists were surprised that they were now hindered to move to valleys belonging to Afghanistan or China, as they had always had freedom of movement before (see Zajcev 1903: 49). British India and Russian Turkestan were separated only by Afghanistan's narrow Wakhan strip, and Britain as well as Tsarist Russia produced mutual suspicions on encroachment plans by the respective other power. The Russian administration emphasized that the boundary served the military purpose of protecting against the sudden intrusion of 'foreign' forces or people in general (see Skyes/Sykes 1920: 144). In the numerous accounts of Russian explorers, scientists and officers describing the new acquisition of the Pamirs, guaranteeing security to the local population was emphasised. This narrative was retained even during the Soviet period (see Masov 1985: 235; Serebrennikov 1899). Additionally, long distance trade between Kashgar and Badakhshan traversing the Pamirs was affected by mutual suspicion of political enemies (see Hedin 1899: 99; Serebrennikov 1899: 222). At the same time, the regular needs of the local population were satisfied by Russian goods brought by external traders. This increasingly channelled the source of supply from Kashgar to Osh (see Serebrennikov 1899: 235).

5.2   Soviet Modernisation: Internal economic integration, external delimitation

After the October Revolution, when Soviet forces gained power in Russian Turkestan, administrative units were reconfigured several times. As a result, in 1925 the Pamirs got the status of an autonomous province, the 'Gorno-Badachshanskaja Avtonomnaja Oblast' (GBAO), and were joined to the Tajik Soviet republic in 1929 (see GosArchiv-GBAO 1992: 6f). Now the region, which was historically connected to Kashgar and Osh, was attached to the poorly accessible lowlands of the Tajik Soviet Republic.

After settling the administrative structure, the major goals pursued by the Soviet power were to persuade the local population of the advantages of an integrated rural development and to convince them of the utility of producing in collective farms. Every endeavour was made to improve the supply of foods and goods, channelled via the railheads of Andizhan and Osh. For example, more than 7,500 tons of goods had to be brought into the Pamirs in the planning year 1936/37 to supply about 29.000 people who were living in the region in 1935[95]. The crossing of a *de jure* international border caused no restrictions.

A higher degree of relevance was attributed to the Tajik Pamir's boundaries with Afghanistan and China. In the aftermath of the October Revolution, a struggle for power broke out in the region. Both communist party commissars and counter-revolutionary forces infiltrating from Afghanistan, tried to convince the local population of the advantages of one or another politico-economic system (see Taipov 2002: 48f). In addition, subsidised, and therefore cheap, goods from the emerging Soviet supply organisations became preferred items for smuggling. Furthermore, numerous people escaped the Tajik Pamirs to avoid their compulsory dispossession by the Soviet authorities (see Audouin-Dubreuil 2008: 182). These factors made the enforcement of the closure of the external borders to Afghanistan and Xinjiang the top priority of the Soviet power in the 1930s, resulting in the total closure in the 1940s. Supply and emerging economic integration of the established collective farms were organised within the boundaries of the Soviet Union. Therefore extraordinary efforts were made by the Soviet state to build a road from Osh in the Fergana valley via Murghab in the eastern Pamirs to Khorog, the provincial centre of the GBAO. The so-called 'Pamir Highway' was opened in 1934 (see Popov 1935). The efforts were

---

95   Although the official state statistics claim more than 55,200 inhabitants in 1932 (see Bushkov/Kalandarov 2003: 106), regional archive documents show a population of 39,320 for 1935, and only of 28,924 for 1936 (GosArchiv-GBAO: 1/3/27). The data were collected by a special brigade activated jointly by the communist party and the government of the Tajik Soviet republic that was sent in order to speed up collectivisation in the Pamirs. The sharp decline gives a hint for the amount of forced migrations during the high time of the repression.

continued by building another challenging engineered road to connect Khorog, the administrational centre of the Tajik Pamir, with the capital of the republic in Stalinabad (Dushanbe). Although opened in 1940, its disadvantage was its regular closure during several months of the winter season due to large amounts of snowfall. Accordingly, the Pamir Highway, crossing the border, continued to be the main supply channel for the Pamirs.

The population of the Soviet Pamirs experienced different restrictions and opportunities arising from the new situation, depending on the socio-economic status of its members. Most of the few wealthy leaders of lineage groups tried to escape before the borders were sealed, anticipating losing their status or even their integrity. The majority of the tributary households and forced migrants from the Basmachi conflict-torn regions had not much to lose and were open to the collective experiment. Formerly depending in their nutrition on the grace and the successful economic exchange of the lineage leaders, they could now rely on the absolute commitment of the Soviet system to supply the geopolitically important region to keep the inhabitants loyal.

A special case is the Sino-Soviet boundary, which was delimited legally binding only in parts. To take the watershed of the Sarikol range as the dividing line was agreed upon in 1884, but only in the northern part. Russia then occupied all territories west of the range also in the south; ignoring China's claims of large parts of the area (see Garver 1981: 115). In the aftermath of the Sino-Soviet border conflicts in the Far East, the tensions increased in all regions with disputed territories. Consequently the Pamir border guards were restructured and reinforced again in 1973. The result of these measures is visible still today: Beginning in the 1970s, an electrically secured, barbed-wire fence was set up along the external boundaries of the Soviet Pamir. Due to the unsettled territorial claims it was set up with a distance of several kilometres from the Sarikol range, constituting the de-facto border (fig. 23).

This buffer zone excluded the collective farms from substantial pasture areas, comprising about 14 % of the district's territory (fig. 22). Later, access was granted, but remained strictly restricted to *sovkhoz* workers approved by the Committee for State Security. Only in 2004, Sino-Tajik negotiations resulted in a final demarcation of the provisional boundary between the states. One item of the agreement was the cession of a territory of about 980 km² to China, with disagreeable effects for the pastoralists of the sub-district Rang-Kul who used the pastures now handed over to China (fig. 22). Furthermore it excluded the biggest part of the population, military and security forces as well as border guards used it as some kind of a resource. Behind the fences they hunted unique wildlife unobserved like the world renowned Marco Polo sheep (*Ovis ammon polii*) and the endangered snow leopard (*Uncia uncia*) – then and now.

Fig. 23: Surreal appearance of closure in an open mountain landscape: The electrically secured, barbed-wire fence, called *sistema elketrosignalizacija* (vernacularly 'the system'), delimits the buffer zone of the Sino-Tajik border (near Kara-Kul Nov 2007)

In contrast, the internal border between the Kyrgyz and the Tajik Socialist Soviet Republic functioned as a demarcation line. The biggest share of supplies for the Pamirs continued to be transported from the economic centres of the Fergana valley. The Soviet Union made extraordinary efforts to increase the living standards of the population in the Pamirs as a territory of highly geopolitical interest. For a region traditionally used by pastoralists this implied the construction of the complete civil infrastructure. Enormous amounts of building materials, foodstuffs, goods and fuel had to be brought in regularly. To fulfil this task a special transport organisation, the 'Pamirskoe Avtotransportnoe Upravlenie' was established, financed and controlled by the supranational administrative level. Running hundreds of trucks on the route of Osh-Murghab-Khorog, the transport of supplies was of highest priority and crossing the border caused no problems. Accordingly, the Soviet Pamirs was almost entirely dependent on the flows of trade.

Former exchange relations of the local population with regions now beyond the Soviet Union's external border were effectively cut. The source of the goods – previously Kashgar or Tagarma in China – was substituted by the well-developed Fergana valley. Another change concerned the involvement of the local population. Where in pre-Soviet times exchange was organised individually, all transportation of goods was now under the control of the state. Individual trans-border trade, even in small quantities, was banned as *spekulacija*.

6 Independent Tajikistan's borders: Revived but restricted exchange

The dissolution of the USSR and the independence of Tajikistan resulted in significant structural changes of the political and socio-economic frame conditions. As a result of the hyperinflation of the Russian Rouble and the Tajik civil war regular interregional trade relations were discontinued. The basic supply was maintained for some time by the state farms bartering their livestock in direct exchange for fuel and flour in the Fergana valley.

The mass exodus from Tajikistan's war-torn south-west resulted in a dramatic increase of the Pamir population just at the moment when the local economy could not cope at all. Including the official figures of 54,800 displaced people (see Herbers 2006: 213), the population rose by one third according to official sources (the real figures likely being higher), just when the former state supply structures had collapsed. During the Soviet era, agricultural production and the economy of the region were transformed to meet external needs; in exchange the Pamirs were supplied with all necessary goods from outside. The effects of this production system were low rates of self sufficiency: Less than 20 % of the cereal needs could be met by local agriculture production (see Breu 2006: 80; Herbers 2006: 231)

In order to alleviate the disastrous supply situation, the Aga-Khan Foundation attracted several international donors for the disastrous situation and organised humanitarian food supplies within the framework of the '*Pamir Relief and Development Project*' (see Bliss 2006: 300ff.). This meant transporting a yearly supply of 300 to 1800 tons of foodstuff for the district Murghab. Beginning with these provisions the exchange relations on the basis of the Soviet system ceased entirely.

Private trade was only slowly established and several years later. One reason is that the Soviet proscription of private trading activities as *spekulacija* was fixed in the minds of the Murghab population. Even 15 years after the turnover of the ideological frame conditions, interviewees recurred to the negative connotation of private trade. Secondly, the basic food supply was secured during the years of humanitarian aid. Thirdly, many obstacles hampered personal journeys. During the time of the civil war the passage to the centre of Tajikistan was dangerous because different warlords controlled the main transport routes. The alternative, to go to the previous supply markets in the Fergana valley, was hard to reach because Russian forces were policing all the traffic in the Pamirs. The deployment of Russian border guards in Tajikistan substituted the Soviet military structures. This was agreed bilaterally in 1993 because of Russia's fear of infiltration by the *Mujahidin*, the acrimonious enemies of the Soviet forces during their Afghanistan occupation (International Crisis Group 2004: 17). Immediately after independence, Tajikistan was caught up in a civil war and its state forces were unable to deal with border control, especially in the remote Pamirs. Russia feared the exploitation of the weak state control in the newborn republics of Central Asia that could give Islamic movements the opportunity to gain hegemony. In practice, the presence of the Russian border guards meant rigorous searches on frequent road blocks along the Pamir highway. In addition to these difficulties, the official status of the Tajik-Kyrgyz border was not clear before the regulations were decreed by the re-strengthened Tajik state in the late 1990s (idem. 2001: 3). This caused confusion concerning permissiveness, checking and customs clearance of traded goods beyond the humanitarian and military supplies at the border. This situation made it very risky to transport livestock to Osh in order to buy goods to bring home, resulting in very infrequent private trading activities.

In one case the high risk is rewarded with the possibility of enormous profits. The weakened border infrastructure made the smuggling of Afghanistan's most valuable products feasible (ibid.: 19). Opium and opiates were abundant because poppy production rose in Afghanistan when the Soviet army loosened control and left the country (see Kreutzmann 2004: 57). The so-called 'northern route' leading to the huge Russian market opened up through the Central Asian countries. The biggest share of this drug flow of yearly 95 t (2008) goes through Tajikistan which ranked first with 1.5 t (2007) annual heroine seizures ahead of Turkmenistan and Uzbekistan. The Pamir route to Osh/Kyrgyzstan is still one of the major ones crossing the country (see Madi 2004; UNODC 2010). Respondents reported that in the mid 1990s opiates were easily available in Khorog at low prices, and that the value could be multiplied when sold in Osh[96]. Due to the absence of individual traffic at this time, ironically, the empty trucks going back to Osh to pick up the next load of humanitarian goods were used by

---

96   Madi (2004) numbers enormous profits for the transborder trade – 1996 prices: Badakhshan
      (Afghanistan) 60-100, Dushanbe (Tajikistan) 1,000, Osh (Kyrgyzstan) 3,000-4,000 USD per
      kg heroine; 2003: Badakhshan (Afghanistan) 240-400, Dushanbe (Tajikistan) 1,500-2,000,
      Osh (Kyrgyzstan) 4,000-5,000 USD per kg heroine. The updated estimates of UNODC (2010)
      show similar price differences for 2009: Afghanistan (farm gate) 64, Tajikistan border 250,
      Dushanbe (Tajikistan) 750 USD per kg heroine.

both drivers and passengers to smuggle drugs, usually in small quantities. Rumours circulate that some people gained resources to start up new businesses, while several dozen people who were caught at one of the numerous checkpoints are still serving their sentences in Tajik and Kyrgyz prisons. Informants from security forces stated that the trafficking of drugs ceased when the state structures were reinforced and professionalised. In fact, individual small-scale trafficking seems to persist, as ongoing cases of seizures from individuals show. Respondent's observations from the population strongly suggest that most of the drug trafficking is currently organised by a small number of businessmen, who avoid search by including border guards through profit sharing. This observation is backed by the UNODC (2010).

The transformation of the post-Soviet Tajik-Kyrgyz border from a boundary controlled by external forces to a 'regular' border operated by state authorities made regular trade with goods possible. More traders became active in the last years of the 1990s. Since the passage was still not easy, people gathered in shared transport. Some shared a hired truck; others used a somewhat regular bus service offering the roundtrip Murghab-Osh-Murghab journey. A former operator of this kind of bus service remembered:

> "I wanted to have a regular timetable, but it was hard to keep; ... The journeys to Osh were no problem. ... The return journeys were awful. Imagine: 10-20 trade women in the bus, each of them with two, three or more packages full of different goods. Usually the customs officials made a search to get an overview, what the traders were carrying. They tried to assess the amount and value of the goods for assigning the custom fees. The back of the bus was full of bags and boxes up to the ceiling, often we had to unload the entire bus. ... When they [the customs officials] started to ask for custom fees, the discussion started, with every single trader. ... Sometimes we were at the border for more than 24 hours!"[97]

As described, these first attempts at trade match with the description of petty trade. Yet after some time, the transportation of goods was organised differently. A growing share of the journeys was executed at the expense of a single trader who acted in the capacity of a freight forwarder. He offered the transportation as a service: in Osh the goods were handed over to him by different individuals and the entrepreneur was solely responsible for transportation and settling trouble at road blocks and borders. As the freight forwarders do the passage fairly regularly, they have good opportunities to establish which goods they can smuggle better and for which it pays off to make arrangements at road blocks and border crossings in order to avoid time consuming searches and official fees and taxes. Several interviewed drivers reported the payment of agreed informal payments depending on the amount and especially the kind of goods. Figure 24

---

97   Azimbek (14.04.2008); names are changed.

shows that the difficulties of trans-border transport results in enormous price
differences of several food items.

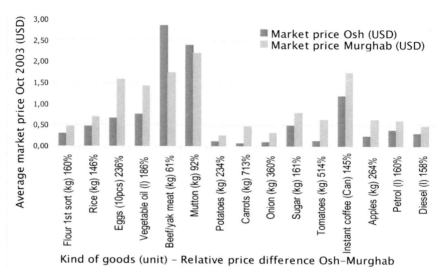

Fig. 24: Price differences between the markets of Osh and Murghab in October 2003 (own survey)

This system of international freight transport proved to be a reliable transport
service, regardless of import/export regulations or taxation policies. This can be
demonstrated with the obstacles of the trans-border trade flows. Although not all
households were successful in livestock breeding after privatisation, total
numbers recovered and many herders were able to sell the herd surplus. Animal
prices in this exclusively livestock region are expectably low; therefore the
breeders seek to sell their livestock in Kyrgyzstan, predominantly in Osh, where
meat is in demand. Therefore, wealthy herders and professional traders are the
second group of individuals that undertake roundtrips to Osh on their own
account for selling the livestock and supplying the household. However, the
Tajik government looks somewhat differently on these exports. Since 2000, the
local administration has refused to issue export permits; for yaks entirely, for
sheep and goats in very limited numbers. In the opposite direction, several goods
are banned from import, basic ones like fuel, as well as stimulants such as
alcohol and tobacco products. Likewise, basic foods are temporarily banned for
export from Kyrgyzstan, as e.g. flour in late 2008 when world market prices
rocketed.

Normally, all these bans would lead to an economic or supply crisis in the Murghab district. However the symbiosis of ambitious freight forwarders together with underpaid border officials enables a steady flow of foods and goods, notwithstanding changing import/export policies. The fact that no amenities in taxation and customs duties are granted to the comparatively disadvantaged region together with the underpayment of state employees encouraged the establishment of a culture of informal operations at the border. Possible public revenues from international trade are now diverted to the pockets of border police and customs officials. Figure 25 shows that traders can save money in comparison to follow official procedures if they find informal arrangements with border officials.

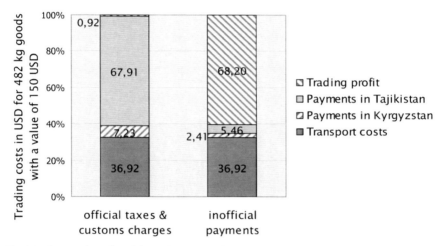

Fig. 25: Costs and profits of the trade between the markets of Osh and Murghab in October 2003 (own survey)

In 2004 a new border crossing with China was opened at the Kulma pass, which connects the Pamir Highway with the Friendship Highway between China and Pakistan. It is the only direct connection of Tajikistan to the Chinese market. In comparison to the Kyrgyz-Tajik border, much more goods cross the Sino-Tajik border, meaning a bigger importance of the informal border economies. However, the organisation of the border procedures leaves fewer opportunities to the employees at the border crossing itself. The main customs operations take place at a terminal near Khorog, thus a position there is highly valued. The local population rarely participates in this border trade, as the traders are usually businessmen from the central regions of Tajikistan, where most goods are transported to.

7 Conclusions

In the last 120 years, the mobile pastoralists roaming through the Pamirs have witnessed processes that have restructured the remote mountain region they live in. First they did not know boundaries that confine their mobility. Usually the pastoralists perceived the restrictions as borders that they faced when tempting to access the markets in order to exchange livestock for supplies. When in the late 19th century imperial interests culminated in agreements between the Russian, the British, and the Chinese empires, the Pamir frontier was delimited with boundaries, thus constraining the mobility of the Kyrgyz pastoralists for herding and trade. They became dependent on the terms of trade of the predominantly Russian traders. The economic benefits of bargaining at the bazaars that they could use only if transgressing the border to gain access to the markets can be seen as a resource that disappeared.

The Soviet power transformed the dividing lines between colonial spheres of influence into hermetically closed nation-state borders of the Soviet Union. While the former trade mobility patterns of the Kyrgyz pastoralists remained discontinued, new opportunities opened up. The Soviet system showed an absolute commitment to supply this geopolitically important region in order to maintain the population's loyalty. Consequently the inhabitants could benefit from multiple supplemental resource allocations that substitute for lost mobility resources. On the other hand, the restrictions of the pasture use in the extensive buffer zone demonstrate that the borders are still contested. Although Murghab district's status of an ideologically charged frontier zone implied a lot of constraints affecting the everyday life of the population and the regional economy as a whole, the existence of the geopolitically attributed border can be regarded as an indirect resource that resulted in benefits for the population.

The dissolution of the Soviet economy and the Tajik civil war caused an isolation of the Pamirs and led to a discontinuation of supply and exchange. On the other hand, a number of local households could benefit from small-scale drug trafficking, since the weakened Afghan-Tajik border became permeable. Although the policies of Russian border guards tried to limit interregional exchange, this trade can be seen as a new resource that the border people used. After the Tajik state regained its sovereignty, the crossing of the Kyrgyz-Tajik border began to function as a regular border crossing thus enabling private trade on a small-scale basis. Likewise, previously hermetically closed borders gained permeability with the opening of border crossings to China and Afghanistan.

Despite reopened borders, the trade vital for the population of such a disadvantaged region is constrained by inscrutable import/export regulations. This urged traders to avoid customs regulations and tariffs by smuggling or making informal payments to border officials. Only frequent traders gained enough knowledge and connections to perform cross-border trade in a profitable manner under these conditions. Consequently, only traders well-equipped with resources and connections as well as the border officials can use the border as a resource. The majority of the population has to pay the higher prices at the Murghab bazaar.

This border study from a historical perspective showed that the boundary-making processes first of all restricted the opportunities for local livelihoods. However, if hegemonic interests towards boundaries are translated into external inputs, it can compensate for the restrictions. Nevertheless, after the recent reconfigurations of independent Tajikistan's Pamir borders only few people can use the borders as a resource, whereas the majority has to live with the disadvantages.

References

Albert, M. (1998): "On boundaries, territory and postmodernity: An international relations perspective". In: Geopolitics, 3, 1, pp. 53-68.

Anderson, J. / Wever, E. (2003): "Borders, border regions and economic integration: one world, ready or not". In: Journal of Borderland Studies, 18, pp. 27-38.

Audouin-Dubreuil, A. (2008): Expedition Seidenstrasse: mit den ersten Geländewagen von Beirut bis Peking, die legendäre Expédition Citroen Centre-Asie 1931-1932. München: Frederking & Thaler.

Bichsel, C. (2009): Conflict transformation in Central Asia. Irrigation disputes in the Ferghana Valley. London [u.a.]: Routledge.

Bliss, F. (2006): Social and economic change in the Pamirs: (Gorno-Badakhshan, Tajikistan), London: Routledge.

Boggs, S. W. (1940): International Boundaries. New York: Columbia University Press.

Borcke, A. v. (1994a): Spannungen an der afghanisch-tadschikischen Grenze und das russische Krisen-Management. Volume 1. Köln: Bundesinstitut für Ostwissenschaftliche und Internationale Studien.

Borcke, A. v. (1994b): Spannungen an der afghanisch-tadschikischen Grenze und das russische Krisen-Management. Volume 2. Köln: Bundesinstitut für Ostwissenschaftliche und Internationale Studien.

Boulger, D. C. (2004[1878]): The Life of Yakoob Beg: Athalik Ghazi, and Badaulet, Ameer of Kashgar. Whitefish/Montana: Kessinger.

Breu, T. (2006): Sustainable Land Management in the Tajik Pamirs: The Role of Knowledge for Sustainable Development. Dissertation, Universität Bern.

Bushkov, V. / Kalandarov, T. (2003): "Le passé et le présent des populations du Pamir occidental". In: S. Jacquesson (ed.): Les montagnards d'Asie Centrale. Cahiers d'Asie centrale; 11/12, Tashkent: EDISUD, pp. 103-118.

Caney, S. (2005): Justice Beyond Borders: A Global Political Theory. Oxford: University Press.

Curzon, G. N. (1888): "The 'Scientific Frontier' an Accomplished Fact". In: Nineteenth Century, 23, pp. 901-917.

Curzon, G. N. (1908): Frontiers. Oxford: Clarendon Print.

Di Cosmo, N. (1993): Reports from the Northwest: a Selection of Manchu Memorials from Kashgar (1806 - 1807). Bloomington: Indiana University Research Institute for Inner Asian Studies.

Djalili, M.-R. / Frédéric, G. / Akiner, S. (eds.) (1998): Tajikistan: The Trials of Independence. Richmond: Curzon.

Ellis, S. (1995): "Frontiers and power in the early Tudor state". In: History Today, 45, 4, pp. 35-42.

Garver, J. W. (1981): "The Sino-Soviet Territorial Dispute in the Pamir Mountains Region". In: The China Quarterly, 85, pp. 107-118.

Gerstle, D. (2006): "Bridging the Panj: Forging a Peacebuilding Livelihoods Strategy on the Afghan-Tajik Border". In: Journal of peacebuilding and development, 2, 3, p. 35-48.

Giddens, A. (1984): The constitution of society. Cambridge: Cambridge University Press.

GosArchiv-GBAO: fond 1, opis 3, delo 27, Chorog: Gosudarstvennyj archiv GBAO.

GosArchiv-GBAO (1992): Spravočnik po istorii administrativno-territorial|nogo delenija GBAO. Chorog.

GosKomStat: Unpublished statistical recordings and reports. Murghab.

Halbach, U. (1993): Rußlands Wacht am Pamir. Köln: Bundesinstitut für Ostwissenschaftliche und Internationale Studien.

Halbach, U. (1997): Rußlands weiche Grenzen (I), Köln: Bundesinstitut für Ostwissenschaftliche und Internationale Studien.

Hartshorne, R. (1936): "Suggestions on the Terminology of Political Boundaries". In: Annals of the Association of American Geographers, 26, pp. 56-57.

Hauner, M. (1989): "Central Asian Geopolitics in the Last Hundred Years: A Critical Survey from Gorchakov to Gorbachev". In: Central Asian Survey, 8, 1, pp. 1-19.

Hedin, S. (1899): Durch Asiens Wüsten: Drei Jahre auf neuen Wegen in Pamir, Lop-Nor, Tibet und China. Volume 1. Leipzig: Brockhaus.

Herbers, H. (2006): Postsowjetische Transformation in Tadschikistan: die Handlungsmacht der Akteure im Kontext von Landreform und Existenzsicherung. Erlangen: Fränkische Geographische Gesellschaft.

Holdich, T. H. (1916): Political frontiers and boundary making, London: Macmillan.

International Crisis Group (2001): Tajikistan: An uncertain Peace. Osh, Brussels: International Crisis Group.

International Crisis Group (2004): Tajikistan's Politics: Confrontation or Consolidation. Dushanbe.

Iskandarov, K. / Lewington, R. (2009): „Grenzmanagement in Tadschikistan". In: Zentralasien-Analysen, 15, pp. 1-9.

Jones, S. B. (1943): "The Description of International Boundaries". In: Annals of the Association of American Geographers, 33, 2, pp. 99-117.

Kolossov, V. / Glezer, O. / Petrov, N. (1992): Ethno-territorial conflicts and boundaries in the former Soviet Union. Durham: IBRU Press.

Kolossov, V. (1999): "Ethnic and political identities and territorialities in the post-Soviet space". In: GeoJournal, 48, 2, pp. 71-81.

Kolossov, V. / O'Loughlin, J. (1998): "New borders for new world orders: territorialities at the fin-de-siecle". In: GeoJournal, 44, 3, pp.259-273.

Kreutzmann, H. (2004): „Opium für den Weltmarkt: Afghanistans Schlafmohnanbau". In: Geographische Rundschau, 56, 11, pp. 54-60.

Kreutzmann, H. (2005): "The Significance Of Geopolitical Issues For Development Of Mountainous Areas Of Central Asia". Paper presented at the workshop: Strategies for Development and Food Security in Mountainous Areas of Central Asia, URL: http://www.akdn.org/akf_rd_mountains_papers .asp (last access: 20.01.2011).

Kristof, L. (1959): "The Nature of Frontiers and Boundaries". In: Annals of the Association of American Geographers, 49, 3, pp. 269-282.
Lattimore, O. (1950): Pivot of Asia sinking and the Inner Asian frontiers of China and Russia. Boston: Little, Brown & Co.
Leimgruber, W. (2005): "Boundaries and Transborder Relations, or the Hole in the Prison Wall: On the Necessity of Superfluous Limits and Boundaries". In: GeoJournal, 64, 3, pp. 239-248.
Mackkinder, H. J. (1904): "The Geographical Pivot of History". In: The Geographical Journal, 23, 4, pp. 421-437.
Madi, M. (2004): "Drug Trade in Kyrgyzstan: Structure, Implications and Countermeasures". In: Central Asian Survey, 23, 3, pp. 249-273.
Masov, R. M. (ed.) (1985): Očerki po istorii Sovetskogo Badachšana. Dusanbe: Izdat. Donis.
Megoran, N. (2004): "The critical geopolitics of the Uzbekistan-Kyrgyzstan Ferghana Valley boundary dispute, 1999-2000". In: Pplitical Geography, 23, 6, pp. 731-764.
Newman, D. (2006): "The lines that continue to separate us: borders in our 'borderless' world". In: Progress in Human Geography, 30, 2, pp. 143-162.
Newman, D. / Paasi, A. (1998): "Fences and Neighbours in the Postmodern World: Boundary Narratives in Political Geography". In: Progress in Human Geography, 22, 2, pp. 186-207.
Ohmae, K. (1990): The Borderless World: Power and Strategy in the Interlinked Economy. New York: Collins.
Perkmann, M. (1999): "Building Governance Institutions across European Borders". In: Regional Studies, 33, pp. 657-667.
Perkmann, M. / Sum, N.-L. (eds.) (2002): Globalization, Regionalization and Cross-Border Regions. Basingstoke: Palgrave.
Polat, N. (2002): Boundary issues in Central Asia. Ardsley/NY: Transnational Publishers.
Popov, T. T. (1935): "Istorija strojki". In: M. M. Slavinskij (ed.): Sbornik stat'ey o stroitel'stve Pamirskogo i Velikogo Kirgizstanskogo Traktov. Frunze: Kirgosizdat, pp. 17-35.
Poulsen, T. M. (1959): "Centrography in Russian Geography". In: Annals of the Association of American Geographers, 49, 3, pp. 326-327.
Prescott, J. (1978): Boundaries and Frontiers. London: Croom Helm.
Raffestin, C. / Guichonnet, P. / Hussy, J. (1975): Frontières et Sociétés. Les Cas Franco-Genevois. Lausanne: L'Age d'Homme.
Ratzel, F. (1897): Politische Geographie. München/Leipzig: R. Oldenbourg.
Reeves, M. (2005): "Locating Danger: 'Konfliktologiia' and the Search for Fixity in the Ferghana Valley Borderlands". In: Central Asian Survey, 24, 1, pp. 67-81.
Scott, J. (2000): "Euroregions, Governance and Transborder Co-Operation within the EU". In: European Research in Regional Science, 10, pp. 104-115.
Serebrennikov, A. G (1899): "Ocherk Pamira". In: Voennij sbornik. St. Petersburg (1899:6-12): 6:432-444; 7-8:219-236, 442-464; 9:216-226; 10:447-466; 11-12:227-236.
Sykes, E. C. / Sykes, P. M. (1920): Through Deserts and Oases of Central Asia. London: Macmillan.
Taipov, B. (2002): Sary Kol tarychyndyn kyskača očerkteri. Murghab.
Teschke, B. (2003): The Myth of 1648: Class, Geopolitics, and the Making of Modern International Relations. London: Verso.
Turner, F. J. (1928[1920]): The Frontier in American History. New York: Holt.
UNODC – United Nations Office on Drugs and Crime (2010): World drug report 2010. New York: United Nations Publications.
White, G. (2004): Nation, State, and Territory: Origins, Evolutions, and Relationships. Lanham: Rowman & Littlefield Publishers.
Zajcev, V. (1903): Pamirskaja strana - centr Turkestana. Istoričeskij geografičeskij očerk. Volume 3. Novyj Margilan: Tip. Ferganskoj pravlenija.

Scales of trade, informal economy and citizenship at Georgian-Azerbaijani borderlands

Lale Yalçın-Heckmann and Nino Aivazishvili

1 Introduction

"26 April 2009
Today I was travelling to Georgia with the minibus. There were six students from Əliabad und Mosul[98]; some had food and wine, others money with them for other fellow students in Georgia. Sitting next to me and behind me were two women in their 40s and 50s. Soon Leila and Guliko engaged all of us on the minibus in their affairs, as they were chatting away loudly and constantly using their mobile phones. They looked like rural women with their headscarves, simple clothes and rubber shoes, and had large bags with them. Leila did not talk much to me at the beginning, but then started asking me questions and soon was already asking me for help: "I have some walnuts with me that I want to take across the border. I put them all in various small bags. I could give you one of them; one should help one another."
The women were selling walnuts in Georgia and crossed the border weekly from Azerbaijan to Georgia. Leila told me her adventures and struggles during these trips in an upset way:
Leila: The Azerbaijani side allows us to cross. With ours (meaning, Azerbaijani customs officers) one can talk directly; but the Georgians do not allow us in. Twice they have sent me back, saying I have extra luggage. They also change this rule very often; sometimes it is five kilos, sometimes seven...
Aivazishvili: Perhaps they don't want to break the rules?
Leila: What kind of rule is this? This is simply bullying people, is this the rule? I begged, I said I have children; but they simply said it makes no difference between a woman and a man, they would not allow it.
At the Azerbaijani border post Leila and Guliko could indeed pass without any fuss: they were only asked what they had in their bags. Once we arrived at the bridge and the in-between zone between the two countries, the women opened up their bags, took out the smaller bags with 5 kg of walnuts (they had prepared 10 bags, hence 50 kg altogether) and distributed them among all the other passengers. I also received a bag with the words: "Don't worry, you will not have any trouble, five kilos are allowed!" So once we had the bag of walnuts across, I heard one student and fellow passenger mumbling unhappily "I have enough of these people; the same bugging each time ..."
We gave the bags back in Georgia and the women thanked us all. I asked Leila where she was taking the walnuts to and she replied she would sell them in Tbilisi in front of the railway station. When I asked her about the price, she was evasive: "I don't know. I have not been to Tbilisi for a long time." She forgot at that moment how she had earlier told me about her weekly travels being full of agony. Apparently she did not want to talk much more. She had

---

98   These are villages in northwest Azerbaijan, in the rayon (district) of Zaqatala, close to the Georgian border.

arrived in Georgia and probably had other important things to do. She took her mobile phone and made a brief call, reporting that all was well and she would soon be in Tbilisi."

(From field notes of Nino Aivazishvili)

This story of petty traders seeking markets across the border between Azerbaijan and Georgia is typical for border regions and also for post-socialist economic formations. Azerbaijani traders were known during late socialism in the former Soviet Union (SU) as having a special inclination and even talent (if not disrepute) for engaging in petty trade and informal economy and for travelling to many parts of the Soviet republics, from Moscow to Vladivostok. Caroline Humphrey (2002, chapter 4) and Georgi Derlugian (2005: 150-154) write that Azerbaijani traders were specialized in trading certain agricultural products or sold illegal products such as alcohol during the late socialist era and immediately after the dissolution of the Soviet Union (see also Yalçın-Heckmann 2010). In this paper we focus on their activities primarily across the Azerbaijani-Georgian border. Nino Aivazishvili has worked in a border region in Northwest Azerbaijan and Lale Yalçın-Heckmann has been studying petty-trade and scales of trade in Ağstafa, a West Azerbaijani small town, also close to the Georgian border.[99] Yalçın-Heckmann's focus on scales of trade follows the classical studies on scales and social organization (such as Barth 1978) but also more recent studies which trace the development of debates on scale especially in political ecological approaches (see Paulson/Gezon 2005) or argue for rethinking the relevance of scale for urban and migrant studies (see Glick-Schiller/Çağlar 2011). These studies underline the primacy of paying attention to scale i.e. size and numbers of the social organizational phenomenon one takes as the unit of study but at the same time draw attention to the dangers of using overly static concepts and missing the dynamics of space and scale: Grönhaug (1978) for instance proposed early on to use the concept of 'social fields' in order to delineate scalar differences of social organization. In her study Yalçın-Heckmann prefers to use the term scales of trade to internally differentiate the economic field of organizing trade activities, where significant scalar differences can be found in terms of actors, institutions, goods, products and turn-over involved.

In this article scales of trade are secondary but complementary to our concern with comparative patterns of border trade and border livelihood. We discuss how these two regions with their petty-traders are integrated into the local and larger scale, national, transnational and global economies. We argue that these economic relationships and processes around petty-trade render the Azerbaijani

---

99   Nino Aivazishvili carried out her PhD research in the rayon of Zaqatala for nine months in
      2009 and Lale Yalçın-Heckmann spent two months each in the years of 2007 and 2008 in
      Ağstafa and hopes to continue research in the same district.

citizens to become aware of the borders and citizenship regimes (see Anderson 1996; Verdery 1998; Torpey 2000) in these sites, and to get engaged in and to transform existing citizenship practices. The borderlands as special locations certainly play a significant role. Even if trade, petty-trade and informal economy have become the major arenas in post-socialist countries (see Ledeneva 2006; Olimpieva et. al. 2007) for articulations of economic citizenship (see Woodiwiss 2008; Yalçın-Heckmann forthcoming), the fact that we are dealing here with a borderland phenomenon certainly needs further attention. The borderlands have often been discussed as spaces where state laws and systems of normative orders could be perceived as being weak or especially strong (as it was the case in border regions during the Cold War period; see Berdahl 1999, also Pelkmans 2006). In our field sites the border regime is particularly inscribed by contestations and encounters in the everyday life of petty-traders and border crossers. These encounters and contestations have the double effect of enacting the state's border regimes (similar to the way Mitchell talks about 'state effects', see Mitchell 1999). But at the same time they subvert them and develop the citizenship practices from below.

The case of the two women above can be interpreted at the common sense level as petty-traders engaging in this trade because they lack other income and resources. Leila argues that she needs to earn her living in this way as she has to look after her children and make ends meet. At an analytical level, however, one can interpret the existence of this trade as simply following the logic of supply and demand, hence of rational choice and market prices, and mechanisms of micro-economics. The two women could equally be motivated to profit from better prices and stable demand for their product in Tbilisi. They seem to follow the trade route regularly. Whatever their motivations may be, what is anthropologically significant in this case is that they take an active part in the shaping of border regimes. Their weekly activities are registers of citizenship regimes played out, where they and other actors along the border enact social roles, articulate citizenship notions and impact the regulations of their economic livelihood. Their economic activities are, therefore, articulations of as well as a consequence of the border dynamics and the actions of various local and supra-local actors and not simply actions and concepts imposed by state laws from above.

After this theoretical and contextual background to our work, in the following we explore the consequences of living on the border and remembering the former regimes of the border especially in Aivazishvili's field site. We then examine the new markets and trade relations in these markets as spaces for experiencing state-citizen relations in everyday life as well as for community building and explicate the gendered aspects of these relations and of the new public space. In the following section we discuss state and large-scale trade relationship on the basis of a case study of a businessman from Yalçın-Heckmann's field site and point out to the kind of experiences such large-scale traders might have of borderlands. After returning to the case of Ingiloy petty-traders' perceptions on lived-in states and those across the border, we conclude our discussion with highlighting our comparative points and conclusions one can draw concerning the intertwining links between engagement in trade and experiences with different citizenship regimes in borderlands.

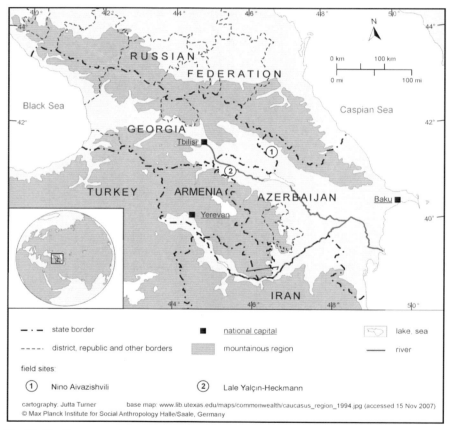

Fig. 26: The Caucasus region

2   Living on the border OR remembering the weak border

Living on the border between Azerbaijan and Georgia evokes memories of the past border regimes and these memories are part and parcel of everyday strategies and constructions of the border regimes. The village of Mosul, where Nino Aivazsihvili had been staying for her anthropological study, is only 15 km away from the Muğanlı Bridge, which is for crossing the Alazan river, the physical border between Azerbaijan and Georgia for some hundred kilometres. During the Soviet period the bridge was a main crossing point for both the Georgians and the Azerbaijanis. Today one can cross the bridge with small cars or on foot, but nevertheless not many people know about this. In 2003 during the Rose Revolution in Georgia the bridge was closed to traffic, as the Georgian government accused the Azerbaijani side for allowing corruption and smuggling when using the bridge. Two years later the bridge was opened to traffic again but according to the village governor in Mosul not many people know the details and are aware of the border crossing possibility.[100]

The closure of the Muğanlı bridge is remembered as a significant event in village life and history, in this and other villages where mostly Ingiloy live.[101] As the border was closed from the Georgian side, borderland people felt the strength and plasticity of the border as a physical thing for the first time, even if such perceptions of the border as a borderland only became common after independence in 1991. Immediately around the early 90s the two countries were going through primarily chaotic political times; the borderlands were not any different. As Aivazishvili's host, Ramil once noted sarcastically "at that time you could bring a tank across the border, as if it was 'invisible'" (Ramil, born in 1975). From the mid-1990s some of the border crossing points across the river, such as the one over Mazımçay[102] became harder to pass, however in general the Alazan river had many points for allowing petrol and crude oil to be traded from Azerbaijan to Georgia. The villagers of Mosul remember this period as a 'crazy time', when the police at these crossing points simply took money as bribes.

---

100   Indeed, apart from the village governor and a few other officials working in the administration no one knew about the border post being open again. Aivazishvili was told that it was closed. The ambiguity concerning this information could also be due to the new Georgian regime's strict measures of demanding official permits and documents for border crossing, unlike in former times when there were informal practices for the local population.

101   The Ingiloy are an ethnic group living in Azerbaijan, who speak a Georgian dialect and have a mixed religious affiliation, some are Muslims and others Orthodox Christian. Those who are Orthodox are locally depicted (etically as well as emically) as being 'Georgian' (Gürcü in Azerbaijani), even if the ethnic border between the Ingiloy and Gürcü within Azerbaijan seems to be fluid.

102   Mazımçay crossing point is to the west of the Balakan district, on the creek of Mazımçay.

Everything was uncomplicated, either morally or physically for any of the parties, as one smuggler of those times described the situation to Aivazishvili:

> "Smuggling then was different in comparison to the current situation. Today smuggling is practised at higher levels and is finely covered up. In those times, smuggling was a source of profit for the people, for everyone; today it is only for the state"[103]

Muğanlı Bridge was a special leeway, a loophole in the system of border control, where many could travel across without proper papers, but with 'protection from above', hence using political networks. In this landscape of highly permeable or less permeable border posts, people referred to different categories of crossings and borders: the one at Mazımçay was the legal or formal border crossing, whereas Muğanlı Bridge was often referred to as the 'old one', 'ours', 'the one below', or the 'nearby'. Similarly the verbs for describing the act of crossing over differed: for crossing at Mazımçay, they used the word *gadasvla* (in Georgian/Ingiloy language), meaning 'border crossing', whereas for Muğanlı Bridge, it was *gadaparva* (in Georgian/Ingiloy language) meaning 'gliding through'. These different categories of permeable borders have hence become part of the linguistic and vernacular cosmologies and mental maps (see Migdal 2004).

The rise to power of Mikail Saakashvili in 2003 in Georgia has fundamentally changed the quality of and practice in the borderlands: there are hardly any regular and casual visits across the border. The often cited reason for this change is the demand from the Georgian side for new documents (*sabutebi* in Georgian/Ingiloy language), the new passports, which not many people possess.[104] Therefore people speak nostalgically about the 'old' bridge; there is also some sense of having been adventurous with those earlier border-crossings. Comparatively the official border crossing at the Mazimçay bridge evokes more associations with strict control, inhuman laws and anxieties related to them.

---

103 Even if Aivazishvili's interlocutor talked about the state, he meant the power-holders in the upper ranks of the political class.

104 The residents of Mosul refer to the identity document as the 'small passport' (patara pasporti) and the international passport as the 'new passport'. After the independence of both countries from 1991 until 2003 the Ingiloy could travel to Georgia using the identity documents alone. After the Rose Revolution in 2003 the regulations concerning the valid documents were changed and now border crossing is only possible with the international passport.

3   Borderlands, markets and traders

In this section we turn our attention to the border town of Ağstafa, to its markets and traders. Administratively Ağstafa had been a part of the larger and wealthier *rayon* (district) of Qazax during most of the Soviet period and only in 1991 did it become a *rayon* of its own. The *rayon* borders Georgia and Armenia to the west and southwest and in 2008 it had a population of some 78,000 people, the city itself had 12,000. The city is adjacent to the village settlement with some 5,000 people and this differs from the city section primarily through the existence of large gardens, previously given to *sovkhoz* (socialist state farms) and *kolkhoz* (collective farms) workers, extremely dilapidated infrastructure (roads, water system and housing quality) and surrounding fields and agricultural land. Hardly any of the earlier economic institutions exist; the railway, schools, hospitals, the police and local and central state administrative bodies continue to be the main source of state employment. Other than the single furniture factory, a small dairy factory, several construction firms, and a clothes manufacturing factory which opened in October 2008, there were no private industries in the city. Trade seemed to be the most flexible and accessible kind of livelihood to many urban as well as rural people from the village part of Ağstafa and the surrounding rural area.

Ağstafa has a daily market which starts at about six in the morning and lasts until 2 pm every day. It has been located on the market place since 1995, has an area which is walled in towards the main street but open towards the back streets. In 2000 it was privatized, i.e. bought by the former head of the bazaar administration. According to the managing director (*bazarkom*) of the bazaar, which has a covered and open section as well as the space around it used for villager traders, there were some 160 traders in the bazaar. This was the number of traders who have regular sales counters assigned by the management. The products sold were diminishable processed food products, agricultural products, as well as manufactured household consumables, such as telephones, cutlery, porcelain, plates, cups, but also technical household equipment, construction goods, etc. The major item sold in the market was, however, clothes, for women, men and children.

Apart from the salespeople and small shops in and around the major bazaar, which all closed at around 2 or 3 pm at the latest, there were shops on the main street, many of them, especially those closer to the railway station and parks, stayed open until late in the evening. Finally there were small sales cabins (*butka*) in many parts of the city and village sector selling food products and mostly open according to the needs and life patterns of the neighbourhood residents.

3.1 Everyday life cycle in the market

The market place (*bazar yeri*) is a place where rural and urban spaces overlap and people encounter one another. The traders are villagers who come every day to either sell their own agricultural produce or they are villagers and townspeople who simply sell the products of others (*alverci*). Those villagers selling agricultural produce come earliest and stay the shortest; they leave as soon as they have sold their goods either directly to consumers or to petty-traders - *alverci*. They come by busses and cars from the surrounding villages, occupy the peripheral area of the market place and sell their goods with the simplest display modus, simply on sheets of plastic on the ground, in buckets or wooden cases if they have any. This is the most direct kind of sale; customers prefer them for major events when they need large quantities of vegetables for pickling or processing them for winter, or for food for major celebrations. The best quality produce is available early in the morning; so one has to be an early shopper, if one needs good quality in large amounts and often for good prices. The later one gets to the bazaar, the higher the prices are and the quality/price ratio changes to the disadvantage of the customer.

On early mornings, therefore, the market is busy with incoming cars and busses, early and eager customers, many of them petty-traders (*alverci*) themselves; there is a lot of commotion. The transactions are definitely guided by competitiveness, calculative reason as the shared culture of the market (see Gudeman 2008: 149), the desire to establish the best price, quality relationship, for buyer and customer. There are, of course, partnerships as buyers and sellers, especially between producer-seller villagers, petty-traders and buyers. Nevertheless, these partnerships are voluntary and flexible, and buyers do not hesitate to buy elsewhere, if they feel the goods are of better quality and price. There is not much time to waste in bargaining for and looking around for goods; the buyers know that if they do not buy after their first glance of the produce, there may not be a second time around, to come back and buy the good, as it could be sold out.

In the early daily phase of the market, speed, quick decisions, skills in recognizing good quality goods, knowing the relation of prices and having either good judgment about the seller's character and honesty or having trust relationships between sellers and buyers are important. In other words, this is the phase and space for calculative reason and economic skills in taking advantage of knowledge, bargaining skills and speed in buying. At the same time, it is seen as the least sociable, most strenuous kind of trade; people fear being cheated or enjoy getting the best deal by being an early buyer. Petty-traders have to compete among one another for getting the best deal the quickest, so that they can go back to their shops or sales' places and start selling the goods they have just bought. It is the phase and space for urban-rural encounters; the rural sellers may wait until they have sold their own goods and then stay on for doing their own shopping in other parts of the bazaar.

Even if this phase and space of the bazaar is occupied with calculative reason and competition, it has a negative relationship with other social relations and attributes like conspicuous consumption, taste and social class. The early trade of food products involves people from a rural background, *alverci* who sell these produce either in the market or in shops and occasionally higher social class consumers who need certain produce for some special need, such as preparing preserves for winter, preparing a special hosting ceremony, a morning ritual, wedding, circumcision ceremony and the like. The competition against time, quality and other consumers and sellers is seen as a negative aspect of the bazaar; petty-traders who work in the bazaar are hence considered to have acquired and internalized these qualities and are seen as 'strugglers', and if they are women, they often risk being 'immodest' in a gendered way, or simply being too poor and unsupported, for having to survive in this competitive, tense, tricky and 'uncivilized' social surrounding. Therefore, for instance, young rural female producer-sellers are usually the first to sell their goods (not always for the best prices for themselves), as they are keen on staying as briefly as possible in this chaotic and competitive atmosphere.

The second phase of the daily market starts at around 9 am, when the regular traders of non-food goods arrive and open up their stalls. These are the so-called 'professional' petty-traders, *alverci* or *tuccar*, trader. They sell manufactured food stuff, household goods, clothes, cloth, electronic gadgets and equipment and other small personal and household items. Female sellers are dominant in numbers in selling clothing items, household ornaments, china and kitchen utensils, as well as in cheese and other milk products, which they buy in villages, from villagers and sell it in the bazaar. They all have stalls which they need to pay a starting sum for to the bazaar manager (*bazarkom*) in addition to a daily due. The goods they sell are mostly bought in local or in Baku's wholesalers. Some traders were also border-crossers, buying goods in Tbilisi until about 2008 when the border became stricter. A petty shoe-trader Yalçın-Heckmann knew well, for instance, used to bring shoes made by Armenian artisans in Tbilisi and these were highly valued and desired for having a good quality and reputation. The trader cannot bring shoes from Georgia anymore because of the hassle from the Azerbaijani customs' side and now has to offer the Chinese made shoes he started bringing from Baku's wholesale market. This means he needs to travel some 450 km to the east, instead of some 100 km to the west, back and forth.

The atmosphere and the social space occupied by this petty-trade and traders are dominated by sociality. The traders set up their stalls in the morning and there is hardly any rushing around; they spend substantial time chatting with one another and with their customers, many of them may be friends, neighbours and acquaintances. There is room and time for walking around themselves, by asking the neighbouring stall-keeper to look after one's own stall, especially if there is not much happening at that moment. Petty-traders go and take care of their other chores, see friends and colleagues, or do not come on certain days at all, then the neighbouring stall-keepers are informed of their absence.

Following Steve Gudeman's (2008) arguments, one can say that this kind of community building is necessary as sales are done primarily on credit relations (*nisiye*). Credit relations work in the following way: when one is a petty-trader in the bazaar with a stall, and especially if she/he does not sell the very cheap items but rather expensive clothes, china and household utensils, it is commonplace that the sum is not fully paid. The customer asks the seller whether he/she could have the good on credit; that a partial sum is paid at the time of sale and the rest will be paid depending on the arrangement between the seller and the customer. These kinds of relations are obviously heavily socially contextualized and multi-dimensional, but not always. Sometimes the credit relationship is only such a relationship; the seller and customer know one another as trustworthy business partners, do not have any extra relationships through neighbourhood, kinship or the like. Nevertheless, these credit relationships 'cascade', in the sense Gudeman (2008) uses it, that once one is known to a seller as trustworthy customer, i.e. paying back under acceptable conditions and within a reasonable time period, the credit relations could be extended to other persons, other sellers and customers. This usually happens when one seller who knows the customer, recommends the same customer to his/her friend seller as a trustworthy person, that the seller could sell a good per *nisiye* (on credit) to the customer, even if they were not previously acquainted. In this way, social reputation as a trustworthy seller and customer and trust relations spread out within the bazaar, making it into a community of controlling 'greed' and other 'immoral' interests. Not only a trustworthy reputation is communicated, of course negative reputations as an unreliable customer or seller quickly spreads around as well.

The cascading extends to the formation of credit unions between sellers: there are micro-credit associations, mostly initiated by various projects in Azerbaijan through the World Bank in cooperation with the Azerbaijani government, which work in the city. These give credit to bazaar traders, and other small businessmen, to shop owners or owners of small repair shops, restaurants, and other businesses. The petty-traders of the bazaar usually get together as groups of five to apply for a credit which they share equally among themselves, but at the same time they take the responsibility of being a guarantor for one another. Again, these types of relationships are not based on previously existing ties of kinship and neighbourhood alone, very often they seem to be based on tight relations of trust traders have developed among themselves. The amounts taken out are usually substantial for the petty-traders; hence the risk they take in trusting their credit partners is significant as well.

The specificity of these economic transactions and how they can be related to citizenship themes could be summarized as follows: The petty-traders come to the bazaar with little prior investment but also with little hope of making substantial gains; hence they are found at the lowest scale of trade relations. For many it looks as if trade in the market place is a self-fulfilling activity; they spend equally long hours socializing with one another (men have long backgammon sessions, for instance) as they put their energy in selling their goods at good prices and making an earning. Nevertheless, this is the only public space where women can enter with few former 'connections', where they can spend the whole morning until early afternoon, and where they have to establish a name for themselves, where they are under social observation for becoming a potential trustworthy trade partner or not. They also have to establish their sexual reputation, for non-bazaar traders and people in other occupational sectors in the city (especially those with state jobs) bazaar women's reputation is on the verge of being daily tested, observed and renewed, re-established. Yalçın-Heckmann was for instance usually pointed at the deplorable fate of female former high-school teachers who 'had to become an *alverci'* in the bazaar (for comparative works on female petty-traders of the post-socialist era, see Kaneff 2002 and Heyat 2002). This was seen by many as social degradation and as an indicator of the decline of the state support. Hence the bazaar is a place where one makes friends and foes, becomes involved with people from all walks of life and has to test one's own capacity to cope with intrigue, gossip as well as economic competition.

The link we see between this kind of sociality and citizenship is the following: the bazaar allows a certain sector of society as well as mostly lower and middle class women as the discriminated gender category access to economic livelihood. It is a social space for developing skills and networks but at the same time it is a sphere where the limits of upwards mobility is tightly controlled and re-instigated. Men and women who want to become or who have managed to become traders of a higher scale or businessmen are our next topic. The activities in the bazaar define the limits of citizenship as well as making them public to people who otherwise have no public life (young women especially) other than in the market place.

4   Looking inwards and outwards beyond the border: Businessmen in Ağstafa and the state

It is not only in the eyes of the others that Azerbaijani people in general were known as petty traders already during late socialism. In Azerbaijan many see their own people as also having a tendency and inclination for engaging in trade; yet who judges who for being a petty-trader (*alverci*) and the degree petty-trade is socially accepted or valued changes according to the social class of the speaker. Some of the local bureaucrats Yalçın-Heckmann interviewed in Ağstafa, for instance, referred to petty-trade as supporting and even being the engine of the market economy. These bureaucrats saw the rural people and residents of small towns as being potential petty-traders, admitting, however, that petty-trade can hardly be seen as an economically viable way of accumulating any substantial capital: *burda halq hirda ticarete meyillidir, ama böyük pul yoxdur* (lit. 'people here have a tendency for petty-trade; but there is no big money in it'). Anthropologists working in the post-socialist countries have pointed out the moral hazards of becoming involved in petty-trade, especially shortly after the end of socialist regimes (see Mandel/Humphrey 2002). This trade was seen as a way of survival, yet debasing and shameful, especially for the educated and urban women, as we discussed above.

In seeking answers to the character of petty-trade and its possibilities for accumulation and mobility, let us turn to the case of a successful businessman in Ağstafa. When talking to the local advisor for economic affairs in the town, the trader's name was mentioned as the prime and showcase example for possible growth from being a petty-trader to a real businessman (a bit like 'from rags to riches'). Giving his name, the local economic advisor to the governor emphasized that: "The market economy is open to all; there is no restriction to anyone who wants to expand (*böyüməyə gidənin engəli yoxdur*)". The advisor, however, was also cautious about the conditions of open market economy and the extent of expanding markets for petty-trade, especially in this border town. Ağstafa is only 50 km away from the Georgian Azerbaijani border and the distance to the Georgian capital is some 100 km. Similar to the situation further north, where Aivazishvili has been doing her research, border trade is said to have flourished and Georgian customs' officers to have been almost equally as corruptible as their Azerbaijani counterparts roughly until Saakashvili's ascent to power. Goods bought in Tbilisi could be brought in relatively small amounts and sold in local markets. Furthermore Tbilisi was a convenient market for local agrarian produce such as fruit and vegetables; some other smaller cities were attractive as the market for animals from this border district with large sheep herds.

Yet, informal economy and petty-trade were severely limited soon after the Rose Revolution, as the new government took effective methods for controlling the borders and border crossings. Ağstafa's petty-traders, similar to the ones further north, have been finding it difficult since then to bribe the Georgian customs' officers and have been having difficulties taking produce and goods either way. Hence the economic advisor sees limitations in a growing market: for Ağstafa he said, if anyone wants to grow his business, the market is limited (*bazar mahdud*). People from Ağstafa go to Baku or to Russia if they want to expand their business. The traders in the *rayon* can only carry out their transactions in this *rayon*, or could go to the neighbouring *rayons* of Qazax, Tovuz, or Şəmkir. However any expansion of trade to Georgia is no longer possible, he said, as customs regulations and controls have become stricter (*qırağa çıxmak lazım, gömrük postları möhkəmləndi, Gürcüstan'a çıxabilmir*).

The answer to the above question concerning the limits of petty-trade, seems to be, in the words of the advisor, related to the potential of being a border region in a positive as well as a negative sense: the borders could be soft or hard, as scholars like Thomas Wilson and Hastings Donnan (1998) have argued or could be perceived as 'boundaries' where the division of 'we' and 'they' begins, as Joel Migdal (see 2004: 5f.) has suggested. It was soft and porous, for the informal economy and petty-trade until early 2000 and border trade functioned as a survival strategy for some and for accumulating for others. Presently, however, it is hard; border-crossing is no longer economically feasible for petty-traders, who do not have the capital to lucratively bribe for the small amount of goods they are able to trade. The border and the market then have been integrated into larger economic and political structures, where 'law and order' is assumed to hold (see also Humphrey 2002, chapter 4) and only those who have access to power-holders' networks manage to 'trade' in a larger scale.

How does the successful businessman, who turned from an *alverci* (petty-trader) to a factory owner in Ağstafa, explain his own success?

Təymur says that he has always been interested in business; in fact, he claims, he was more than only interested in it, it was 'in his blood' (*hevəsi vardı, kanda vardı*). He comes from a village close to the Georgian border, which is known as formerly being the home village of religious *ulema* (the learned people in Islam), later of many educated persons, intellectuals and bureaucrats. He had some college level law education in Russian via distance learning in Tbilisi and at the crucial and politically volatile years at the end of SU, independence and war over Karabagh (1988-1994), he worked as a policeman in the town. In 1994 he quit the police and started with petty-trade, he says. His first trade was with flour, especially the flour brought from Turkey during and shortly after the war years, where there was an acute shortage of food products. He worked with a Turkish

businessman who was then importing flour to Azerbaijan; he sold this flour in
Ağstafa on the market. He then moved on to selling construction material which
he brought from Baku to Ağstafa; later on came the trade with mobile
telephones, Xerox machines, electronic gadgets, then he opened up a restaurant
… As his starting capital he remembers to have taken 4000 US $ from a private
person which he had to pay back at 40% interest rate per month (he did not say
this, but private persons giving credit at such high rates are usually known to be
usurers, of which there are still plenty in Azerbaijan). Seeing Yalçın-
Heckmann's surprise about the high interest rate on the loan, he answered her
question about how he was able to pay back, with: "There was lots of money in
small trade, I paid it back" (*alverdə para çoxdu, qaytardım*).

Today Təymur is seen as the most successful and only businessman from the
locality. He no longer lives in Ağstafa permanently, although he still has a house
there and often comes for his business. He has his furniture factory just at the
city border, almost opposite the city's market place, which considerably
expanded in 2007-2008 when Yalçın-Heckmann was visiting the *rayon*. The
furniture is sold in a big shop next to the factory and Təymur has other major
furniture stores in Baku (two of them) and in the second largest city in
Azerbaijan, Ganja. His stores are often shown on TV advertisements in the local
television. The size of his business can be estimated with the last loan he took,
which he said was 500 thousand US Dollars in 2005; he had to repay it by 2010.
This was a loan he took from the state Economic Development Fond (*Iqtisadi
Inkişaf Fondu*); suggesting that his business is in the accounted economy.

One can interpret Təymur's success as being purely an economic one; that he
had the skills, social and monetary capital and ability to start and expand his
trading business and then to go on into the production sector, being the first and
most successful businessman in his *rayon*. Furthermore, he had the possibility of
using the advantages of the temporal conjuncture: The border was weak and
permeable in the early 1990s and he must have benefitted from the cross-border
trade. He himself, however, has explained the expansion of his business with
extra-economic and basically political factors. Təymur says that he was able to
expand his production unit without the intervention of any third parties after the
president, Ilham Aliyev, came to visit his factory in 2005. He explained his
situation as follows: "*Prezident buraya geldi, ondan sonra bizə her türlü imkan
açıldı, indi həç kimə bir qepik pul verməyirik*" (The president came here to visit
us; thereafter we had all the possibilities open for us; now we don't pay a single
penny to any one). What Təymur here points out is the clearest indicator
concerning the existence of monopolies in production and trade and that these
control the economy and polity. Təymur was, in fact, with his own example
pointing out the widely-known and publicly discussed practice of local and

regional bureaucrats extorting payments from businessmen when these establish or expand their business, as well as extracting regular payments from such businessmen as 'donations' to various *rayon* and city works and projects. He meant that for establishing his factory he had to pay to these various authorities, and for expanding it he then sought access to the presidential apparatus, and once he managed to arrange him visiting his factory, he says, he is now immune from any pressure for extortion.

Təymur's case exemplifies the upper limits of expanding local trade, cross-border economic relations and small industrial production. Other wholesale traders Yalçın-Heckmann talked to also mentioned feeling restricted in their efforts to expand their business, not due to lacking capital or skills, but due to informal and power politics of monopolistic networks of politicians, higher bureaucrats and large businesses, as well as the more recent border regimes of controlled movement of goods and trade.

Petty-trade is then open-ended at the lower level of the scale: I.e. it is relatively easy to enter and there is now even the possibility of expanding it with state and private sector support through micro-credits. Nevertheless, one could argue that the unaccounted economy is an integral part of all trade in Azerbaijan, as the wholesale markets largely (but not solely) work with informal credit relations, where payments and debts are not registered and oral communication and trust relations are essential.

On the part of the state, transparency and formality in economic transactions seem to function top down: the state oil company (SOCAR) has created a social fund (after a decree in 1999 by the former president Heidar Aliyev) from the national oil income for supporting the economically weak in the contemporary society and to offer economic security for future generations (SOFAZ, State Oil Fund). This fund has been highly praised for its transparency; in 2007 it even received a UN Public Service Award for its commitment to transparency (RFE/RL 2010).[105] Yet between this level of accountability and the local level of economic structures there is of course a large space for local interventions and agency of local actors as well as competition between the local and national level enterprises and social actors. Local construction firms for instance complained that any public sector investment in road construction or a large construction project (like the recent culture centres for the former president Heydar Aliyev or

---

105   For a discussion and comparative analysis of oil income, oil funds and investments from these funds in Azerbaijan, Kazakhstan, Alaska and Norway, see Lücke (2010). Concerning the cases of Kazakhstan and Azerbaijan the author writes that: "The oil funds in both Kazakhstan and Azerbaijan strengthen presidential control over oil-related revenues to the detriment of parliaments. At the same time, there are no legal provisions that limit the discretionary power of presidents regarding the use of oil revenues" (ibid: 22).

the Olympic Sports Complexes) was impossible to bid for given their local economic and political networks. It was almost always companies based in Baku and often with links to Azerbaijani oligarchs abroad.

5   Crossing the borders and looking at the two states: Contemporary border regimes

The fields of action across the borderlands are complex, as our example of the female petty-traders in Aivazishvili's case above or Ağstafa's small traders at the bazaar have shown. The actors and border-crossers have to develop complex and multiple strategies concerning the border posts on each side of the border. These strategies are sometimes contrary to one another and raise perplex reactions from each side. The Georgian side, especially since Saakashvili's rise to power is seen in the eyes of the Ingiloy as having attained some quality of being the 'educator' and 'civilizer' state, resonating Gramscian notions of control being internalized as civilization. The Georgian state is perceived as operating 'according to a plan' hence urging, inciting, soliciting and punishing (see Gramsci [1971] 2006: 77) when eradicating corruption, hence at the same time, modernizing the state along the Western defined ideals of governmentality and transparency. At the Georgian border post, the officers were, according to Aivazsihvili's experience and also shared by her interlocutors, always factual and serious; they hardly chatted or were informal with anyone. They would weigh the produce in utter silence and indifference, showing no emotions at all; due to their habitus of dispassion and graveness as representatives of the state, some saw the officers as deaf and dumb, as Oktay, one of Aivazishvili's interlocutors, an Ingiloy and a citizen of Georgia, commented to her once.

The Azerbaijani side on the other hand was 'familiar' and the border-crossers found them as 'close' and 'familiar', in all senses. The accompanied luggage was checked outside in front of everyone. Everyone knew how to behave and what to do. The sellers from the Georgian side paid the bribes[106] (stavka) in order to take their produce across the Azerbaijani post. The minibus drivers paid their share[107] in order to be passed through swiftly.[108] As in the case of Leila and Guliko, when they were crossing to Georgia, the Azerbaijani officers asked briefly what they had in their luggage, if beans, walnuts or

---

106   Either 1 AZN or 2 GEL per person. In 2009 one Azerbaijani Manat was worth app. 0.90 EUR and one GEL was worth app. 0.43 EUR.
107   10 AZN or 20 GEL per minibus driver.
108   The driver collected all the passports and went to the border post counter. The passengers received their stamped passports either at the counter or the driver brought them all back and gave each to its owner.

anything else was in their bags this time, joking and laughing with them, as if they were already well-known to the officers. Nothing was weighed. Interestingly enough, even if the Ingiloy villagers talked about the existence of 'more democracy and order in Georgia' compared to Azerbaijan, at the Azerbaijani border the state seemed to be more human and familiar. What the border-crossers mostly resented at the Azerbaijani border was the excessive 'time' they needed to spend there; they would prefer to pay something (bribe) and avoid the official controls, which cost them so much time. The passage of goods across the border meant for many petty-traders simply costing them nerves and strategies, instead of any direct and open exchange and behaviour. To what degree the 'laws of the border were really fair' was a constantly open question for many. The unfairness of the Georgian side, that 'laws' there are inhumanly applied causes discontent among the Ingiloy. They associate their discontent with their own ethnic historical status, and accuse the Georgian (state) with 'treachery', for having left them on their own, for having drawn the border unfairly, leaving the Ingiloy in Azerbaijani territory. Now it is impossible to correct this historical injustice; the border-crossers hence project their frustration on the border officers and soldiers, on their inhumane and agonizing treatment of the petty-traders.[109]

6   Concluding remarks

In this article we have explored the kinds of trade and informal economy which exist in the border regions of Azerbaijan, the borderlands between Azerbaijan and Georgia. In one of the field sites we observed that petty-traders from rural backgrounds are not only dependent on the border trade for their modest economic livelihood, they also assess their border-crossing activities and experiences as the basis for understanding the border regimes, their own and other states around them. They actively take part in shaping the border regimes, even if their influence may be judged as limited. Their ethnic identity often plays a significant role in their judgement of each state which is involved in making laws for border crossing as well as installing the border officials who are seen to be humane or inhumane, depending on one's own access to them.

---

109   Madeleine Reeves (2007a, 2007b) reports about similar negative feelings and associations people have concerning the soldiers at border posts between Uzbekistan, Tajikistan and Kirgizia. She notes that: "The border guards and customs officers who nationally guard the border are often perceived by border villagers less as a guarantor of security than as a threat" (Reeves 2007a: 73).

The second site of field work was in a larger setting, in a small town of West Azerbaijan, where different scales of trade could be observed. Petty-trade here is seen to be the source of livelihood for many, and some border-crossing existed for petty-traders until the change of regime at the border posts to Georgia. Petty-trade could also be seen as the basis for community building in this small town, creating the sociality for women especially, who otherwise would have been excluded from public and economic life in the small town. It could also be interpreted as providing the social basis for developing ideas about economic citizenship and possibilities of economic mobility in post-socialist and economically developing Azerbaijan. The activities of traders provide the analysis with many indicators for the conjuncture between economy and polity in Azerbaijan, suggesting how economic mobility through trade could be alleviated or hindered, be it national or international, depending on economic and political networks and access to them in this western borderland of the country.

References

Anderson, D. G. (1996): "Bringing Civil Society to an Uncivilised Place: Citizenship Regimes in Russia's Arctic Frontier". In: C. Hann and E. Dunn (eds.): Civil Society: Challenging Western Models. London, New York: Routledge, pp. 99-120.

Barth, F. (ed.) (1978): Scale and Social Organization. Oslo, Bergen, Tromsø: Universitetsforlaget.

Berdahl, D. (1999): Where the World Ended: Re-unification and Identity in the German Borderland. Berkely, Los Angeles, London: University of California Press.

Derlugian, G. M. (2005): Bourdieu's Secret Admirer in the Caucasus: A World-System Biography. Chicago, London: The University of Chicago Press.

Glick Schiller, N. / Çağlar, A. (eds.) (2011): Locating Migration: Rescaling cities and migrants. Ithaca: Cornell University Press.

Gramsci, A. ([1971] 2006): Selections from the Prison Notebooks. New York: International Publishers, transl. by Q. Hoare and G. N. Smith; reprinted in: A. Sharma and A. Gupta (eds.): The Anthropology of the State: A Reader. Malden: Blackwell, pp. 71-85.

Grönhaug, R. (1978): "Scale as a Variable in Analysis: Fields in Social Organization in Heart, Northwest Afghanistan". In: F. Barth (ed.): Scale and Social Organization. Oslo, Bergen, Tromsø: Universitetsforlaget, pp. 78-121.

Gudeman, S. (2008): Economy's Tension: The Dialectics of Community and Market. New York, Oxford: Berghahn.

Heyat, F. (2002): "Women and the Culture of Entrepreneurship in Soviet and Post-Soviet Azerbaijan". In: R. Mandel and C. Humphrey (eds.): Markets and Moralities: Ethnographies of Postsocialism. Oxford: Berg, pp. 19–31.

Humphrey, C. (2002): The Unmaking of Soviet Life: Everyday Economies after Socialism. Ithaca, London: Cornell University Press.

Kaneff, D. (2002): "The Shame and Pride of Market Activity: Morality, Identity and Trading in Postsocialist Rural Bulgaria". In: R. Mandel and C. Humphrey (eds.): Markets and Moralities: Ethnographies of Postsocialism. Oxford: Berg, pp. 33–51.

Ledeneva, A. V. (2006): How Russia Really Works: The Informal Practices that Shaped Post-Soviet Politics and Business. Ithaca, London: Cornell University Press.

Lücke, M. (2010): Stabilization and Savings Funds to Manage Natural Resource Revenues: Kazakhstan and Azerbaijan vs. Norway, Kiel Institute for the World Economy (ifw). Kiel Working Papers, No. 1652, October 2010.

Mandel, R., / Humphrey, C. (eds.) (2002): Markets and Moralities: Ethnographies of Postsocialism. Oxford: Berg.

Migdal, J. S. (2004): "Mental Maps and Virtual Checkpoints: Struggles to Construct and Maintain State and Social Boundaries". In: J. S. Migdal (ed.): Boundaries and Belonging: States and Societies in the Struggle to Shape Identities and Local Practices. Cambridge: Cambridge University Press, pp. 3-26.

Mitchell, T. (1999): "Society, Economy, and the State Effect". In: G. Steinmetz (ed.): State/Culture: State-Formation after the Cultural Turn. Ithaca, London: Cornell University Press, pp. 76-97.

Olimpieva, I. / Pachenkov, O. / Ejova, L. / Gordy, E. (2007): Informal Economies of St. Petersburg: Ethnographic Findings on the Cross-Border Trade. Jefferson Institute, URL: http://www.jeffersoninst.org/sites/default/files/Informal%20Economies_0.pdf (last access: 20.06.2010).

Paulson, S. / Gezon, L. L. (eds.) (2005): Political Ecology across Spaces, Scales, and Social Groups. New Brunswick, New Jersey, London: Rutgers University Press.

Pelkmans, M. (2006): Defending the Border: Identity, Religion, and Modernity in the Republic of Georgia. Ithaca, London: Cornell University Press.

Reeves, M. (2007a): "Unstable objects: corpses, checkpoints and 'chessboard borders' in the Ferghana Valley". In: Anthropology of East Europe Review, 25, 1, pp.72-84.

Reeves, M. (2007b): "Travels in the Margins of the State: Everyday Geography in the Ferghana Valley Borderlands". In: J. Sahadeo and R. G. Zanca (eds.): Everyday Life in Central Asia: Past and Present. Bloomington: Indiana University Press, pp.281-300.

RFE/RL – Radio Free Europe/Radio Liberty (2010): Caucasus Report: Data on Azerbaijan's Oil Revenues Incomplete, Inconsistent. 16 April 2010, URL: http://www.rferl.org/content/Data_On_Azerbaijans_Oil_Revenues_Incomplete_Inconsistent/2 015871.html (last access: 20.06.2011).

Torpey, J. (2000): The Invention of the Passport: Surveillance, Citizenship and the State. Cambridge: Cambridge University Press.

Verdery, K. (1998): "Transnationalism, Nationalism, Citizenship, and Property: Eastern Europe since 1989". In: American Ethnologist, 25, 2, pp. 291-306.

Wilson, T. M. / Donnan, H. (1998): "Nation, State and Identity at International Borders". In: T. M. Wilson and H. Donnan (eds.): Border Identities: Nation and State at International Borders. Cambridge: Cambridge University Press, pp. 1-30.

Woodiwiss, A. (2008): "Economic Citizenship: Variations and the Threat of Globalization". In: E. F. Isin and B. S. Turner (eds.): Handbook of Citizenship Studies. Los Angeles, London, New Delhi, Singapore: Sage, pp. 53-68.

Yalçın-Heckmann, L. (2010): The Return of Private Property: Rural Life after Agrarian Reform in the Republic of Azerbaijan. Halle Studies in the Anthropology of Eurasia, vol. 24, Berlin: LIT.

Yalçın-Heckmann, L. (Forthcoming): "Re-thinking Citizenship in the South Caucasus". In: Europe-Asia Studies, Special Issue on the Caucasus, 2011.

Crossing conflicting state boundaries: The Georgian-Abkhazian Ceasefire Line

Andrea Weiss

1 Introduction

In a global perspective state borders are very often contested, remain contested or at least are not demarcated and unfixed by bi- or multinational treaties for decades. However, of particular rigour in this respect are ceasefire lines, which so far have been under-researched, if not unresearched, especially as a particular type of border. As ceasefire lines are the result of interstate or secessionist conflicts, for the most part other international or third states have been involved either in the settlement of these conflicts or are even an integral part of the ceasefire line (CFL) management, sometimes in the form of a de-militarized zone. As Dan Rabinowitz and Sliman Khawalde (2000) have outlined, suspicion is part of the everyday life regime in a de-militarized zone, which is certainly the case for the Georgian-Abkhazian CFL. States and their agents pay particular attention to movement and residents in these zones with a priori sceptical attitude, and very often see their own citizens as aliens. Border-crossers or residents of these zones arouse constant suspicion of disloyalty or even treason in their everyday life. Even more, the irony of de-militarized zones is very often that they are in turn located in a highly militarized environment, very often with and under the surveillance of third parties.

This article addresses the issue of resourcing borderlands in an area of halted armed conflict, with a special emphasis on permeability and notions of licitness. The underlying understanding departs from a borderland perspective, but takes into account that my research is based on research on the Georgian side of the CFL, so to speak the current periphery of Georgia proper[110]. As the material is based on ethnographic research, the article will for the most part be empirical and carry out a micro-level analysis. The article pursues the following question: How does differential permeability impact on how people resource on the Geo-Abkhaz Ceasefire Line? I want to look in more detail at the kind of narratives that come with the resourcing, which also includes the contested legal

---

110 'Georgia proper' is used predominantly in diplomatic language to distinguish between the Georgian claim to its entire Soviet territory and to denominate the territory which the Georgian government de-facto governs (excluding Abkhazia and South Ossetia).

framework. Further, I focus on permeability differentials and on how these differentials impact on resourcing. The underlying theoretical problem deals with the differential permeability and the contested terrain of legality and illegality at a ceasefire line.

Nugent (2002) as well as Feyissa and Hoehne (2008) have outlined that 'borderlanders' (see Feyissa/Hoehne 2008: 6) are not only the victims of state borders and the respective states, but they also face obstacles they might eventually turn to their advantage. Particularly Feyissa and Hoehne (2008) argue that prior social science contributions on borders have neglected the perspective of opportunities and emphasized the obstacle perspective. Although I agree with Feyissa and Hoehne (2008), such a view seems to be an obvious choice, as narratives such as 'to be the victim of state policies' and 'the need to overcome multiple obstacles' correspond to the narratives of 'borderlanders'. These narratives frame and represent the experience of 'borderlanders'. Very often the narratives can be of a conflicting nature, but not only: for instance official narratives used by state agencies might go against other narratives that portray daily life at the border as a struggle. The Georgian-Abkhazian CFL is a case in point where such conflicting narratives are likely to coexist. Nevertheless, even in a state of halted (sometimes called 'frozen') conflict, where narratives of loss and deprivation flourish, people sometimes succeed in resourcing on borders.

Nevertheless, some people are more successful in resourcing on borders than others. I argue that examining the differential permeability of a border brings more insights than talking about soft and hard borders. In looking at the resourcing from a permeability perspective, I partly draw on Feyissa and Hoehne (2008), but also on Reeves (2007). Their approach looks at the border not just as a line in the sand, but as a borderland area with specific and often contradictory normative frameworks on either side. Permeability takes the borderland perspective into account, which according to Donnan and Wilson (1999) has been a concern in border studies at least since the 1990s. The borderland perspective criticizes and amends the common view, which regards borders and the adjacent territories as a state's periphery (as opposed to see these peripheries as a space in itself) and thereby contributes to a state-centrist discourse (see Brenner 2003).[111] For the most part permeability is mentioned in the literature as a term that little analytic attention is paid to (for instance Donnan/Wilson 1999). From Madeleine Reeves (2007: 111) I borrowed the term 'differential permeability' to point to the differentials and selectivity of permeability. By deploying the term 'differential permeability' I want to point to and name the

---

111   State-centrism is a critique that has been mostly brought forward by post-colonial political geography (see Brenner 2003). State-centrism denominates the perspective whereby the nation-state is taken as the unquestioned research and container unit of social science research.

fact that in the everyday life of 'borderlands' different categories of people have different opportunities to cross borders and consequently can also resource on borders to different degrees, as I show below. As borders very often entail quite informal proceedings and procedures, potentials for resourcing also depend for instance on the possibility of activating resources such as personal relations.

Differential permeability is not the only characteristic of 'borderlands'. As Willem van Schendel and Itty Abraham (2005) have outlined, a multiplicity of very often contradictory laws and social norms proliferate in border areas. Therefore they rightly question the notions of legality and illegality and introduce the term 'licit', which in their terminology refers to actions that are illegal from the standpoint of law, but deemed legitimate by the population through informal norms. A CFL has an open (armed) conflict in the background and therefore is even more likely to be a normatively loaded space. Particularly in the case of a CFL probability runs high that state policies of the two adjacent states will rather contradict each other than concur. At the same time 'borderlanders' will look for and find ways to accommodate contradictory narratives and practices.

Feyissa and Hoehne (2008) have outlined multiple ways of resourcing on borders; even though they have pointed out that resourcing opportunities depend on the way these are appropriated and used, they have not pointed out the differentials that exist also in terms of permeability. Different categories of persons cross easier than others, which creates additional differences in terms of resourcing potential. My emphasis will be on these permeability differentials.

2   Methodology

Borders are sensitive areas for nation states, almost any movement in the vicinity of a CFL is of potential interest to the adjacent states. Given this situation research activity is considerably more difficult. I conducted a large part of the research for this article in 2007 when my physical presence at the border was certainly noted, but less problematic than after the 'Georgian-Russian war' in August 2008. Such an arena of suspicion as a borderland, and even more the borderland of a CFL, creates unfortunate conditions for research. Ethical difficulties have been mentioned elsewhere, particularly in anthropology a large body of literature on the ethics of research and its dilemmas exists (see Nordstrom/Robben 1995). The promise to gain knowledge does not justify endangering the well-being of interview partners, therefore everyday research in such border areas becomes a constant effort to balance, it seems that in spaces where the border is more immanent, border-crossers are under more pressure, so that they are less likely to talk about their crossing in the immanence of the border. My research included a combination of observation on the border and since 2008 it has rather been based upon getting in touch with border-crossers on the Georgian side of the border. On the one hand, my interview partners were comprised of acquaintances and relatives of my friends and people I worked with in Zugdidi[112], where I lived during my fieldwork and the main town close to the Georgian-Abkhazian CFL. Some of them themselves were refugees from Abkhazia. On the other hand, I also randomly interviewed people who crossed the CFL, some of them quite often. The first group of people I interviewed mostly at the homes of my friends, where the crossers were guests; and the second group I interviewed in what Marc Augé (1995) would have called 'non-places', where they were in transit and waiting for movement, particularly on the Tbilisi-Zugdidi night train. This train offers convenient travel hours, affordability and a discount based on internally displaced persons (IDP) benefits. In this atmosphere of certain anonymity and un-traceability some of them offered quite insightful short spontaneous accounts of their lives, problems and border-crossing strategies. Apart from a combination of these two different groups and the fact that I interviewed them outside the tensest zones, the method I used involved informal conversations rather than structured interviews. While regarding content they all related to the crossing experience, the related obstacles and opportunities, I realized that a more formalized form of interviewing made my interview partners less at ease.[113] This approach, to create a less formal interview setting, in combination with an open statement that I (among other things) am researching the border and the movement across it, proved to be the most useful approach in my setting.

3   The Georgian-Abkhazian Conflict and the Emergence of a New Border Zone

The ceasefire line (CFL) between Abkhazia and Georgia (proper) is not only a peculiar state boundary, but also a quite recent border (in this paper I use border and state boundary interchangeably). Since the secessionist conflict between Abkhazia and Georgia in 1992/93 and a subsequent ceasefire agreement concluded in 1994, the cease fire line has turned into a de-facto border. From an

---

112   Zugdidi is the capital of the province Samegrelo-Zemo Svaneti. It is also the main town of the historical region of Mingrelia – as Samegrelo is called in English.

113   Bernard 2005 refers to informal interviews as the kind of informal conversations anthropologists usually start an extensive period of fieldwork with, but also 'hanging out' with people who are involved in some sort of 'illegal' or 'illicit' activities, sometimes only involves informal interviews.

Abkhazian perspective the CFL constitutes its Eastern state border, much more so after the recognition of its sovereignty by Russia, Nicaragua, Venezuela and more recently Nauru, in the course of or after the armed conflict in August 2008.[114] The history of this potential territorial fragmentation at least goes back to Soviet times, when Abkhazia formed an Autonomous Socialist Soviet Republic (ASSR) within the Georgian SSR. The precarious majority-minority demographic relations of the late Soviet Union were reflected in the 1989 Soviet census, after major demographic shifts and policy shifts throughout the 20th century. In this census the Abkhaz only accounted for less than 20% of the overall population of Abkhazia, whereas Georgians accounted for almost half thereof, with Armenians and Russians having the third and fourth biggest shares.115

While from an Abkhazian perspective the recognition of its independence by Russia officially sanctified the current situation, from an official Georgian perspective the CFL is only an administrative boundary. However Georgia legally closed the northern border to Russia on the Psou river (which is no longer under the control of Georgia proper, but under Abkhazian control); according to this logic a controlling point was established at the main crossing, the Enguri bridge. After a brief period of occupation by Russian forces well into Georgia proper during the 2008 armed conflict, the Russian forces retreated back to the "status quo ante", behind the former CFL to Abkhazia (except for the Kodori Valley in the mountainous upper Abkhazia, which Georgia did not recover).

As a result of the Georgian-Abkhazian conflict the largest part of the pre-war Georgian population of Abkhazia has been driven out. Apart from single individuals, mostly in mixed marriages, the only remaining Georgians in Abkhazia live in the Gali district, which is the district that borders with the adjacent Georgian region of Mingrelia. In fact, the population of Gali and Mingrelia possess a strong regional identity, fostered by a distinct language - Mingrelian. While being Mingrelian does not pose any loyalty conflict to their Georgian identity for Mingrelians living in Georgia, two facts prevent this

---

114   See http://www.ng.ru/cis/2009-12-16/7_abhazia.html (last access: 23.02.2011).
115   Certainly historiography itself has played a crucial role in the conflict, particularly in the sense that already during Soviet times, well in the 1950s, particular historiographies laid claims on a particular interpretation of history, and subsequently on the claim to the 'historical right' to this territory (in ethnic terms). Similar to national historiographies two – when confronted - mutually exclusive categories of international law – the right to self-determination and the right to territorial integrity – have played a similar role. The argument regarding statehood and international law at least goes back to the question whether the Abkhazian and the Georgian territories were annexed by the Soviet Union with an equal – the Abkhazian take – or whether the Abkhazian had a subordinate status, which is the Georgian take on it; changes in status within the Soviet ethno-federal system of both entities does not contribute to clarity. For more on the historical dimension of the Georgian-Abkhazian conflict see for instance Gerber 1997.

automatically applying to the Gali population.[116] First, it has to be noted that Mingrelians, who were educated in Russian schools in Abkhazia, do not necessarily master Georgian, but some rely on Russian as their first language of literacy and Mingrelian as their colloquial mother tongue. Secondly, the Abkhazian government, apparently with little success, has undertaken attempts to foster the Mingrelian identity not as a regional identity, but as a national identity distinct from a Georgian one. The residence of Mingrelians in the Gali district is anchored in the 1994 ceasefire agreement, officially as the first step in the future repatriation of internally displaced persons to Abkhazia; further steps have never been taken. In practice the Gali district had already been exclusively populated by Mingrelians by the end of the Soviet Union.[117] According to estimates roughly 45,000 Georgians lived in Abkhazia in 2003.[118] This population segment is, according to the regulations, only comprised of Mingrelians who were officially registered as residents of the Gali district before the war in Abkhazia in 1992/93.

The CFL, for the most part, is nicely delineated by geography; it runs in the riverbed of the Enguri river, which comes from the Caucasus mountain range and flows into the Black Sea. The geographical outlays of the border pose a natural impediment to crossing, as the river for the most part of the year cannot be crossed without some support, be it a (pedestrian) bridge or a vehicle such as a tractor. Apart from the Enguri bridge, several smaller bridges over the Enguri and the dam of the Enguri power plant serve as crossing points. The water level plays a decisive role for crossing opportunities. For three months during winter the river bed almost runs dry as most water is withheld and channelled for electricity production purposes. During the other months of the year the constant search for and later abandonment of passages across the river is an ongoing business. These physical-geographical conditions frame and shape the passage of people and often require a creative and flexible approach on how to transit. This knowledge of potential crossing opportunities is crucial for the residents of the Gali region, some of whom often cross into Georgia proper mostly to purchase goods that are more expensive or unavailable in Abkhazia or to make use of public services, for instance health care or IDP subsidies.

The emergence of a ceasefire line in the form of a border regime was not the only factor that hit the economy in Mingrelia hard; the collapse of the Soviet

---

116   Throughout this article I use rather Georgian than Mingrelian, which they are, too, except for situations when their particular regional identity is in focus.

117   I have to note that the administrative boundaries of the Gali district has been changed by the Abkhazian government – the Soviet Gali district was divided into the Tkvarcheli district and the Gali district, with all Abkhaz now living in the Tkvarcheli district.

118   See http://www.ethno-kavkaz.narod.ru/rnabkhazia.html (last access: 23.02.2011).

Union and the subsequent deep economic changes away from the command economy, aggravated by the Georgian civil war, also had an effect. The region's (Mingrelia and Gali's) economy relied heavily on sub-tropical agrarian produce that was exported to other parts of the Soviet Union – either by plane or mostly via the land route crossing from Abkhazia into Russia. This export of citruses was not only embedded into the planned economy, but very often a private endeavour and as such formed one of the main mechanisms of wealth accumulation. The above-mentioned chain of events had a heavy impact on the region's economy. The region lost its privileged position in the market, particularly in Russia, as citruses from outside the Soviet Union could now be imported into the former Soviet Union (in large quantities). Roughly at the same time the closure of this route for easy transit, due to civil war, but even more due to the Georgian-Abkhaz war, altered trade and the whole production – and subsequently, had an important impact on impoverishment.

De-militarized zones are clearly instigated with fear and suspicion (see Khawalde/Rabinowitz 2005). In the case of the Georgian-Abkhazian conflict we are dealing with a former de-militarized zone (between 1994 and 2008) that again became a hotspot in August 2008. Apart from the CIS peace-keeping mission, which manned the CFL with up to 2,500 soldiers and had posts at various spots on both sides of the CFL (see Lynch 1998), the UNOMIG (Unites Nations Observer Mission in Georgia) was present in Zugdidi and Gali and patrolled on both sides of the CFL.[119] The CIS peace-keeping mission, although nominally organized by all CIS countries, was in practice exclusively made of soldiers from the Russian Federation. The UNOMIG's mandate expired in 2009 and was not renewed, mainly due to the opposition by the Russian Federation. The EUMM (European Union Monitoring Mission in Georgia), which was seconded by European Union member states, has a more restricted mandate than the UNOMIG had, but has in practice partly replaced some of the tasks the UNOMIG previously performed. Many narratives among the population portray the presence of the internationals as a presence that either brings corruption or at least show that the officials of the international organisations drain off or even embezzle resources that are destined for the local population. Despite these narratives resourcing on their presence is equally an option. This option is however less present in the narratives about these forces.

---

119   The UNOMIG was a pure monitoring mission with no peace-keeping functions, but it also performed many humanitarian and development tasks in the region mainly as a donor organisation.

4 Smuggling and Earning a Living: Legal and Licit Categories

Borders are zones where the legal and the illegal are contested (see van Schendel 2005). As outlined earlier, due to the Georgian-Abkhazian conflict, this statement counts even more so for the nature of a secessionist state or quasi-state (see Jackson 1990) – where legal and illegal categories are even more blurred. Although the CFL is only an administrative boundary for the Georgian administration, from the Georgian central perspective and perception (meaning the administrative units located in the capital Tbilisi) this administrative boundary serves to isolate Georgia from the danger that the uncontrolled flow of products, or even worse dangerous items, such as weapons poses. Particularly the aspect of being uncontrolled (by Georgia) serves to give Abkhazia the touch of being an 'outlaw territory'. While from a Georgian legal perspective the CFL remains a purely administrative boundary, the border crossing at the Psou river, which separates Abkhazia and Russia, is officially closed. According to the Georgian legal point of view this entails that anybody with or without goods crossing the Psou border can be prosecuted and punished for the violation of the Georgian border regime. The Georgian perspective entails that all goods brought into Abkhazia via the Psou are branded as contraband. At the same time this border crossing is frequently used not only by residents of de-facto Abkhazia, but sometimes also for transit from Russia into Georgia proper. From the perspective of de-facto Abkhazia and also from the Russian one (at least since the recognition of Abkhazia's independence) the closure of the Psou border is a mere farce, as it is purely Georgia's proclamation. Even more, for Abkhazia the Psou border is the main entrance point for imports (see Kukhianidze et al. 2003; Weiss 2007).

As a logical consequence of the Georgian-Abkhazian antagonistic relationship and the different conceptualization of legal and illegal there is very little cooperation on a national and inter-state level. In fact, the Enguri hydro power plant complex is the only working inter-governmental cooperation between Georgia and Abkhazia.[120] The electricity generated is distributed among the two parties, 60 percent go to Georgia and 40 to Abkhazia.[121] The vehicles of the Enguri power plant, which have a special permit to cross the Enguri bridge

---

120 The dam of the power plant complex is located on Georgian territory, while the generator to produce electricity is situated on the Abkhaz territory (see Garb 2001). The operation of the plant resumed operation shortly after the war and mainly the EBDR (European Bank for Development and Reconstruction) financed rehabilitation work. While the ownership of the plant lies in the hand of a Russian company, the main employees of the power plant are local Georgians who reside on both sides of the CFL, depending on their place of work respectively.

121 See http://www.eurasianet.org/departments/insightb/articles/eav011609e.shtml (last access: 23.02.2011).

officially, can frequently be seen with Abkhazian number plates in Zugdidi. However they are not the only vehicles with Abkhazian number plates in Zugdidi. In practice an administration preoccupied with sovereignty and the subtleties of international law tolerates the trappings of a country whose sovereignty it heavily denies. The pragmatics of border micro-management triumph over the principles and vehicles with Abkhazian number plates can be seen so frequently in Zugdidi and other areas close to the CFL that none of the local residents expressed any surprise.

For Georgia smuggling, particularly of (Russian) cigarettes, and the alleged transit of 'illegal' goods such as drugs, weapons and radioactive material (see Kukhianidze/Kupatadze/Gotsiridze 2004) have been and remain an important issue. Particularly before 2005, Abkhazia was portrayed as a stronghold for the transit of 'illegal' goods. I would like to refer to two products, which definitely cross the CFL, each in the other direction, and their implications for the wider context: cigarettes and hazelnuts. Apart from cigarettes, clothes and food products are also traded: clothes are bought almost exclusively in Georgia, to be marketed further in Abkhazia, whereas the trade of food products depends on the prices, which can affect and change the flow direction for single goods, even though they mostly flow to, and not from, Abkhazia.

Cigarettes are still a widespread good that flows from Abkhazia into Georgia. These cigarettes – either produced directly in Russia or allegedly only the boxes, which are then filled in Abkhazia with cigarettes produced there – have an Abkhazian excise stamp on the cellophane wrapper. Despite the fact that in most other parts of Georgia Russian cigarettes, which are imported without paying tax, have virtually disappeared, in Zugdidi and the surrounding area, they are probably bought more often than the Georgian ones, which could be observed by the public on the sales stalls around town. Even the residues of the 'smuggled' cigarettes can be traced in many places – in the form of plastic wrappings with Abkhaz excise stamps on it, which were thrown on the ground wherever the buyer walked by. These cigarettes are mainly brought from the Gali district to Zugdidi in the company of just a few other packets of cigarettes, transported and carried by women, who take part in pre-arranged chains of distribution. These very often seem to be elderly women, who can cross the CFL with more ease than men.

Hazelnuts, next to citruses, have been virtually the only crop grown in Mingrelia and the Gali district in the latter part of the last decade, which is and are exported abroad in large quantities. Particularly during their harvest season, political tensions rise. Hazelnuts are virtually the only cash crop in the Gali district; they are kept and stored for months instead of money. Taxes are also collected in hazelnuts by the Abkhazian de-facto authorities (see Champain et al.

2004: 127). Different numbers are spread around, but amounts of ten per cent of the entire foreseen harvest being a realistic proportion mentioned by several interview partners. Best quality hazelnuts of the area are grown in the lower part (closer to the seaside) of the Gali district. The market in Zugdidi was the centre of commerce where people delivered their harvest to. Before the Rose Revolution[122] local power structures procured the delivery to the local market in Zugdidi. A special bus terminal with doors was constructed and bus drivers were 'instructed' not to stop on their way to the terminal. Upon arrival there the harvest had to be sold to the bus terminal owner at a fixed price, unless the owners of the harvest wanted to and could invest money and effort to carry the heavy bags somewhere else in town. After the Rose Revolution a new hazelnut processing factory was built in Gali. Now the Abkhazian government has exerted pressure, particularly on the population of Lower Gali, to deliver their produce to the hazelnut processing factory in the town of Gali. Due to the importance of the hazelnut harvest especially for the Gali population, and to a lesser extent for the population of Mingrelia, the hazelnut harvest season is a time of particular tension. Gali residents try to get a good price for their harvest and at the same time they try to leave the exact amount of their harvest unclear to Abkhazian de-facto authorities. In Georgia proper the delivery of Gali hazelnuts to Zugdidi is deemed important not only for economic, but also for political reasons.

While the existence of differing categories and notions of legality and illegality are a common phenomenon of most borders, even more so of the disputed ones, particularly CFLs seem to be more prone to an even wider gap in terms of different legalities on both sides. As in CFLs either the border itself, its location or even the very existence of the other state is deemed illegitimate at least by one of the two involved parties. In fact, the way notions of legality and illegality are constructed and executed form part of the very way and nature how a (formerly) violent conflict is prolonged. The importance of these notions of legality and illegality is manifested for instance in the constant efforts to use legal categories in order to justify one's own pretensions. While Georgia deploys the right for territorial integrity in international law to accommodate its claims, Abkhazia does the same with the right for self-determination.

Still different from the gap between the legal and illegal, there is a broad variety of moral categories lived at the border. While the narratives both states deploy in and through their policies, the populations contest not only the 'other' state, but also their own. These moral categories, such as for instance to deploy narratives of poverty along with narratives of corruption, allow people to frame

---

122   The events in November 2003 that led to the peaceful resignation of the then Georgian president Edward Shevardnadze and subsequent demonstrative 'reform' politics by following president Mikhail Saakashvili have received the name 'Rose Revolution'.

their stories and actions in a flexible and situational way. As van Schendel (2005) points out illegal activities might very often be perceived as legitimate. He calls these illegal activities that are deemed legitimate 'licit'. On the other extreme legal actions might not always be perceived as illegimate, and can be called illicit. At a CFL these differences between (il)legality and morality force actors to manoeuvre between different categories of (il)legality and licitness as they overlap or digress. However, sometimes the different special qualities and distribution of (il)legality and licitness facilitate opportunities for manoeuvring. For instance the Abkhazian de-facto state does not care about the export of cigarettes from its territory into Georgia (proper), yet is not necessarily at ease with the constant flow of the Gali population to and from Georgia. This unease is mirrored in the attempt to obstruct movement of the Gali population to Zugdidi, for instance by not allowing the circulation of direct buses from villages in the lower (Southern) zone of Gali to Zugdidi. While the Georgian government is rather positive about the movement of the Gali population into Georgia proper (and back), the fact that cigarettes are imported without paying taxes and via the 'closed' Psou border is problematic and fought with (sometimes draconian) measures of punishment. Border-crossers in their everyday life movements have to manoeuvre around these two conflicting frameworks.

Smuggling is one of the activities that the state regards and sanctions as a crime. At the same time smuggling and trade with smuggled goods is well accepted as a means of survival among the region's population and therefore seen as perfectly licit. Yet another dimension why smuggling is regarded as perfectly licit might be the fact that the very CFL is not a border in the eyes of the borderland population, as this delineation was of minor administrative importance and never involved any limitation of movement. The closure of the Psou border with Russia is a rather abstract notion and this border today is a far away and unreachable space at least for the population in Mingrelia. The cigarettes that cross this boundary are brought into Georgia by others than the ones who then carry them to Georgia proper. Due to this task division the customs evasion as an illegal act becomes still more abstract to the ones who transport the cigarettes into Georgia proper. However, the main objective – in the sense of being objected – is the fact that in everyday life the struggle for economic survival and well-being weighs more in deeds than abstract principles of territorial integrity and sanction politics.

Even though the terminology of 'contraband' as a denomination for the cigarettes and other goods transported across the CFL into Georgia proper is widely accepted and used in everyday conversations, the narratives of crossing are constructed using rather neutral terminology: for the simple fact of crossing the Georgian word '*gadasvla*' is used, which means only to cross (or literally go over), while for any payments made in order to facilitate the crossing the word *'pasi'*, in English simply price, is applied. The word price, which is very neutral as to the direction this money flows, be it into private pockets or the state budget, means neither bribe nor tax. While the terminology displays a seemingly indifference in terms of what happens to the money after it leaves one's private pocket, it reflects very much a daily reality – even if this money would end up in some state budget – there would be no tangible benefit on the ground for the individual.

The simple expression of price also shows that something else is important – namely what is the price to cross – whoever benefits from the money is less important; in other words a stress on differential quality of permeability is made. In June 2007 upon my first visit on my own at the Enguri bridge crossing, I was 'welcomed' after about five minutes by two 'border guards' in plain clothes, who upon a short inquiry about my goals were 'eager' to show me (a certain take on) the procedures and their smoothness of their border. I paid particular attention to the passing vehicles, which were only very few: Two vehicles from the power plant, a Georgian ambulance, and two private cars. In each of the cases I inquired into their status, why particular vehicles could pass the bridge and what kind of papers they needed to do so. In the case of the first private car, I got the answer that the owner had obtained permission, after further questions about where he obtained the permission from, the answers became very vague and evasive. In the second case, an older European medium-sized Opel manned by a middle aged man, I became more insisting and inquired, not only where the owner had obtained 'permission' from, but also how they knew he had a permit, because no papers were shown or handed over. As an answer I received a smile of the kind I would also get on numerous other occasions when pressing for answers about formal ways where there were mainly pragmatic ones, be it with or without the exchange of money. The smile indicated to me a certain degree of complicity that people were aware that I knew that procedures in this situation were highly flexible and informal, but also that I did not know what exactly was going on.

While this section has outlined that in the case of the Georgian-Abkhazian CFL, (il)legality and (il)licitness entail spaces to be manoeuvred in and in which actors sometimes find creative potential to resource on, differential permeability is also an issue that ranks high and will be addressed in the next sub-chapter.

5   Differential Permeability

Citizenship and the fact which passport a person holds, have been discussed particularly in literature about migration (see Wimmer/Glick Schiller 2002;

Jansen 2009) as facilitators or obstacles of border crossing (or in other words permeability). Nevertheless, in the case dealt with here I want to draw attention to the 'informal', less obvious and less addressed part of differential permeability. Feyissa and Hoehne (2008: 6) for instance point to the 'arbitrariness' of border permeability, however, arbitrariness – as opposed to selectivity – does not go far enough into the patterns behind the 'arbitrariness'. Even though the contingency element has to be reckoned, the border crossing criteria are not necessarily arbitrary, but based on differentials and selectivity. Differences made between different categories of people, which are not obvious at first sight and still less transparent. In other words, in the arbitrariness or differential permeability there are patterns which can be researched and exposed. These patterns should be analysed to gain insights into how far borders pose obstacles and above all – to whom. In order to understand these permeability differentials – and ultimately to comprehend border resourcing better – I turn next to the importance and meaning of documents, age, gender, money, personal relations and networks. Particularly, I want to draw attention to how permeability elements, which facilitate or hinder crossing, are turned to one's own advantage.

The specific importance of documents I outline in this section is not necessarily a phenomenon tied to the Georgian-Abkhazian conflict, as is the importance of 'national' – read 'ethnic' – classifications.[123] The Soviet federal system was comprised of SSRs, some of which also included national entities, such as autonomous republics (ASSR) or autonomous regions (AO), belonging (often but not always) to a national group. Where-ever these national groups were institutionalized in a territorial way, this institutionalisation also included access to certain economic privileges. Among those privileges was above all the opportunity to obtain a job based on one's nationality, because some jobs were distributed according to a quota system privileging the nationality the autonomous entity 'belonged' to. The nationality, as distinct and specific from Soviet citizenship, was also fixed in people's passports (see Martin 2001; Hirsch 2005). While these economic privileges were non-existent through long periods of the Soviet era, and sometimes even to the contrary; to be Abkhaz offered access to the above-mentioned economic advantage at least since the 1970s.

Tamuna, who grew up in Sokhumi, vividly described in a conversation how once during Soviet times she had to get a new passport, but was given an 'Abkhaz' one, meaning a Soviet passport with 'Abkhaz' as the nationality entry. This incident happened in the late 1970s, early 1980s when Tamuna was still a young, unmarried woman. Tamuna routinely obtained a new passport, because her old one had expired. When she opened the passport, she realized that

---

123   I use the term 'national' here in a way the meaning is used in post-Soviet countries to denote affiliation to a recognized ethnic entity.

'Abkhaz', instead of 'Georgian', was entered in the nationality section of her passport. According to Tamuna the registry office had simply committed an error. When Tamuna returned home and told her mother about the error, her mother went crazy (*'gagizhda'*). Her mother argued that all Tamuna's siblings were registered as Georgians and that it would be improper and cannot be (*'ar sheidzleba'*) that she was Abkhaz in her papers. The error did not happen out of the blue, but was quite comprehensible. Tamuna's surname was originally etymologically an Abkhaz name, which had been Mingrelized by adding an '-ia' ending. Her forefathers a few generations back were forcefully resettled to a Mingrelian populated area in the 19th century. However, this surname, even in its Mingrelianized form, was ambiguous enough, because some bearers of this surname lived with the nationality label 'Abkhaz' in their passport, while others had an entry as Georgians.

While this error apparently shocked her mother, Tamuna was less preoccupied for yet another reason. On her father's side Tamuna had an Abkhaz grandparent, to whom she was very close in her childhood. So she did not object to the entry as fiercely as her mother did. However upon her mother's insistence she changed her passport back to a Georgian one. Nevertheless Tamuna seemed slightly sad that she changed her passport, as it could have changed her life during the war and also eased the passage to Abkhazia. While she repeated the words of her mother, that it would be improper (*'ar sheidzleba'*[124]), she smiled. Having talked to her on other occasions about her ancestry, her smile expressed a mixture of things to me. Probably the smile indicated to a lesser extent the missed opportunity, but rather more the experience and unspoken belief that documents were in many instances less a marker of identification than an indicator of political circumstances; and also that documents could serve to achieve goals.

While the possession of such a passport would be of great value in Tamuna's situation today, her situation highlights some features that also reflect the contemporary value of documents and reflects the often pragmatic ways in which documents, be they Soviet, Russian, Abkhaz or Georgian passports, are dealt with[125]. In Tamuna's case her ethnic affiliation also depends on contingency and on choice, as opposed to natural(ized) belonging. Some roots of the current multitude in documents and perception lie with Soviet passport politics, as I will outline in Lela's case.

Lela, whom I met on a night train to Tbilisi, was originally from Sokhumi, but fled during the war and settled in the Ukraine a little later in the early 1990s.

---

124   Literally one cannot and should not.
125   See also F. Mühlfried (2010): "Citizenship at war: Passports and nationality in the 2008 Russian-Georgian conflict". In: Anthropology Today, 26, 2, pp. 8–13.

She lived in the Ukraine, but occasionally returned for summer holidays and stayed with relatives in the Gali region. During a summer holiday in Gali in the mid 2000s her daughter was bride-kidnapped (*caartves*) and therefore she and her son moved back to Abkhazia.[126] However as they could not go to Sokhumi, and she wanted to stay close to her daughter, they settled in Gali. She tried to not cross the CFL too often, and if she considered it necessary to do so (for her small-scale trading business, mainly in clothes) she avoided the official crossing at the bridge. Then she used unofficial ways to cross, which were for the most part downstream of the Enguri bridge or 'paid money'. She still possessed an old Soviet passport. Even though the Soviet Union had long disappeared and the passports had expired, many people like Lela still had to rely on the Soviet passport as their only means of identification. Due to the lack of other documents, particularly documents accepted by both Georgian and Abkhazian border guards, in practice border crossing was possible with the Soviet passport. However, the Soviet passport also revealed a detail that was not so convenient to be apparent to border guards: the place of registry prior to the demise of the Soviet Union and the war in Abkhazia. Therefore Lela avoided using it at the border control. "I am afraid" she said "that they will take it away". As she had Sokhumi as her place of residence in the Soviet passport, she was officially not allowed to cross into Abkhazia and feared for the loss of her precious document.[127] However, as she did not have a Gali registration, she had so far been unable to arrange for an Abkhazian identity document.

Similar to Lela, many IDPs from the Gali region still cross back into Abkhazia with their old Soviet documents. At the same time they possess Georgian documents in order to come frequently into Georgian territory and pick up their IDP allowance or make use of medical care facilities. These IDPs sometimes might leave their Georgian documents with relatives or friends on Georgian territory. Lela's story illustrates two patterns: the multiplicity of documents used and the value of certain documents on the one hand, and the unconventional patterns of movement and migration many IDPs follow on the

---

126 'Bride kidnapping' or 'marriage by abduction' has a historical tradition in many parts of the Caucasus. The future groom and/or his friends or relatives abduct the bride and hide her from her parents at least for one night, for the social assumption then is that she has lost her virginity and should stay with her new husband. While the current practice is multi-faceted – depending on whether the abduction takes place with or without the bride's consent (for instance in case of the non-consent of the bride's parents this can be a feasible way for the couple to enforce marriage) – the abduction is punishable by law (information drawn from personal communications).

127 According to the 1994 ceasefire agreement only residents of the Gali region (who were registered there as residents before the war) are allowed to enter Abkhazia, those Georgians who lived and were registered in other parts of Abkhazia are not.

other. These two patterns lie at the heart of the differential permeability that characterizes the Georgian-Abkhazian CFL. IDPs, some of whom rather move back- and forwards from Gali to Georgia proper than stay in one place, necessarily possess Georgian documents. Parallel to their Georgian papers they hold other documents: old Soviet passports and/or Abkhazian documents, which are called passports, and they might also be in the possession of a Russian passport.

However, there is an important aspect, which is not as obvious in Lela's story, but still plays a role: gender. In comparison to men of her age Lela can move relatively easily. Georgian men from the Gali district potentially run into more difficulties, as do young men or boys who approach the majority age. Men of Lela's age would be scrutinised by the Abkhaz for having potentially fought in the 1992/93 war or for having been involved in guerrilla activities in the Gali district. Generally, more respect is paid to elderly people in Abkhazia and Georgia, for example elderly women are more likely to cross the CFL without problems.

Furthermore, differential permeability might not only depend on the kind of documents one is able to produce, but also on money or ties to other people that one is able to produce and demonstrate. Money is only one currency among various 'currencies' to ensure the crossing, next to documents (the weakest) or some sort of knowledge/information (about where to cross). Particularly as the CFL was announced to be closed very often, the prices in hard currency rose. It is also remarkable that the term people used in conversations to refer to crossing of the CFL, no matter in which way, was the simple and neutral term 'to cross' (be it related to the river or to the newly established boundary is hard to tell). Also the reference to the money that had to be given in order to cross with goods or when the border was 'closed', was simply 'price', as I have already outlined. However, price is not necessarily the only crossing facilitator, but might be substituted by relations, as I will outline with Tina's funeral attendance in Abkhazia.

Tina is from Sokhumi, Abkhazia, and lived with her husband and children in Zugdidi. She is in her 50s and had a well paid job in Abkhazia. Tina's mother and other members of her family of origin have continued to live in the Gali district throughout the conflict. As Tina has escaped death by chance several times during the war, she is afraid of trips to Abkhazia. When one of her close relatives in the Gali district died, she decided to attend the funeral, as funerals are of particular importance for social life among Mingrelians. To pay respect to a dead person and his/her living family is of crucial importance in order to maintain social bonds. Misha, a cousin of Tina's in the Gali region, a very close relative to the deceased, made an arrangement for her and other relatives, who are IDPs from Sokhumi. Without problems and any checking of documents they passed and were picked up by car by a friend of Misha's. The same procedure happened on the way back. She explained to me that the following arrangement was behind this easy transit into Abkhazia: Misha underwent his whole education in the Russian sector of Sokhumi University, where he had befriended many Abkhaz. As one of his university colleagues was an Abkhazian minister, this minister guaranteed for the whole entourage Misha had brought to the funeral and facilitated an easy entry. As Tina formulated it, she crossed into Abkhazia for free (*upasod*). Tina explained that Misha's friend was a respectful man (*pativiscemuli katsi*) and that he in turn paid respect to Misha.

Differential permeability depends at least on two persons involved in crossing: the border-crosser and the border guard. The factors involved are the status of a certain person and his or her relationship to a particular person with influence on the one hand; and the decision-making status this particular person with influence or border guard has on the other. However, mostly protection and intervention from a higher level figure less prominently in everyday movements across the CFL, but rather the relationship to a particular border guard or group of border guards. This relationship is usually rather one based on friendship, kinship or neighbourhood ties. When we consider the analytical tool Feyissa and Hoehne (2008) offer us with their resourcing on borders, we should always have in mind that the permeability differentials are more than worth paying attention to.

6   Conclusion

Borders can be seen as resources, but these are in most cases neither automatically procured nor easily available resources. The resourcefulness of borders is not available to everyone to the same extent, but they have a permeability differential. In which ways differentials in permeability work has to be considered in the examination of resourcing on each individual border. In the case of the Georgian-Abkhazian CFL particularly macro-political factors – the fact of an unsettled conflict – and resulting questions of legality and illegality frame the permeability of the CFL. Subsequently, the CFL is in a zone that the adjacent states handle as a 'dangerous' territory with an omnipresent suspicion towards the loyalty of their own citizens/subjects. These citizens in turn handle the notions of (il)legality in a flexible way and try to make them match or subvert their own actions in subtle ways. Subsequently, the interesting part is not necessarily the manner in which states restrain the population, but more insightful is to pay attention to the means people are still able to resource upon even in otherwise constrained situations. Differential permeability impacts on the way people resource on the Georgian-Abkhazian CFL. The kind of techniques citizens use in resourcing is based on the very different personal opportunities and resources and these are often counter-intuitive particularly to official narratives. While the references to crossing the CFL remain largely neutral in terminology, creative ways in which documents or personal relations are activated in a creative way can be observed. An important conclusion is that personal relations trump the regime that the state apparatuses have imposed and to a large part determine the differential permeability. As I have outlined, one feature of the border regime is to generate and serve as a point to drain off and channel resources under the disguise of taxes (mostly into private pockets). Simultaneously, narratives form international law prescribe the handling of the border in theory, but these narratives have less impact in practice.

I have suggested a focus on differential permeability, which in contrast to soft and hard borders, depends simultaneously on the border regime and on the individual wanting to cross. To put my conclusions into a broader context: by permeability I mean the ways in which people (and their goods) are allowed or able to cross the border and what this permeability tells us about relationships and state effects; and particularly about how notions of (il)legality, (il)licitness, and (in)formality mingle at borders. Therefore, the crucial question that has been posed here on the example of the Georgian-Abkhazian CFL is: Who can cross under which premises? I have highlighted the power of documents, money, relationships, information and their particular relationship at the Georgian-Abkhazian CFL, but I am convinced that these are of vigour even in politically less contested spaces.

References

Abraham, I. (2005): "Introduction: The Making of Illicitness". In: W. van Schendel and I. Abraham (eds.): Illicit Flows and Criminal Things: States, Borders, and the Other Side of Globalization. Bloomigton: Indiana University Press, pp. 1-37.
Augé, M. (1995): Non-Places: Introduction to an Anthropology of Supermodernity. London: Verso.
Bernard, H. R. (2006): Research Methods in Anthropology: Qualitative and Quantitative Approaches. Walnut Creek/CA: Altamira press.
Brenner, N. / Jessop, B. / Jones, M. (2003): State/Space: A Reader. Oxford: Wiley-Blackwell.
Champain, P. / Kleine, D. / Mirimanova, N. (2004): From War Economies to Peace Economies in the South Caucasus. London: International Alert.
Donnan, H. / Wilson, T. M. (1999): Borders: Frontiers of Identity, Nation and State. Oxford: Berg.
Garb, P. / Whiteley, J. M. (2001): "A Hydroelectric Power Complex on Both Sides of a War: Potential Weapon or Peace Incentive?". In: J. Blatter and H. Ingram (eds.): Reflections on

Water: New Approaches to Transboundary Conflicts and Cooperation. Cambridge: MIT Press, 213.

Gerber, J. (1997): Georgien, nationale Opposition und kommunistische Herrschaft seit 1956. Baden-Baden: Nomos Verlagsgesellschaft.

Hirsch, F. (2005): Empire of Nations: Ethnographic Knowledge & the Making of the Soviet Union. Ithaca/N.Y: Cornell University Press.

Hoehne, M. V. / Feyissa, D. (2008): Resourcing State Borders and Borderlands in the Horn of Africa. Max-Planck-Institute for Social Anthropology Working Papers.

Jackson, R. H. (1990): Quasi-States: Sovereignty, International Relations, and the Third World (Cambridge studies in International Relations 12). Cambridge: Cambridge University Press.

Jansen, S. (2009): "After the Red Passport: Towards an Anthropology of the Everyday Geopolitics of Entrapment in the EU's 'Immediate Outside'". In: Journal of the Royal Anthropological Institute, 15, 4, pp. 815-832.

Kukhianidze, A. / Kupatadze, A. / Gotsiridze, R. (2003): Smuggling through Abkhazia and Tskhinvali Region/South Ossetia. Research report for the American University's Transnational Crime and Corruption Centre.

Lynch, D. (1998): The Conflict in Abkhazia Dilemmas in Russian 'Peacekeeping' Policy. London: Royal Institute of International Affairs.

Martin, T. (2001): The Affirmative Action Empire: Nations and Nationalism in the Soviet Union. 1923-1939. Ithaca/N.Y: Cornell University Press.

Mühlfried, F. (2010): "Citizenship at war: Passports and nationality in the 2008 Russian-Georgian conflict". In: Anthropology Today, 26, 2, pp. 8–13.

Nordstrom, C. / Robben, A.C.G.M. (1995): Fieldwork Under Fire: Contemporary Studies of Violence and Survival, Berkeley: University of California Press.

Nugent, P. (2002): Smugglers, Secessionists & Loyal Citizens on the Ghana-Togo Frontier: The Lie of the Borderlands Since 1914. Oxford: James Currey.

Rabinowitz, D. / Khawalde, S. (2000): "Demilitarized, then Dispossessed: The Kirad Bedouins of the Hula Valley in the Context of Syrian-Israeli Relations". In: International Journal of Middle East Studies, 32, 4, pp. 511–530.

Reeves, M. F. (2008): Border Work: An Ethnography of the State at Its Limits in the Ferghana Valley. Cambridge: University of Cambridge.

Sasse, G. (2001): "George Hewitt (ed.), The Abkhazians. A Handbook". In: Nations and Nationalism 7, 2, p. 254.

Van Schendel, W. (2005): "Spaces of Engagement: How Borderlands, illicit flows, and territorial states interlock". In: W. van Schendel and I. Abraham (eds.): Illicit Flows and Criminal Things: States, Borders, and the Other Side of Globalization. Bloomington: Indiana University Press, pp. 38-68.

Weiss, A. (2007): "Probleme der wirtschaftlichen Entwicklung in den De-facto-Staaten Abchasien, Südossetien und Berg-Karabach". In: H.-D. Wenzel (ed.): Der Kaspische Raum. Ausgewählte Themen zu Politik und Wirtschaft. Berg Working Paper Series on Government and Growth, 57. University of Bamberg. pp. 41-60.

Wimmer, A. / Glick Schiller, N. (2002): "Methodological Nationalism and Beyond: Nation-State Building, Migration and the Social Sciences". In: Global Networks, 2, 4, pp. 301-334.

'Winter-tyres-for-a-flower-bed': Shuttle trade on the Finnish-Russian border

Anna Stammler-Gossmann

1 Introduction

'We will figure it out' is a common expression among Russian shuttle traders, which refers to their ability to effectively respond to the new state restrictions regarding the crossing of the border and customary rules. I obtained an insight into how it works in practice during the 'participant observation' part of my fieldwork. I crossed the Finnish-Russian border for the first time in 2006. This year has been viewed as a most significant turning point for the further 'squeezing' of this segment of the economy, since the devastating, sharp devaluation of the rouble in 1998 (see Stammler-Gossmann 2006; Gostev/Kuskov 2006; Nedobitkov 2006). The maximum allowed customs-free import of goods to Russia per person (for one's own need) was fixed in 2006 at 35 kg per month, instead of the previous 50 kg per week. The value of goods that was to be considered tax free was set at 65,000 roubles, approximately 2,200 dollars.

The regulation of 2006, as well as several previous and following ones, has been commented upon by many experts in Russia and in public discourse as 'a birth of a new law that does not work' (see Gvozdetskii 2004; Volodin 2006; Pravo.ru 2009). Our taxi driver joked about it: "We transfer even more goods now". Shortly before crossing the border my observational part of the fieldwork was transformed into a participating one. All passengers in the car were asked by the driver, if necessary, to reply to the Russian customs officials that each of us wants to bring one BMW winter tyre to Russia. All together the driver had four new tyres in his car boot whose weight definitely exceeded the custom-free requirements for the goods imported by one person. In response to my question whether this will be at all possible, the driver ensured me that nobody will ask or check me anyway, because he is not bringing anything prohibited over the border. He suggested me to reply, in case I was asked, that I am bringing the tyre as a present for my friends, who can use it for their flower bed, for example. He tried to comfort me, saying that the "rules of the game" are also known to the officials.

Indeed, the crossing of border points, the Finnish and the Russian one was smooth. The goods were perfectly legal, the divided amount of weight of the tyres among the passengers was not recorded, customs fees were not paid, and the desirable goal of the driver to import the 'trusted' quality tyres from Finland for sale was achieved. The passengers got a comfortable door-to-door service and a low private taxi price. In the following years of my crossing the Finnish-Russian border, the same 'beat-the-system' approach has been evident in devising means of circumventing rules, regulations and other means of state control. Moreover, shuttle traders have been producing even more sophisticated by-passing schemes in order to adapt to the constant toughening of customs rules and regulations.

The definition of shuttle trade is often used interchangeably with a definition of informal activity, where the circumvention of legal regulations is viewed as part and parcel of entrepreneurs' practices (see Hart 1970; Castells/Portes 1989; Williams 2005; Jones et al. 2006; Fernández-Kelly 2006). At the same time, this sector cannot be considered as inherently illegal. Indeed, as we can see it in the 'tyres-for-a-flower bed' case, the line between the articulations of 'formal' and 'informal' in the small-scale trade sector may be placed between 'white' and 'grey' with dots of 'black'. The petty shuttle trade in Russia, started as a mass phenomenon in the early 1990s (see Yakovlev et al 2007; Klimova/Zhsherbakova 2008) has undergone several changes within the last two decades but little of it has resulted in decisive boundaries clearly separating 'informal' from 'formal'.

Despite a decline in size after the rouble crisis of 1998, when the size of the informal labour force in Russia dropped by an estimated 40% (see Klimova/Zhsherbakova 2008: 393), the practice of small-scale cross-border trading a decade later still seems to be surprisingly buoyant. Many factors of the first post-socialist decade (e.g. unemployment, poverty, lack of goods and services) nowadays seem to come out as the most important cause of semi-legal economic practices. It is no longer merely a survival niche for those marginalised by society and neither is it about a scarcity of basic goods and services. Jobs have become available in the public sector and formal private industries have grown, too. This is especially true for the Murmansk region and St. Petersburg, which border Finland. Both of these Russian border regions are highly industrialised and densely populated. Job opportunities, living standards and purchasing power of the population are higher than in other border regions.

Nowadays, northern cross-border petty trade is a dynamic sector that is driven more by trading for 'advantage' rather than by trading for necessity. Shuttle trading activities may even be associated with higher incomes that often exceed those in the formal sector. The border regulations have become harder but not necessarily more efficient in their control over the shades of grey in the petty trade. Despite its limits, informal components of the shuttle trade have overcome multiple economic crises and governmental attempts to bring the shuttle trade under its control.

Fig. 27: Finnish-Russian border (Source: Arctic Centre, University of Lapland)

The persistence of the phenomenon that may take different shapes and acquire varying content over time has been observed in the last decade across other national largely regulated contexts (see Williams/Baláž 2005; Centeno/Portes 2006; Yuekseker 2007; Eder/Özlem 2010; UNECA 2010; Williams 2010). However, as Fernández-Kelly points out, "cogent explorations of the role of the state and popular activism are missing in the maintenance of this segment of economy" (Fernández-Kelly 2006: 3). The shifting nature of the relationship between the 'formal' and 'informal' is still a research field, where the meaning of the 'informal economy' may be interpreted in a sharply polarised way (see Jones et al 2006).

Most of the literature on the informal sector has been mainly interpreted from the perspective of the institutional environment towards informal arrangements. This paper focuses on the different aspects of economic 'informality': Taking an anthropological perspective I investigate the shifting nature of the relations between the 'informal' and 'informal' domains from the little known perspective of Russian petty traders, who regularly cross the border between Finland and Russia. In doing so, the paper draws attention to the articulation of informal practices and their justification in the local context of the Northern border region. It may help to understand why people prefer to trade informally and what the factors are that foster the practice of alternative enforcement mechanisms 'competing' with the regulatory system.

2   Informal – formal: Theoretical and methodological considerations

Due to its moving boundaries, the informal economy, as Castells and Portes state, cannot be captured by a strict definition (see Castells/Portes 1989: 11). In firm economic settings our case would include all unrecorded income-earning activities that are not regulated by the state. Petty trade practitioners in Russia cross the border as 'tourists' on paper and bring small quantities of public merchandise for selling. The informal trade may be combined with tourist and delivery services. The commodities 'carried' across the border are declared as 'goods for personal consumption' that often exceed the weight and amount of goods allowed to be imported without customs payment. The goods' transfer from public to private includes all forms of transactions which evade the tax system. Furthermore, state authorities find it difficult to control and regulate economic practices that cannot be defined in detail.

At the same time, parts of the black market transactions in the small-scale shuttle traders' tactics today have been definitely 'whitened'. The goods and services themselves are perfectly legal. Border crossing practitioners are more concerned with the quantity and monetary value of their commodities than with their legality. Circumventing the legal regulations may be mixed with formal components. Early day practices of bribing customs officers are not exercised on the North Western border as reported by traders 'because nowadays their salaries are high and the anti-corruption rules are tougher'. Analysing the current petty trade activities on the Finnish-Russian border we can join the recognition of the experts who see informal economy as a 'far less clear-cut and much more blurred category than always assumed' (see Leonard 1998; Jones et al 2006).

As mentioned above an interaction between formal and informal aspects is usually considered in the institutional context. This approach has been applied in the research on conditions producing such activity and informality within the formal sector of Russia itself (see Black/Tarassova 2002; Zheltov 2004; Zhuplev/Shein 2004; Radaev 2005; Albats 2005; Yakovlev 2006; Ledeneva 2006; Mukhina 2010; Puffer et al. 2010). Institutional/formal dimensions include government, regulatory agencies, and especially the legal system (see Puffer et al. 2010). In the Russian context-dependent definition the most important formal institution remains the Russian government (see Ayios 2004). The border's framework is viewed here as a main representative part of the state, i.e. as in customs, security forces (see Donnan/Wilson 1999: 4); and as a point of contact between the formal and the informal spheres.

In the field of shuttle traders' practices, the 'formal' also includes institutional arrangements related to registration and licensing activities, formal payments, access to premises, political ties, and public services as well as other regulated units like single enterprises with a legal status. Current research on the Russian institutional economy emphasises the important role of informal 'cultural-cognitive legitimacy' as termed by Scott (2008) in the formal sector (see Zhuplev/Shein 2004; Radaev 2005; Puffer et al. 2010).

It is more challenging to define 'informality' when moving from the 'informal' aspect towards the 'formal'. Very little empirical research has been done to determine the precise nature, extent and implications of governmental regulations on the informal sector from the bottom-up perspective. Anthropological case studies of shuttle trade in the post-socialist era have addressed the issue of informality in the context of challenges as well as opportunities. This approach has shown how different national borders may be negotiated by people of varying class, gender, and ethnicity (see Konstantinov 1996; Thuen 1999; Williams/Baláž 2005; Heintz 2007).

Recent border studies as well as research on petty trade in Russia have highlighted different aspects of informality in the cross-border activities such as its internal dynamics, articulation and output (see Holtom 2003; Stammler-Gossmann 2006; Olimpieva et al. 2007; Holzlehner 2007; Mukhina 2009; Ryzhova/Ioffe 2009). Still, very little is known about the issue of the 'non-formal' among the local actors. The expansion of informal activities in relation to the shuttle trade in Russia is relatively recent and research on informality considering the cross-border petty trading practices in general and in the North West border region, particularly, is still in its infancy.

From my fieldwork among the shuttle traders I have learned that there are not only multiple forms of operating in the informal/formal sector but that there are also different components that constitute the environment in which these forms are articulated. In a movement of goods and people between 'formal' and 'informal' domains, which is dual in its nature itself, we can find multiple argumentations at play. Traders' justification of their informal practices often operates around and between dichotomies of trust – distrust, efficiency – legitimacy, risk – uncertainty, normal – abnormal. Dealing with these dualisms may cause the existence of different logics of evaluation of 'grey' activities.

Seeking for appropriated analytical tools to discuss a diversity of 'grey' economic forms and their justifications, I found a good starting point in Stark's idea of the 'sense of dissonance'. He argues that entrepreneurship is the ability to keep multiple evaluative principles in play and to exploit the resulting friction of their interplay (see Stark 2009: 15). Stark's accounts about the value of play, ambiguity and uncertainty seem to hold a number of important implications for my research on shuttle trade, where different forms of evaluation may act simultaneously. These insights have also been useful to develop an approach for a situation, where grey practices do not necessarily occur in economic or legal gaps.

For the purpose of this paper informality of the shuttle trade is defined as practices of navigating between formal rules and application of norms, which do not necessarily correspond with the formal settings, to certain rules in certain situations. Thus, 'informality' here is recognised as a socially defined category subject to change. By referring to the traders' internal view of their circumventing the rules practices, it is possible to look behind the appearance of informality, and to focus on the social and cultural dynamics underlying the production of such informality.

An examination of petty trade in the context of the local border -where the 'meeting' between state and people is particularly visible- can reveal more about how the structures of the state manifest themselves in people's daily life. Viewing the border as "a part of cultural landscapes" (Donnan/Wilson 1999: 12) my research is addressed to the ways, in which social actors construct meaning by interacting with the national state.

Focusing on informality as it is routinely lived and experienced by ordinary people, this paper departs from the insights into informality within the formal sector. As previous research reveals many informal sector activities have close links with consumption in the formal economy (see Mulinge/Munyae 1998: 27). It has been exemplified in studies on the Soviet planned economy (see Grossman 1977; Lomnitz 1988), business-state interaction in contemporary Russia (see Yakovlev 2006), corporative governance (see Zheltov 2004; Zhuplev/Shein 2004; Puffer et al. 2010), and state structures in 'the shadow of informal economies' (see Radaev 2005; Albats 2005; Ledeneva 2006). Predisposed to this idea, I analyse the intersection of the economic behaviours of informal traders with the regulatory structure and the utilisation of grey modes, assuming that dependent linkages between the two sectors exist within many informal sector activities.

3   Defining invisible: Carriers and shopping tourist traders

Obviously, the practiced informality termed as trader-tourism (see Hann/Hann 1992) does not have a formal definition among the involved people. The naming of this kind of trading activities may be considered as a possible threat for their business, allowing for an easier application of legal restrictions and obligations. The name *chelnoki*, which is commonly applied for Russian petty traders, is not in use in the North Western border regions. It has a rather negative connotation that refers to the Soviet association with commercial speculative activity. The meaning of the term where *chelnoki* have been regarded as victims of life circumstances driven by extreme poverty (see Klimova 2006) cannot be attributed nowadays to the shuttle traders of this region.

During several hours of driving between the two countries and ideal conditions for anthropological participant observations, I learned a lot about identifying those activities. At the same time a long conversation made the desire of the practitioners clear to avert any definition that could make them officially 'visible'. Their involvement in informal economic activities is so diverse in nature and permanently changing that any strict classification would be deficient.

My fieldwork was conducted between 2006 and 2011 mainly in the northern segment of the Finnish-Russian border but also in its southern part. The empirical data was collected using the 'snowball method' in making the contacts and I had the opportunity to communicate with different groups of people participating in petty trade. For the purpose of my analysis a typology of shuttle traders is not essential. However, to facilitate understanding the informal dynamics, I refer to two types of shuttle traders based on their own representation. Both groups constitute a significant part of the informal sector of cross-border trading. They are mainly Russian residents for whom visits to the other side of border have become daily routine.

The 'shuttling' component of the trade may be termed in the specific northern border context with the word 'carriers' (*perevozchiki*) as the one group of traders may say among themselves. In general, many of the traders favour to describe their activities in 'active verb' vocabulary, such as 'going to Finland for businesses', 'carrying goods', 'driving tourists', or 'shopping'. For formal reasons they refer to their quasi-official or semi-official affiliation to a certain unit. In fact, most traders are registered within one or another formal institution 'for calculating the years of work experience and the pension'. However, bringing/selling the goods and providing services is a single or a large part of their 'for profit' activity. The goods that traders buy in Finland for selling in Russia have varied over time according to the changing price differences, consumers' demand and customs regulations. Among the goods that have been continuously 'carried' are new and/or second-hand spare car parts and household appliances. Imported commodities are sold through personal local networks.

For the carriers the informal economy is both their employer and the major source of their consumption. Sometimes they bring the goods on order ("Somebody asked me to buy a car in Sweden."; "My partner in one shop wanted to have a certain style of jacket."). Sometimes it could be furniture, household appliances or spare parts for own use or for the relatives ("I bought a house for my mum in Ukraine and she needed a new fridge."). Some practitioners regularly buy Finnish products to supply their own local enterprise: "I buy Finnish 'Tikurila' colours, tile, tools etc. for my small 'evroremont' [house renovation according to the European standard] company". Occasionally, some goods may be bought in Finland on order from Finnish acquaintances ("We have known each other for many years."): "One day I bought a TV in Finland with a 50 percent discount for me as long-term customer, crossed the border to get the duty free reimbursement and brought it back to my Finnish partner".

All these activities may be combined with providing services for the tourists. The groups are small up to 9 persons to avoid the whole paperwork and payments (license, permission, transport control) for the vehicle's registration as a bus and easier rearrangements of the activities. As one of the 'carriers' described their diverse practices, "all of the societal needs lead to us – commodities, transportation, issues of a visa, knowledge about the foreign country".

While 'carriers' regularly cross the border, commonly twice a week, and make a profit selling the goods and providing the services, another larger group is represented by people who cross the border intermittently, from once a week to a few times in a year. They usually combine local employment with petty trading on a cross-border basis. It is popular among the ordinary Russian residents in the regions neighbouring Finland, mainly because of the relatively high profits available in this sector. Price differences and the possibility to import tax-free purchases are preconditions for considerable profit margins.

Additional profits can be also realized in organized 'shopping' bus tours (see Olimpieva et al. 2007) between Helsinki and Saint Petersburg, which I also participated in, if individuals sell cigarettes and alcohol. While for the 'carriers' the cigarette business does not have economic value, bus travellers may cover the round bus trip by selling one or two packs of cigarettes. At the same time, trading is not necessarily only connected to economic profit for most of the 'shoppers'. Referring to their involvement in shuttle trade we could apply the definition of 'informal social entrepreneurship' or 'favour providers', where according to Williams mostly one-off tasks are undertaken as 'paid favours' for friends, family and acquaintances (see Williams 2004: 7). According to the estimation of the Russian Association of the tourist companies, the organised shopping tours made 10 per cent of all travel abroad in 2009 (see Pravo.ru 2009). The shopping tours which are offered by self-employed non-registered small entrepreneurs are hard to estimate.

The traders in both identified groups started their business without any economic or financial education, without any cultural experience with those countries they travel to and without any foreign language skills. In the mean time, some 'carriers' with whom I worked have a higher academic education for example in financial management or have gained extensive practical experience in this field. The majority of those involved in small-scale trade appears sensitive to the market situation, reacting quickly and flexibly to legislative and organisational changes in the business environment. All of them are confident not only with the national legal regulations but with foreign rules as well.

Parts of the black market tactics in the untaxed and unregistered activities of the early days have been definitely 'whitened'. There is a tendency among expanding traders to register a small part of their activities in order to legitimise the indefinable whole. The 'invisible' professional traders who have been doing their business for more than a decade and the shopping tourist traders with their occasional involvement cross the border with licit goods. The bypassing official rule tends to be more embedded into the formal frame. However, it remains largely outside official control and occupies a considerable 'grey' zone of semi-legality. This grey component of the shuttle trade can be defined here deriving from the motto of shuttle traders formulated by one of them: "Do not violate the law, but know the ways to avoid it".

4   Crossing the border

Crossing the Russian border checkpoint is a culminating point in the efforts of the petty trade business. The state manifests itself here in three offices: the regulator, the policeman, and the customs/tax collector. Since 2006, the Federal Customs Service has been managed and directed by the government of the Russian Federation. The border guard is a sub-division of the Federal Security Service. As any state territorial boundaries are in a perpetual state of transformation, the Finnish-Russian border is a part of the historically contingent processes of territory, meanings and building space (see Paasi 1998).

The border crossing between Finland and particularly the Murmansk region of Russia could be counted to the hardest in the world. The border can only be crossed by transport vehicles and the number of the control check points entering from Finland can be up to eight on the Russian side, depending on where you cross the border: 1) border check point entry control; 2) passport control, 3) customs control, 4) transport control; 5) border point exit control, 6) border crossing zone exit control; 7) border zone exit control; 8) near-to-border territory exit control.

The north western region of the Soviet Union was one of the most heavily militarised areas of the world and place of the world's largest concentration of nuclear weapons (see Luzin et al. 1994). Also today the Murmansk region has more 'closed zones' than any other administrative unit in the country.[128] It is assumed that the influence of the military and other power institutions is still more significant here than elsewhere in Russia (see Hønneland 2006). During the Soviet era the Finnish-Russian border marked a dividing line between two rivalling political, economic and cultural systems and the border was heavily guarded on both sides.

Even nowadays, the old mental borders are still present on both sides in spite of the strong de-bordering influence facilitated by EU and intensive cross-border cooperation (see Scott and Matzeit 2006: 44-45). "Our border is locked and will be locked as our fathers did it", proudly reported the representative of the Murmansk department of the Federal Security Service in a local TV program during my recent visit to the Kola Peninsula in 2011.

The great boundary has a place of prominence in the national consciousness. The barrier function of the border is highly valued not only on the national level. Even the shuttle traders, who may joke about the crossing procedures on the Russian border in comparison to the borders within the EU, do not question the need for this strict control for 'Russian security'.

The modern history of cross-border petty trade in Russia started with the Presidential decree "On the foreign trade liberalization in the Russian Federation" (No. 213, 15.11.1991). The Eltsin's Decree 'On the freedom of trade' (No. 65, 29.01.1992) allowed all enterprises to engage in foreign trade and import goods without customs payments. These regulations created the legal basis for small-scale cross border trade in Russia.

For the north western border of Russia Finland's entry into the EU in 1995 radically changed the functional and symbolic meanings of the border (see Paasi 1998; Hønneland 2006; Marin 2006; Ollus/Simola 2006), and the number of border-crossing points has greatly increased. According to statistics in Finland

---

128   Law of the Murmansk region, No. 1090-01-ZMO, 29.04.2009

Russian tourists were number one visitors to Finland between 2005 and 2009 and had the lead in expenditure statistics for foreign passengers in Finland in 2009 (see Statistics Finland 2009). A record high number of 6.8 million people crossed the Finnish-Russian border in 2010 as Finnish broadcaster YLE reported (see Staalesen 2011). The new Finnish visa centre in St. Petersburg opened in February 2011 with 83 service counters and is the largest in the world. Finland is the country which issues most Schengen visas to Russians (see Staalesen 2011).

The North West Customs Service is the only one in Russia that has a border with the EU. The regional section of the Federal Customs Service has undergone several reforms related to the process of integrating European customs regulations. Thereby problems related to 'grey' trade have been highlighted at the highest levels of its administration (see Ollus/Simola 2006: 45). First of all, the process of integration is related to the introduction of standard European technologies like a 'double corridor system' (green and red lines) and a 'control system of risks' (see Ollus/Simola 2006: 44ff.; Agreement 2010: clause 2f.; Tamozhennyi sbornik 2011: 3ff.). Nevertheless, the North West Customs Service was placed second among seven regional Customs Services in the list of unpaid customs duties in 2010 related to their evasion (Tamozhennyi sbornik 2011: 12).

When examining the discrepancies between Finnish export and Russian import figures, Finland is among the countries that have, as in 2006, the largest discrepancies between their and Russian trade statistics (see Ollus/Simola 2006: 39). How the official statistics may not correspond with the reality of informal practices in trade shows an example of import of computers and other devices as given by Russian sociologists. As it is stated, usually these products were imported as green beans, which were the cheapest commodity in terms of import taxes. The official statistics registered significant increases of green beans in the Russian market in the mid-90s but no import of electronic devices was recorded (see Olimpieva et al. 2007: 3).

According to investigations on Russia's informal economy in the field of household appliances only 20 percent of the goods in 2001 were imported legally. 70 percent of the goods imported were covered by 'grey' schemes (see Radaev 2003). As it was estimated for the Russian-Chinese border shuttle trade, 20 Russian tourists might bring commodities with a value equivalent to one import load of a middle-size officially registered enterprise from China (Nedobitkov 2006). However, existing statistics cannot be considered as an indicator for the amount of grey imports to Russia by petty traders. Due to the confidence of informal practices any attempts to grasp them statistically do not reveal a real picture of the nature and size of this economic sector.

Structural and regulative reforms of the internal Russian border are crucial for border crossing by traders. Crossing the Finnish border point is not seen as challenging as the Russian one: "The Finns are not as strict as long as nothing illegal is exported and they are happy when we buy in Finland and contribute to their economy". Fostering a good reputation with border officers on both sides belongs to the business for people who may cross the border twice or three times a week: "Customs officers already know that everything is fine, I do everything according to the law". At the same time real relief comes after passing all the check points of the border.

5   Between white and grey: Circumventing customs regulations

To bypass all the border controls and bring in commodities that in reality do not abide with the rules of customs duty-free goods may appear impossible. However, there are various ways of circumventing or reducing customs expenses. It is a basic skill of the petty trade business to learn not only about the consumer's preferences and price differences but also about the type of commodities it pays off to bring over the border to Russia and how to do so. The rapidly changing customs laws force them to act fast not only within their established strategies of moving between the formal and informal but also to 'keep their eyes open' in general for any changes in their environment.

Following varying tactics of evading customs payments between 2006 and 2011, I could observe how their patterns can be recombined and altered according to legal changes. For example, I was 'taught' how – without paying customs duties – to import a heavy fridge or sofa as an "indivisible commodity for private use with a weight that does not exceed 35 kg" (Agreement 2010). I also was able to determine why the import of fridges/mobile telephones/cars is not profitable this year any more but importing washing machines still is.

I was able to obtain detailed knowledge about the weight of different items. I learned, for instance, how heavy car tyres with and without metal disks are, what the weight of a fridge or oven without a door is and how many jackets may fit into the 35 kg weight restriction. Illegal 'green beans as computer' schemas of the 1990s are hardly used among the petty traders today and have been modified into 'winter-tyres-for-a-flower-bed' patterns. Traders generally avoid the fundamental replacement of one custom code by another 'cover commodity' code. Thus, the legal status of goods is necessarily considered. While the price of the imported customs - free commodities may be hidden or negotiated, weight is the major concern. Sometimes, it comes down to grams and in such cases the removal of the packaging may play a crucial role.

Basic tactics of avoiding customs duty follow established patterns. The spectrum of their modification is wide and is applied in an elaborative way according to the current stand of the customs requirements. The main tactics classified within the white/grey schemas are:

- weight distribution amongst passengers
- under-invoicing
- commodity disintegration
- replacement of identical goods for the same purpose

Thus, for example, the new dissembled fridge (without the compressor and door) may be imported 'for personal use' to be re-assembled later. All other parts may either be distributed among the passengers, preferably in different cars, or they can be stored on the Finnish side until the next border crossing.

Due to the most recent changes in customs rules this popular household appliance has now become a more cumbersome good for the border-crossing procedure. If the weight of the fridge exceeds the allowed weight by only 100 g, a customs duty of 30% of the whole value and volume may be required. Further, a new item may be 'transferred' to the 'reduced defective' or 'second-hand' category. In this case, the under-invoicing schema may be applied additionally. For this schema traders have to be able to identify new resources for their success not least in the country where they purchase the goods. Such possibilities are discovered by carefully making confidential approaches in Finland, testing them on Finnish people, gathering information about the shops and services with 'good guys', who 'can understand our mentality'.

As a result, it is for example possible to 'personify' car tyres when buying them, whereby each tyre receives a separate invoice with the names of different buyers and their passport details. In this way, the weight of 'personified' tyres is distributed among the passengers to be imported 'more legally'. This practice may work with any 'divisible' product. At the same time, this particular trans-national network is rather fragile, due to its semi-informal nature.

The movement between the informal and formal spheres at the border check point is not always successful. In particular, the practice of replacing identical custom codes (commodity category) may only be effective for a short period of time. Bad-luck stories related to these practices belong to some of the most amusing stories. These replacement tactics require people to apply special communication skills in order to convince border officers. Not seldom, women are found utilising these abilities.

One of them told me her story about bringing a new chic sofa to Murmansk. For this purpose, she first brought an old sofa from Russia and made a custom declaration that the sofa was being taken to Finland 'for cleaning' and accordingly was brought back in a 'cleaned' version. Next time, she was asked by the border officers to declare the piece of furniture 'brought for cleaning' with a precise description of weight, colour and form. Another trader, who was specialised in trading down-hill ski equipment, used the same tactic with his old skis a few times. He was taking a couple of his old skis 'for skiing' in Finland and on the way back he was bringing 'the same' skis but in a 'modernised' version for sale. Well-maintained and repaired second-hand skis were brought for his son's classmates until the 'social entrepreneur' was stopped by the officers. Still it was worth trying and the response to this was "we will figure it out".

6   The rules of the game

The experts on informality in the institutional economy may explain its persistence with an 'institutional vacuum' or with the abundance of formal rules or with the structure of these rules and the way they were introduced (see Radaev 2001). Customs officers may complain about the lack of resources to implement the 'laws' (see Karimova 2010). From the petty traders' point of view, customs procedures are definitely overruled and have been permanently expanding since a policy of 'complete import liberalisation' was declared in 1992. After less than one year this policy was changed and the adopted Decree 'On temporary import customs tariff' (No. 825, 07.08.1992) started the process of permanently revising and diversifying the customs tariff structure and rates. The traders always complain about myriads of permits to register and operate their businesses legally and the high cost for the entrance into the formal world.

As my research resources for viewing the changes of the last years in federal customs regulations were exhausted, the carriers also pointed out the importance of monitoring internal changes at the border. The change in internal customs rules can happen within one week: "When I crossed the border on the way back I had to pay a penalty because during the five days when I was in Finland unexpectedly a new procedure was introduced".

Often changing rules on the border have become a 'rule' itself and adjustment to them is a routine practice in everyday economic activity. Some authors emphasise a circular dynamic produced by this kind of situation when formality creates (see Lomnitz 1988) or breeds (see Fernández-Kelly 2006) its own informality. As observed in the 'tyres-for-a-flower-bed' case, the new customs restrictions produce a number of informal rearrangements among petty traders rather than a subjection to formal rules.

As traders get used to the continuing changes in the border crossing regulations, their particular strategies are shaped, not by 'systemic requirements' (see Stark 2009) but from the urgency of their practical situation. Most effective practices based on monitoring the legal situation are crystallised around knowledge of other rules, rules of the game. The temporality of the regulations is one of the features, which contributes to the common understanding of relations between state control and informal transactions as a 'game'. The term 'rules of the game' is used not only by traders and mass media but also among experts on informality in the Russian formal economy (see Radaev 2005; Ledeneva 2006).

Selectivity of the formal rules is another characteristic, which brings the 'game' component into informal practices. Traders emphasise that the officers' selective behaviour is an inherent component of the border crossing: "If they want, they can always find something wrong". That is why the customs officers as main state agents may be perceived as representatives of a confronting system but also as 'good' or 'bad' guys. Border crossing points between Finland and Russia are characterised by carriers first of all in relation to their staff: "When I go to Finland I take the closest check point, but on the way back to Russia I cross the border there, where the officers are more tolerant or I try to cross when the nice officers have their shift".

Like in any other 'game' there are multiple participants. The border officers are in charge of differentiating a tourist from a trader or what the real value and weight of imported commodities is. In practice, it is not seldom that officers at the northern border and 'professional' traders know each other. Both sides know of the tricks employed to get around the state regulations. At the same time, the Decree 'on goods transfers for personal use' (No 715, 27.11.2003) allows for a person to prove that the imported commodity is not for commercial use. It is within the trader's ability to convince the customs guard that a disassembled fridge is a book shelf or that the price of a new appliance is only 20 Euro instead of 400 Euro and that the customs fee should be charged on the previous amount. Traders emphasise the importance of communication and psychological skills in their business.

From this perspective, a border officer not only represents an institutional entity but is also a 'person like us', confident with the rules of the game. I was surprised about how easy it is to talk with them about the various tricks employed to get through border control. Sometimes, traders cross the border twice a day when they import disassembled goods because if you bring the fridge in separate pieces, it's better to carry them in different cars or even better one piece per crossing, thus no one will ask you why you are crossing the border as a tourist. The discrepancy between words and the formal elements must not be played out deadly serious. As a response of a trader in my field notes states, this is what people may ascribe to the Russian mentality and "what Finnish border officers do not understand".

The existence of parallel structures in the relation between the border officers and petty traders, carries the Soviet shadow, which is seen by experts as an integral component of the national economy, rather than as a marginal appendix to it (see Butler/Purchase 2004; Radaev 2005; Ledenva 2006). Also, two decades after the collapse of the Soviet Union we can still observe the persistence of the *homo Sovieticus* mentality. Back then working around formal rules was a generally accepted norm in society in general and in economic activities in particular.

The diversity of the shadow economy could find its expression in the morally acknowledged, direct use of state resources, sometimes also called *cleptocracy* (see Grossman 1977). Theft of state property, e.g. workers stealing tools from factories, restaurant staff meat and drivers petrol, was a largely widespread practice (see Radaev 1999). As Radaev states, the physical form of resources is not as important anymore in informal activities, but *cleptocracy* has remained and has moved into the financial operations sector. According to Radaev, for example, 2/3 of all Russian residents in 1996 did not declare their income (see ibid.). Only 1.5 per cent of Russian enterprises paid all of their taxes on time in 1998 as reported by the Centre of economic reforms (see Glinkina 1998). The scepticism of petty traders towards formal demands may be regarded as a double standard, which may relate to the institutional economic sector "where people pretend to comply, and the government pretends to regulate" (May 2004: 152).

As the activities of private actors involved in petty trade illustrate, lasting improvements in this double standard logic are difficult to achieve in the short run. As expressed by one trader, there is a common agreement among many Russian residents that this attitude will take generations to change: "We used to live in instability. We may steal from the state for the children's future but we have not learned to rely on the future. We teach them to live the same way".

In the fast-changing environment of petty trading, knowing the rules of the game is a field, where people can adhere in navigating between formal/informal sectors. The rules of the game, however, are not without limits and traders have to know, where and how the rules should be applied. Strategies have not always been successful. Like the 'rules of law' the rules of the game may be selective and personalised. Sometimes, a signal exchange is needed to determine the willingness of officials to 'play' the game. Practitioners may refer to their abilities to identify the officer's acceptance. The main principle of the shuttle traders is that the grey patterns are recognisable but frequently have to be petty and should not obviously violate state regulations.

Traders try to transform the uncertainties of the circumstances into calculable risk. That is according to Stark, the distribution of outcomes, which can be expressed in some probabilistic terms and what uncertainty lacks (see Stark

2009: 14). On typing in 'crossing the Finnish-Russian border' in the Russian search machine yandex.ru one will obtain one million entries, which include practical guidelines on how to make this matter more predictable.

7   Distrust versus trust

Russia is viewed as a prominent example of a low-trust society (see Ayios 2004; Radaev 2005; Kuznetsov/Kuznetsova 2008; Puffer et al. 2010). In the institutional economy's studies the state legislative and regulatory policy is estimated as being non-predictable by the market actors (see Puffer et al 2010). The Fraser Institute's 2008 Index of Economic Freedom evaluates the opportunities to trade internationally in Russia at rank 114 out of 141 countries (see Gwartney et al. 2010: 11).

Also petty traders do not interpret legal regulations in small business as an instrument to support them but as a way of further empowering and legitimizing the powerful. As it was exemplified to me with the currently introduced limitation for the household appliances import, "it means that behind this restriction there are some persons related to the government, who have established a new factory in this sector".

The new framework of customs regulations related to the launch of the Customs Union (Russia, Belarus, Kazakhstan) that came into force in 2010 has significantly relaxed the restrictions on the weight of imported goods and the import frequency. Traders received it with a comment full of distrust: "The state is against us anyway, one restriction is abolished but another has been introduced". They pointed, for example, to the new limitation on the amount of petrol allowed to be brought from Russia to Finland. While Finland, according to the traders, allows crossing the border with up to 60 litres of cheaper petrol from Russia in canisters, Russia limits it to 10 litres.

For a number of carriers, a new restriction, related to the limitation of the tax free movement of goods for Russian residents, who have been living abroad for more than six months, was a big disappointment for those involved in the traders' economy of favour. Harder regulations from previous years on the import of new or second-hand cars (*inomarki*), declared as a support of national car industry, have been noted with severe scepticism. The traders are convinced that the quality of Russian cars has not improved at all and the preferences of customers for *inomarki* have not changed. It is a common argument against the state that the increase of the governmental control over the customs regulations only brings the price increase in the car or other commodity markets and in the end it affects the ordinary people.

In general, there is a high mistrust in the competitiveness of national products. As I have experienced in the last years, the majority of 'shoppers' cross the border to buy the increasingly more demanded, 'trusted' quality goods from Finland. Goods originating from western countries are usually considered to be of higher quality than those produced nationally. Shuttle traders, for example, prefer to purchase coffee in Finland, cloths or even baby nappies, although the same brands are available in Russia. This expresses their non-trust towards pirated products rather than explains their profit motivations with price differences. Russia is often mentioned as one of the key countries for product counterfeiting (see Chaudhry/Zimmerman 2009: 31ff.).

Viewed as a low trust society, Russia can be ranked very high on 'uncertainty avoidance'. Findings from the case studies on the northern Russian border demonstrate a causal relationship between the fundamental lack of trust in the state among small-scale traders and the avoidance of 'as many formal institutions as possible'. This reality exacerbates the tendency to rely instead on what Puffer et al term as 'relational trust' (see Puffer et al. 2010). Studies on informality in the formal economy of Russia clearly demonstrate an importance of high-trust options in such situations on the personal relationship (see Ayios 2004; Ledeneva 2006).

The case of the shuttle traders restates this view. A tendency to distrust organisations that fall outside personal relationships appears to be even stronger. Petty trade relies exclusively on its extended personal network ("Finnish seller, who speaks Russian and can even understand our jokes", "Hotel owner whom I have known since I started the business", "Customs officer with whom I shared the floor in the student dormitory", "My contact in the authority", "My neighbour who now lives in Finland", relatives etc.).

I have taken the argument of reliance on the informal network and embedded practices in the entrepreneurship to accomplish business objectives one step further, suggesting that the difference between 'as it is' and 'as it should be' is not that big. It means that people distrusting the state are not entirely unhappy with the perception they have about the lack of structure in social institutions. If you ask the shuttle traders "why there are so many check points when you cross the border on the Russian side", the people may explain it with the fact that "it is everywhere in Russia".

The border existence is not questioned at all. They can make jokes about crossing the Russian border comparing with the borders between the western countries but I have never experienced any doubt in the need for border control. Informal operations happen rather naturally in the context of institutional distrust but at the same time within trusted personalised relations to the state. While 'institutional' contact is avoided, there is a strong desire to have institutional contacts on the personal level to serve informal activities. This seems to be in line with a widely shared self-representation and very much boasted feature of the Russian residents of being able to improvise (muddle through).

8   Conclusion

The relation between written rules and actual informal practices in petty trade is a mirror of society. Informality operated in this segment of the economy cannot only be limited to the legal shortcomings, high costs of legality or economic marginalisation of the actors involved. For shuttle traders on the Finnish-Russian border the drive to work outside of the scope of ordinary laws and regulations is justified by the 'normality' of informal practices in the society. The interplay of categories of formal and informal, legal and semi-legal, like normal and abnormal is recognisable not only in the economic environment but in other areas and at different points of their everyday life. The informal sector appears not only as a rational 'device' to increase economic rationality but as a phenomenon that acts under cultural and historical conditions. I argue that the informal activities are socially embedded transactions that permit a cultural-moral logic of the society.

Operators of 'micro-enterprises' do not accept the legal targets and opt to beat the system also referring to the feeling of 'being beaten by the system'. The western-based view of basic trust in formal institutions, which is particularly recognisable in Finland, is not yet applicable for Russia. As long as the trust level in the society is low, the uncertainty avoidance remains high. However, the analysis of informal-formal relations among the petty traders illustrates that government entities are not always in opposition to the unregulated sector. The pervasive utilization of informal modes of small-scale trade is constituted by a field where both informal and formal domains act as a 'contradictory unity'.

A 'beat-the-system' attitude is applied by the shuttle traders not necessarily in terms of a conflict with the state but in terms of a competitive environment, created through this contradictory unity. On the one hand, people involved in the grey economy try to bypass state institutions as much as possible. On the other hand, personal relational contacts within these institutions are very much appreciated and even desired. Rules of the game such as in case of the border crossing embody implicit forms that are recognisable to both the traders and the state officials. They reflect the ambivalences of relation between traders and the state which is represented by the power institution but also by a person in power.

As I demonstrate in my case studies, shuttle traders deal with different ambiguities, which act in their environment. Various forms of justification and multiple evaluative practices may occur simultaneously. Traders may switch between the informal and formal sector during the same day or border crossing. The dynamics of trust and distrust is very much person- and content specific. The rules of the game are highly contextualised and may combine seemingly discrepant elements. In such a rapidly changing environment traders also face the problem that taken-for-granted can soon be out-of-date and have to move between the temporality of the customs rules and the stability of their income.

Grey elements of cross border trading are produced in the context of navigating between these ambiguities. From ambiguity traders make an asset. What I learned from my fieldwork among the shuttle traders on the Finnish-Russian border lends support to Stark's idea on generative friction which may emerge as a result of dealing with dualisms. However, in difference to the institutional field, where 'dissonance' according to Stark may be interpreted as 'organised', shuttle traders do not create this disruption but use existing ambiguities to create assets that are ambiguous.

Thus, the desire to avert certain definitions of their activities is almost equivalent to making practitioners invisible. Giving specific performance terms to the undefinable whole would turn them into activities with a legal obligation towards a specific set of rules. Leaving an open semantic field in their definition gives the practitioners the possibility to retain their flexibility. It allows them to be creative and more independent with respect to the formal rules. Otherwise, as is believed, it would curb the needed dynamism. The approach 'we will figure it out' as it was observed at the northern border occupies a stable position in the informal segment of the petty trade.

References

Agreement 2010. About the order of moving of the goods by physical persons for a private use through customs border of the customs union and fulfilment of the customs operations connected with their release. June 19, 2010, ratified in 2011 (Federal Law N 60-FZ, 05.04.2011), URL: http://master-eng.customs.ru/index.php?option=com_content&view=article&id=72&Itemid=1850 (last access: 08.07.2011).

Albats, Y. (2005): The Shakedown State. (Working paper 4). Moscow: State University, High School of Economics GU VShE.

Ayios, A. (2004): Trust and Western-Russian Business Relationships. Aldershot: Ashgate.

Black, B. S. / Tarassova, A.S. (2003): "Institutional Reform in Transition: A Case Study of Russia". In: Supreme Court Economic Review, 10, pp. 211-278.

Butler, B. / Purchase, S. (2004): "Personal Networking in Russian Post Soviet Life". In: Research and Practice in Human Resource Management, 12, 1, pp. 34-60.

Castells M. / Portes A. (1989): "World underneath: The Origins, Dynamics, and Effects of the Informal Economy". In: A. Portes, M. Castells and L. Benton (eds.): The Informal Economy: Studies in Advanced and Less Developed Countries. Baltimore: Johns Hopkins University Press, pp. 11-37.

Centeno, M. A. / Portes, A. (2006): "The Informal Economy in the Shadow of the State". In: P. Fernández-Kelly and J. Shefner (eds): Out of the Shadows: Political Action and the Informal Economy in Latin America. Philadelphia: Pennsylvania University Press, pp. 23-48.

Chaudhry, P. / Zimmerman, A. S. (2009): The Economics of Counterfeit Trade: Governments, Consumers, Pirates and Intellectual Property Rights. Berlin, Heidelberg: Springer.

Gvozdetskii, V. (2004): "'Chelnokov' zastavyat podelit'sya?". In: Novye izvestiya, 13 February 2004, URL: http://www.rgwto.com/digest.asp?id=4419&full_mode=1 (last access: 24.06.2011).

Donnan, H. / Wilson, T. W. (1999): Borders: Frontiers of Identity, Nation & State. Oxford, New York: Berg.

Eder, M. / Özlem, Ö. (2010): "From Cross-Border Exchange Networks to Transnational Trading Practices? The Case of Shuttle Traders in Laleli, Istanbul". In: M.-L. Djelic and S. Quack (eds.): Transnational Communities: Shaping Global Economic Governance. Cambridge: Cambridge University Press, pp. 82-106.

Fernández-Kelly, P. (2006): "Introduction". In: P. Fernández-Kelly and J. Shefner (eds): Out of the Shadows: Political Action and the Informal Economy in Latin America. Philadelphia: Pennsylvania University Press, pp. 1-22.

Glinkina, S. (1998): "Osobennosti tenevoi ekonomiki v Rossii". In: Nezavisimaia gazeta: NG – politekonomia, 5, p.5.

Gostev, A. / Kuskov, O. (2006): "Torgovtsy-'chelnoki' zayavlyayut, chto novye zakony o tamozhennykh platezhakh mogut ostavit' bez raboty ili odezhdy millionov rossiyan". In: Radio svoboda, 6 March 2006, URL: http://www.vch.ru/cgi-bin/guide.cgi?table_code=15&action=show&id=3930 (last access: 11.08.2010).

Grossman, G. (1977): "The Second Economy of the USSR". In: Problems of Communism, 26, 5, pp. 25-40.

Gwartney, J. et al. (2010): Economic Freedom of the World. Annual Report. Economic Freedom Network (The Fraser Institute).

Hann, C. / Hann, I. (1992): "Samovars and Sex on Turkey's Russian Markets". In: Anthropology today, 8, 4, pp. 3-6.

Heintz, M. (2007): "'Nothing has Changed, It Just Turned Illegal': Discourses for the Justification of Illegal Trade and Immigration in the Moldovan Republic". In: Anthropology of East Europe review, 25, 1, pp. 21-28.

Holtom, P. (2006): "Shuttle Trade and New Border Regimes". In: Russian Regional Perspectives Journal, 1, 3, URL: http://www.iiss.org/programmes/russia-and-eurasia/russian-regional-perspectives-journal/rrp-volume-1-issue-3/shuttle-trade-and-new-border-regimes/ (last access: 17.10.2010).

Holzlehner, T. (2007): Weaving Shuttles and Ginseng Roots: Commodity Flow and Migration in a Borderland of the Russian Far East. Berkeley program in Soviet and post-Soviet studies working paper series, URL: http://iseees.berkeley.edu/bps/publications/Holzlehner-fall07.pdf (last access: 24.06.2011).

Hønneland, G. (2006): "Power Institutions and International Collaboration on the Kola Peninsula". In: The Journal of Power Institutions in Post-Soviet Societies, 4, 5, URL: http://pipss.revues.org/index448.html (last access: 25.05.2010).

Jones, T. / Ram, M. / Edwards P. (2006): "Shades of Grey in the Informal Economy". In: International Journal of Sociology and Social Policy, 26, 9/10, pp. 357-373.

Karimova, A. (2010): "Soyuz i minus. Otdel po svyaziam s obzhestvennost'yu SZTU (Severo Zapadnoe Tamozhennoe Upravlenie)". In: Press byulleten, 7, pp. 2-5.

Klimova, S. G. / Zhsherbakova, I. V. (2008): 'Chelnochestvo' i gosudarstvo: Etapy evolyutsii otnoshenii. Rossiia reformiruyuzsaiasia. Moscow: Institut sociologii RAN, pp. 389-405.

Anna Stammler-Gossmann

Klimova, S. G. (2008): "Kontseptualizatsia roli chenoka ee isponiteliami". In: Sociologicheskie issledovaniia, 4, pp.52-62.
Konstantinov, Y. (1996): "Patterns of Reinterpretations: Trader-Tourism in the Balkans (Bulgaria) as a Picaresque Metaphorical Enactment of Post-Totalitarianism". In: American ethnologist, 23, 4, pp. 762-782.
Ledeneva, A. (2006): How Russia Really Works: The Informal Practices that Shaped Post-Soviet Politics and Business. Ithaca: Cornell University Press.
Leonard, M. (1998): Invisible Work, Invisible Workers: The Informal Economy in Europe and the US. London: Macmillian.
Lomnitz, L. A. (1988): "Informal Exchange Networks in Formal Systems: A Theoretical Model". In: American Anthropologist, 90, pp. 42-55.
Luzin, G. / Pretes, M. / Vasiliev, V. (1994): "The Kola Peninsula: Geography, History and Resources". In: Arctic, 47, 1, pp. 1-15.
Marin, A. (2006): Integration Without Joining? Neighbourhood Relations at the Finnish-Russian Border. DIIS Working paper 14. Copenhagen: Danish Institute for International Studies (DIIS).
May, R. (2004): "A Strategic Approach to Improving Corporate Governance". In: D. McCarthy, S. M. Puffer and S. Shekshnia (eds.): Corporate Governance in Russia: A Framework for Analysis. Cheltenham, Northampton: Edward Elgar, pp. 147-168.
Mukhina, I. (2010): "Regulating the Trade: International Peddling in Post-Soviet Russia". In: The Soviet and Post-Soviet Review, 37, 2, pp. 166-186.
Mulinge, M. M. / Munyae, M. M. (1998): "The Persistent Growth in Size and Importance of the Informal Economy in African Countries: Implications for Theorising the Economy and Labour Markets". In: African sociological review, 2, 2, pp. 20-45.
Nedobitkov, A. (2006): "Finish chelnochnogo bega". In: Vashe delo, 16 March 2006, URL: http://altapress.ru/story/9931/ (last access: 24.06.2011).
Olimpieva, I. / Pachenkov, O. / Ejova, L. / Gordy, E. (2007): Informal Economies of St. Petersburg: Ethnographic Findings on the Cross-Border Trade. Jefferson Institute.
Ollus, S.-E. / Simola, H. (2006): Russia in the Finnish Economy. Sitra reports 66. Helsinki: Sitra.
Paasi, A. (1998): Territories, Boundaries and Consciousness: The Changing Geographies of the Finnish-Russian Border. New York: John Wiley and Sons.
Pravo.ru (2009): "Tamozhnia beret chelnokov na abordazh". In: Pravo.ru, 10 July 2009, URL: http://www.pravo.ru/review/crisis/view/13864/ (last access: 21.08. 2010).
Puffer, S. M. / McCarthy, D. / Boisot, M. (2010): "Entrepreneurship in Russia and China: The Impact of Formal Institutional Voids". In: Entrepreneurship Theory and Practice: Special Issue on Institutional Theory & Entrepreneurship, 34, 3, pp. 441-467.
Radaev, V. (1999): "Tenevaya ekonomika v Rossii: Izmenenie konturov". In: Pro et Contra, 4, 1, pp. 5-25.
Radaev, V. (2005): "Informal Institutional Arrangements and Tax Evasion in the Russian Economy". In: S. Koniordos (ed.): Networks, Trust and Social Capital: Theoretical and Empirical Investigations from Europe. Aldershot: Ashgate, pp. 189-203.
Ryzhova, N. / Ioffe, G. (2009): "Trans-Border Exchange Between Russia and China: The Case of Blagoveshensk and Heihe". In: Eurasian Geography and Economics, 50, 3, pp. 348-364.
Scott, J. / Matzeit, S. (2006): EXLINEA Lines of Exclusion as Arenas of Cooperation: Reconfiguring the External Boundaries of Europe – Policies, Practices, Perceptions. Final project report, URL: http://www.exlinea.comparative-research.net/fileadmin/user_upload/reports_and_publications/Executive_Summary.pdf (last access: 07.09. 2006).
Scott, W. R. (2008): Institutions and Organizations: Ideas and Interests. Thousand Oaks/CA: Sage Publications.

Staalesen, A. (2011): "6,8 million people crossed Finnish-Russian border". In: BarentsObserver, 7 January 2011, URL: http://www.barentsobserver.com/68-million-people-crossed-finnish-russian-border.4869398-99350.html (last access: 24.06.2011).

Stammler-Gossmann, A. (2006): "Top-Down and Bottom-Up Globalisation in the Russian North". In: M. Rantaniemi, K. Kurtakko and K. Norvapalo (eds.): Pieces from Peripheries and Centres. Rovaniemi: University of Lapland, pp. 31-53.

Stark, D. (2009): The Sense of Dissonance. Accounts of Worth in Economic Life. Princeton, Woodstock: Princeton University Press.

Statistics Finland (2009): Border interview survey 2009, URL: http://www.stat.fi/til/rajat/2009/03/rajat_2009_03_2010-06-09_tau_006_en.html and http://www.stat.fi/til/rajat/2009/03/rajat_2009_03_2010-06-09_tie_001_en.html (last access: 24.06.2011).

Tamozhennyi sbornik (2011): Tamozhennaia sluzhba Rossiisoi Federatsii v 2010 godu. Moscow: FTS.

Thuen, T. (1999): "The Significance of Borders in the East European Transition". In: International Journal of Urban and Regional Research, 2, 4, pp. 738-750.

UNECA (2010): United Nations Economic Commission for Africa. Assessing regional integration in Africa (ARIA IV report). Chapter 5: Informal trade in Africa. Addis Ababa: UNECA, pp. 143-191.

Volodin, V. (2006): Rynok bez chelnokov. Moscow: Nationalyi institut sistemnykh issledovanii problem predprinimatel'stva, 2 March 2006, URL: http://www.smb.ru/reviews.html?id=189 (last access: 24.06.2011).

Williams, A. M. / Baláž, V. (2005): "Winning, Then Losing the Battle with Globalization: Vietnamese Petty Traders in Slovakia". In: International Journal of Urban and Regional Research, 29, 3, pp. 533-549.

Williams, C. C. (2004): Small Businesses in the Informal Economy: The Evidence Base. London: Small Business Service.

Williams, C. C. (2010): "Re-theorizing the Informal Economy in Western Nations: Some Lessons from Rural England". In: The Open Area Studies Journal, 3, pp. 1-11.

Yakovlev, A. (2006): "The Evolution of Business – State Interaction in Russia: From State Capture to Business Capture?". In: Europe-Asia Studies, 58, 7, pp. 1033-1056.

Yakovlev, A. / Golikova, V. / Kapralova, N. (2007): "Rossiiskie 'chelnoki' – ot predprinimatelei ponevole k integratsii v rynochnoe khoziaistvo". In: Mir Rossii, 2, pp. 84-106.

Yuekseker, D. (2007): "Shuttling Goods, Weaving Consumer Tastes: Informal Trade Between Turkey and Russia". In: International Journal of Urban and Regional Research, 31, 1, pp. 60-72.

Zheltov, A. (2004): "Challenges of Implementing Transparency and International Standards". In: D. McCarthy, S.M. Puffer and S. Shekshnia (eds.): Corporate Governance in Russia: A Framework for Analysis. Cheltenham, Northampton: Edward Elgar, pp. 223-242.

Zhuplev, A. V. / Shein V. I. (2004): "Corporate Governance in a Cultural Context". In: D. McCarthy, S. M. Puffer and S. Shekshnia (eds.): Corporate Governance in Russia: A Framework for Analysis. Cheltenham, Northampton: Edward Elgar, pp.110-136.

List of Authors

Nino Aivazishvili has studied history in Tbilisi, Georgia and is currently a PhD student (since 2007) in social anthropology at the Martin Luther University in Halle-Wittenberg and an associate member of the Research Group "Caucasian Boundaries and Citizenship from Below" (2006-2009) at Max Planck Institute for Social Anthropology in Halle. Her field research was in North-West Azerbaijan, where she worked with the Georgian speaking ethnic group *Ingiloy* and is completing her dissertation on themes of ethnicity, citizenship and nationality in everyday life of the Ingiloy.

Rory Archer works as an assistant at the Centre for South-East European Studies and is a doctoral candidate of history at the University of Graz, Austria. He holds a MA in Nationalism Studies from Central European University, Budapest and a BA in International Relations from Dublin City University. His main research interests include social anthropology and contemporary history of Balkan Europe, nationalism and ethnicity in Europe and Balkan ethnomusicology.

Just Boedeker studied Ethnology, Scientific Studies of Religion, Islamic Studies and Near Eastern Archaeology in Heidelberg (Ruprecht-Karls- Universität) and Berlin (Freie Universität). In 2006 he completed his Master's thesis on "Ritual and Identity in Iranian Zoroastrian Occasions" which was based on a number of researches in the Iranian city of Yazd. Currently he is based in Berlin at Zentrum Moderner Orient working in the Competence Network *Crossroads Asia* on the topic "The Baloch Borderlands: The Conflict of Tribe and State in a Globalized World". His main focus is on religions and cultures of Central Asia. He experienced several fieldworks, language courses and workshops in Iran, Afghanistan, Armenia, the former Soviet Central Asian Republics and Pakistan. Recent publications include "Begegnungen mit den Luri in Sistan und Belutschistan – Eine Kontrastkultur innerhalb einer Kontrastkultur?" in *Tsiganologische Mitteilungen* (15.August 2010; Special Volume, pp.11-17) and "An Inter-Ethnic Conflict in the Cultural Environment of the Baloch National Movement in Present-day Afghanistan" in *Iran and the Caucasus* (13, 2, 2009, pp. 357-364).

Bettina Bruns, Dr. phil., Schumpeter fellow at the Leibniz Institute for Regional Geography, Leipzig, in the project "Within the 'ring of secure neighbours' – regional and local effects of the extra-territorial involvement of the European Union in Belarus, Ukraine and the Republic of Moldova". Prior to this, she was a research assistant in the project "Geographie[s] at the edges of the European Union". Her research interests include borders, informal economies in Eastern and Central Europe and ethnographic methods. Recent publications comprise "'Grenze als Ressource' – Die soziale Organisation von Schmuggel am Rande der Europäischen Union" (Wiesbaden: VS-Verlag, 2010) and „Moral an der Grenze? Theoretische Überlegungen und empirische Befunde zur Moral im Alltag an der östlichen Außengrenze der Europäischen Union" in *Geographische Revue* (1, 2010, pp. 21-36, together with Helga Zichner).

Martin Doevenspeck is an assistant professor at the Department of Geography of the University of Bayreuth, Germany. His research focuses on mobility, territoriality, conflict and risk in West and Central Africa and the borderland between Rwanda, Uganda and DR Congo.

Kapitolina Fedorova, Associated Professor at the Department of Anthropology, European University at St. Petersburg, Russia, specializes in sociolinguistics. Her kandidatskaya (the Russian equivalent of PhD) degree in philology was obtained from St. Petersburg State University in 2002; the topic of her dissertation was "Language behaviour strategies in conversing with foreigners (based on the Russian language)". Her current research interests include: Sociolinguistic of schooling (the book "School, language, and society" is going to be published in 2011), interethnic communication in the border regions (field studies on the Russian-Chinese and Russian-Finnish borders), analysis of speech practices relevant for social studies (book chapter on linguistic analysis of Russian friendship published in 2009; book chapter on the term 'society' usage to be published in 2011).

Gulcan Kolay is a doctoral candidate in Political Science at Institut d'Etudes Politiques (Sci Po d'Aix) in Aix-en Provence; focusing on cross-border commerce between Turkey and Iraq more precisely between two Kurdish regions and its consequences on the relation between two sides. After graduating from Istanbul University (journalism and Public Relations) in 1999 she started to work as a journalist. She wrote numerous published articles on the economic policies of Turkey. Also she lived and worked in United Kingdom (2000-2001) before coming to France. Her main interests are nationalism, national minorities, and socioeconomic consequences of conflicts, transnational networks, and border issues. She is member of The French Political Science Association.

Tobias Kraudzun, Dipl. Geogr., graduated from the Universität Hamburg after his studies of geography, anthropology and computer science. Currently, he works as research assistant in the Centre for Development Studies of the Institute for Geographical Sciences at Freie Universität Berlin.

Nene Morisho Mwanabiningo is a PhD student at BIGSAS, Bayreuth International Graduate School of African Studies, University of Bayreuth. In his dissertation project he explores the politics of cross-border trade between Congo and Rwanda.

Judith Miggelbrink, Dr. phil, head of the research unit „Productions of Space between State and Society". The research unit comprises projects as "Geographie[s] at the edges of the European Union" (2007-2009), "Power technologies' production of Space: Indigeneity and Territoriality of the Sámi" (2008-2012) and "Within the 'ring of secure neighbours' – regional and local effects of the extra-territorial involvement of the European Union in Belarus, Ukraine and the Republic of Moldova" (2011-2016). Her research interests include social geography, spatial theory, practice theory, visual geographies, discourse analysis, borders and informal economies. Recent publications are: "Hier so, dort anders. Raumbezogene Vergleiche in der Wissenschaft und anderswo" (Münster: Westfälisches Dampfboot, 2010, edited together with Bernd Belina) and „Am Ostrand des ‚wettbewerbsfähigsten Wirtschaftsraums der Welt'. (Raum-)Theoretische Überlegungen zur Produktion der EU-Außengrenze als Territorialisierungs- und Skalenstrategie" in W. Łukowski and M. Wagner (eds.): Alltag im Grenzland. Schmuggel als ökonomische Strategie an der EU-Ostgrenze (Wiesbaden: VS-Verlag, 2010, pp. 215-230, together with Bernd Belina).

Enza Roberta Petrillo is Research Fellow at the Sant' Anna School of Advanced Studies of Pisa, International Laboratory on Conflict Development and Global Politics. She is carrying out research in the area of post-conflict peace-building. Her main current research lines focus on Eastern European politics, critical geopolitics, institutional transitions, transnational organized crime and international migrations. Her researches have combined backgrounds in international relations and geopolitics with interdisciplinary expertise in the social sciences and empirical research methodology, doing field research in Kosovo, Albania, Slovenia, Bosnia and Herzegovina, Belarus and Ukraine. She was Policy Analyst Consultant for several think tanks and International Organizations, working as electoral observer for OSCE/ODIHR, providing short-term technical assistance to United Nations Human Rights Council; designing and managing research projects and policy briefs for the International and European Forum of Migration Research –FIERI- and the Italian Senate of Republic, Foreign Policy and Defence Department. In 2009 she obtained a Ph.D. in Geopolitics at the University L'Orientale in Naples. Her most important publications include "Narconomics" (Roma: Lantana Editore, 2011), "Empirical Trends and Characteristics of multi-stakeholder partnerships in Afghanistan, Kosovo, and the DRC" in A. de Guttry, W. Benedek and O. Green (eds.): Peace-Building And Human Security After Conflicts: The Significance of Multi-Stakeholder Partnerships (Routledge, forthcoming, together with K. Pishchikova) and "Elezioni senza democrazia. I casi della Croazia, della Repubblica federale di Serbia e Montenegro e del Kosovo" in O. Cappelli (ed.): Oltre la democratizzazione. Il problema della ricostruzione dello stato nello spazio politico post-comunista (Napoli: ESI, 2010).

Abel Polese is Research Fellow in the Institute of Geography of the University of Edinburgh. Prior to this endorsement he has been Marie Curie Research Fellow at the Hannah Arendt Institute of Dresden and Civic Education Project Visiting Fellow to Ukraine. He has been teaching as visiting lecturer in several universities (University of Warsaw, Corvinus University, Marmara University, Moscow Higher School of Economics). Dr Polese is co-editor (with D. O'Beachain) of the recently published "The Colour Revolutions in the Former Soviet Republics: Successes and Failures" (London and New York: Routledge, 2010) and his articles have been published in journals such as: Journal of Communist Studies and Transition Politics, Comparative Education and Nationalities Papers. He is currently working, together with Peter Rodgers, on a special issue of the International Journal of Sociology and Social Policy in the framework of a research project on informal economies in Turkey and Ukraine.

Krisztina Rácz holds an MA in English language and literature from the University of Szeged in Hungary, and an MA in Sociology and Social Anthropology from Central European University in Budapest, Hungary. She is a PhD candidate at the Balkan Studies doctoral program at the University of Ljubljana, Slovenia (Thesis: "The All-In-One Myth: Deconstructing Multiculturalism in Vojvodina", expected year of defence 2013). Her main research interests include multiculturalism, collective memory and anthropology of youth. Recent publications include "Trauma ili zabava: Sećanje na bombardovanja u diskursu Simposiona" in G. Đerić (ed.): Pamćenje i nostalgija (Belgrade: Institut za filozofiju u društvenu teoriju, 2009), "Krvotok od benzina" in Ž. Miloš (ed.): Antimemorandum-dum (Belgrade: VBZ, 2009) and "Virdžina u helankama" in Ž. Miloš (ed.): Antimemorandum-dum. (Belgrade: VBZ, 2009, with Dragan Nikolić).

Anna Stammler-Gossmann, PhD, is a Senior Researcher for the Anthropology Research Team (www.arcticcentre.org/anthropology) at the Arctic Centre (University of Lapland, Rovaniemi, Finland). Her main interests are post-socialist socio-cultural transformation, cross-border relations, resource governance, local community adaptation to social and environmental changes; the concept of the North in politics, economics, and culture; and indigenous and non-indigenous identities. She carried out her research in 1995-2002 at the University of Cologne, Seminar für Osteuropäische Geschichte, Germany; and as visiting scholar at the Scott Polar Institute, University of Cambridge, UK in 2003-2004 and in Centre for Northeast Asian Studies, Sendai Tohoku University, (Japan) in 2009. Her research sites are in different parts of Fennoscandia – Finland (Lapland), Northern Norway (Finnmark), and the Russian North (Murmansk region, Nenets Autonomous District, Republic of Sakha Yakutia, Kamchatka). Dr. Stammler-Gossmann has been conducting fieldwork in the Russian North since 1995.

Andrea Weiss graduated from Vienna University in Social Anthropology and Political Science; she also holds a M.A. in Central Asian and Caucasian Studies from Humboldt University in Berlin. Currently she is a PhD candidate at Central European University in Budapest in Sociology and Social Anthropology with a thesis project on political anthropology in Western Georgia.

Lale Yalçın-Heckmann studied sociology in Istanbul and anthropology at the University of London (PhD 1986). Since 1988 she has been living in Germany and had taught and carried out research projects at various universities. From 2000 to 2009 she was a senior researcher and head of research group at the Max Planck Institute for Social Anthropology in Halle/Saale. Currently she is a docent at the University of Pardubice and adjunct professor at the Martin Luther University of Halle-Wittenberg. Her research interests range from Kurds in Turkey, migration to Europe and in the former Soviet Union, the anthropology of the South Caucasus, postsocialism and informal economy. She is the author, co-author or co-editor of the following books: "Tribe and Kinship among the Kurds" (Frankfurt/M., 1991), "Die Kurden. Geschichte, Politik, Kultur" (Munich, 2000, together with M. Strohmeier), "Caucasus Paradigms: Anthropologies, histories and the making of a world area" (Berlin, 2007, edited with Bruce Grant) and "The Return of Private Property: Rural Life after Agrarian Reform in the Republic of Azerbaijan" (Berlin, 2011).

VS COLLEGE
REVIEWED RESEARCH: KURZ, BÜNDIG, AKTUELL

VS College richtet sich an hervorragende Nachwuchs-wissenschaftlerInnen, die außergewöhnliche Ergebnisse in Workshops oder Abschlussarbeiten erzielt haben und die ihre Resultate der Fachwelt präsentieren möchten.

Dank externer Begutachtungsverfahren fördert das Programm die Vernetzung des wissenschaftlichen Nachwuchses und sichert zugleich die Qualität.

Auf 60 - 120 Druckseiten werden aktuelle Forschungsergebnisse kurz und übersichtlich auf den Punkt gebracht und im Umfeld eines hervorragenden Lehrbuch- und Forschungsprogramms veröffentlicht.

___ Soziologie
___ Politik
___ Pädagogik
___ Medien
___ Psychologie

VS College